Top Bikini Pictures

Taylor Timms

Author Online!
For updates and
seduction resources visit
Taylor Timms page at

www.foreverlaid.com

Top Bikini Pictures
by Taylor Timms

ISBN 978-0-9866426-3-0

Printed in the United States of America

Free Online Seduction Course

As a thank you for buying this book, I would like to give you access to my online seduction course.

To claim your free spot, please go to
www.foreverlaid.com
and enter your valid email address now.

Also by Taylor Timms

Forever Laid Formula
Best Ways To Get Women To Sleep With You
ISBN 978-0-9866004-2-5

Best Gift Ideas For Women
Perfect Gifts Ideas For Any Special Occasion
ISBN 978-0-9866004-4-9

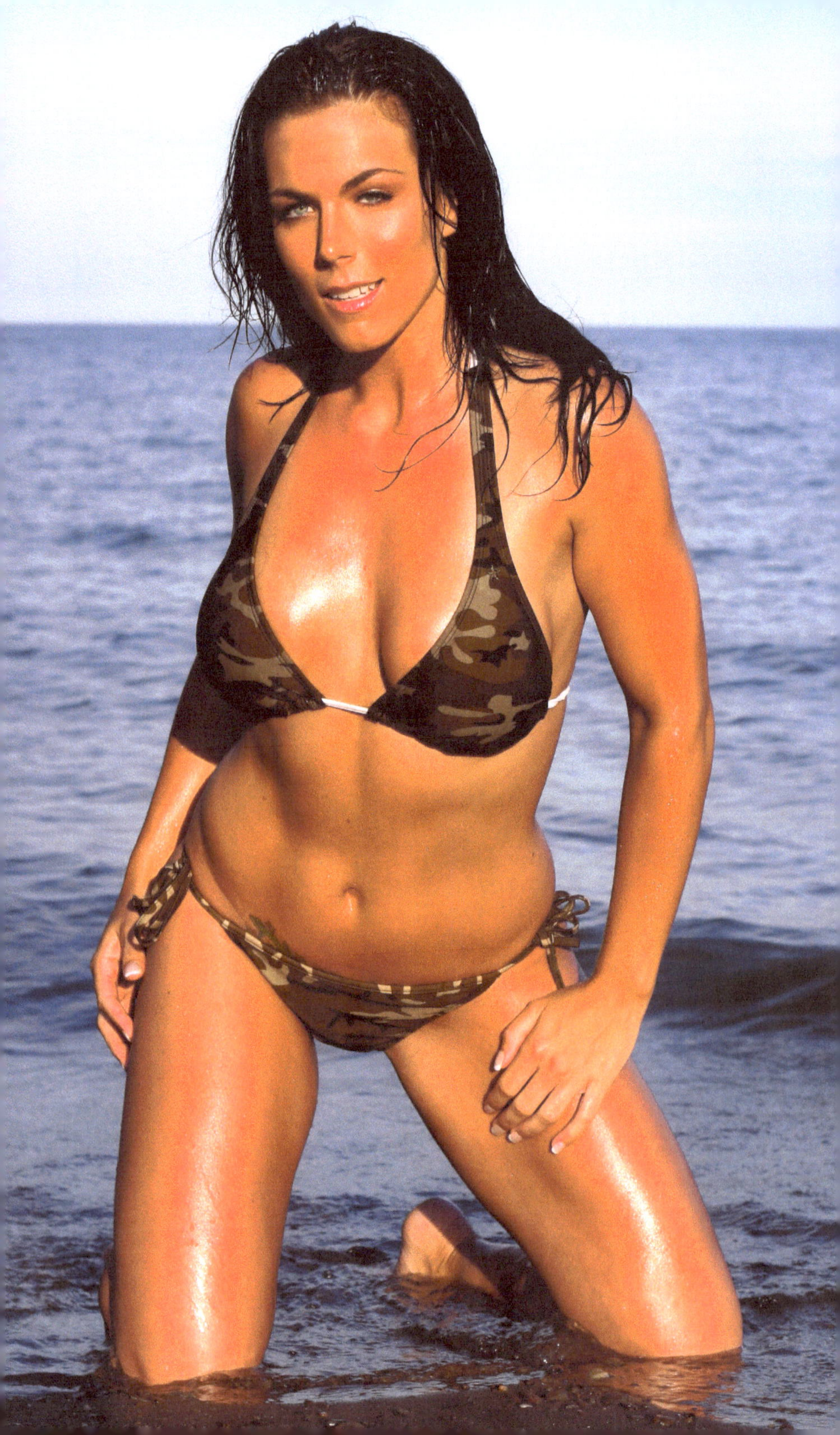

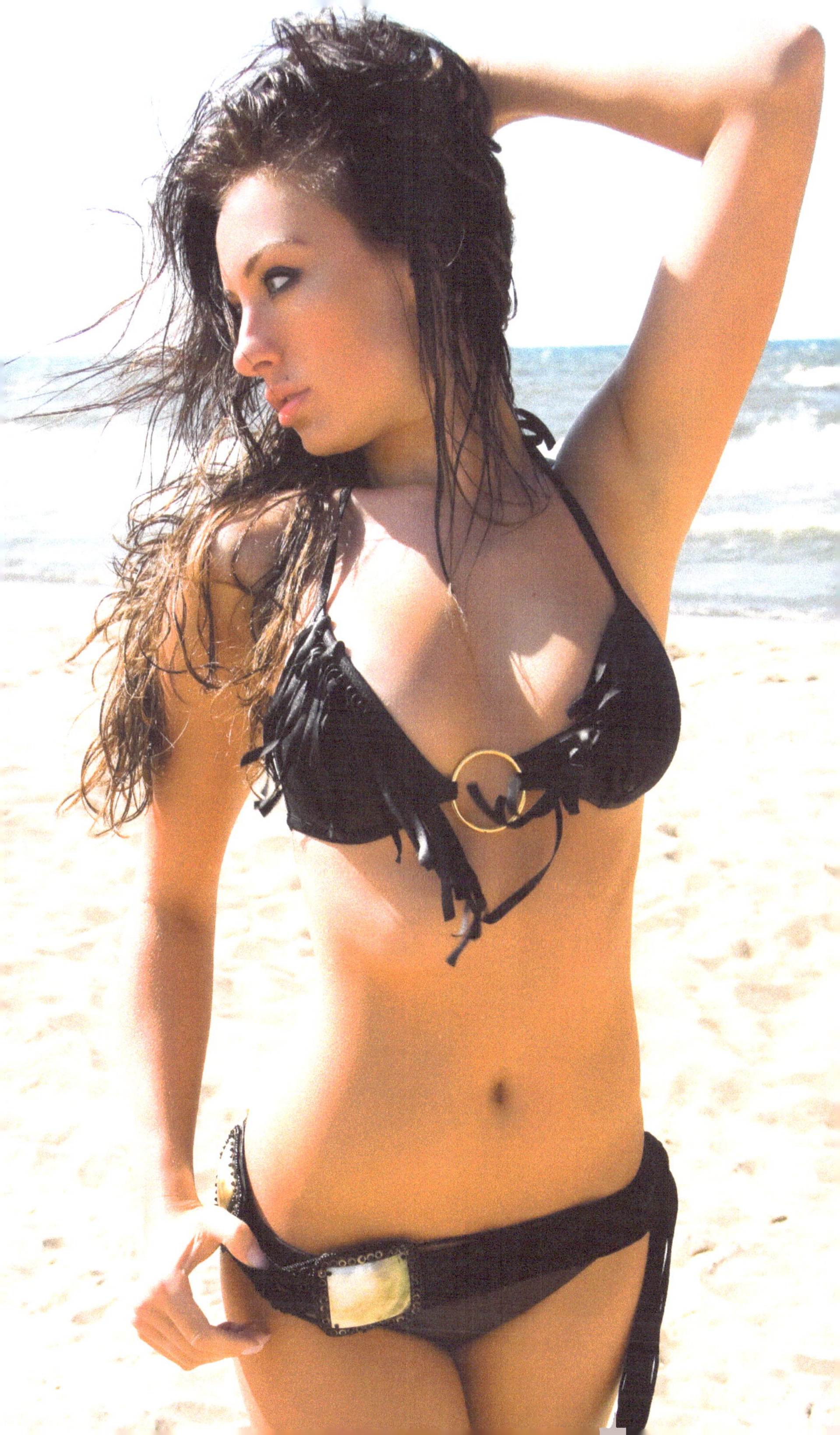

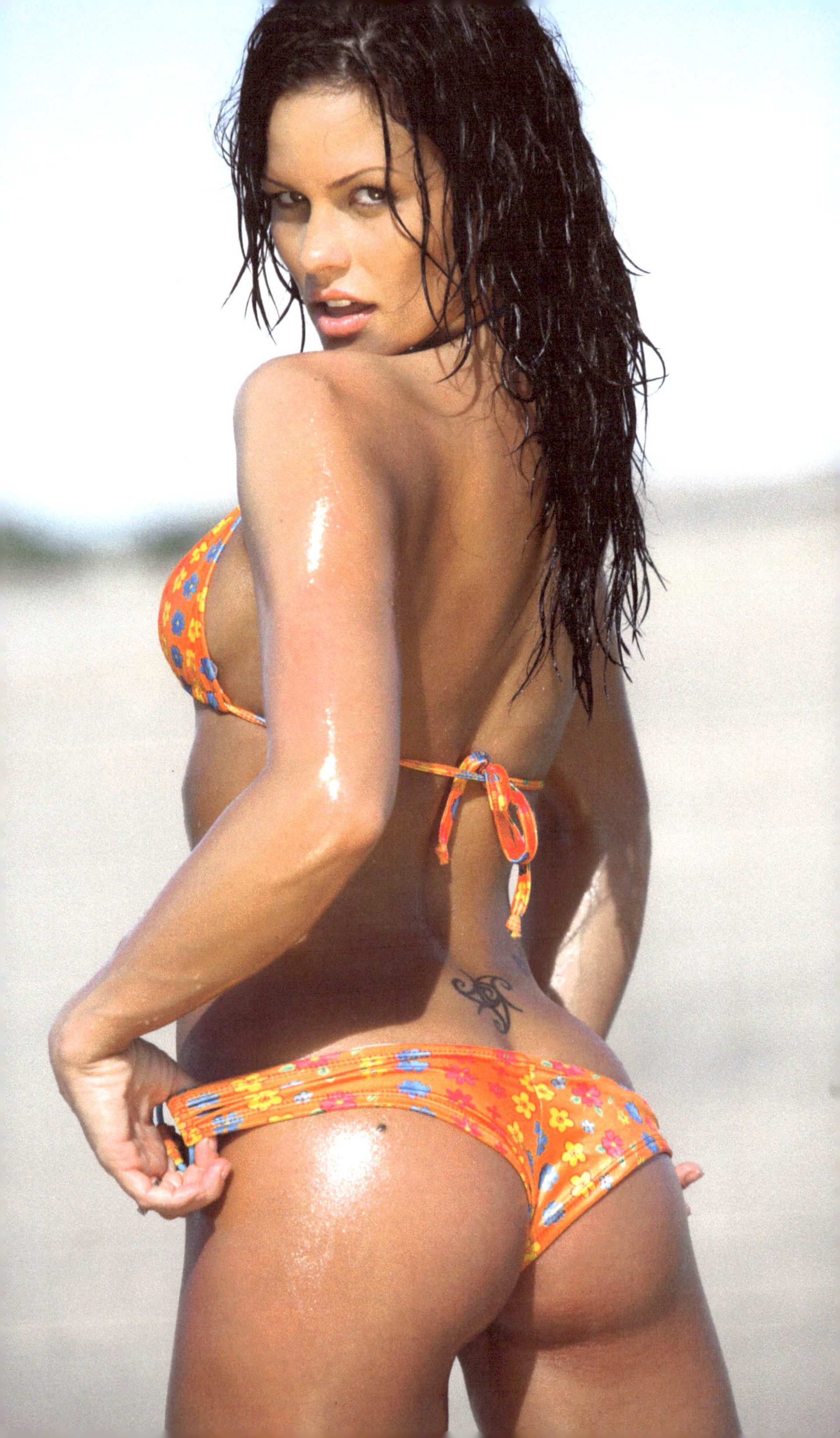

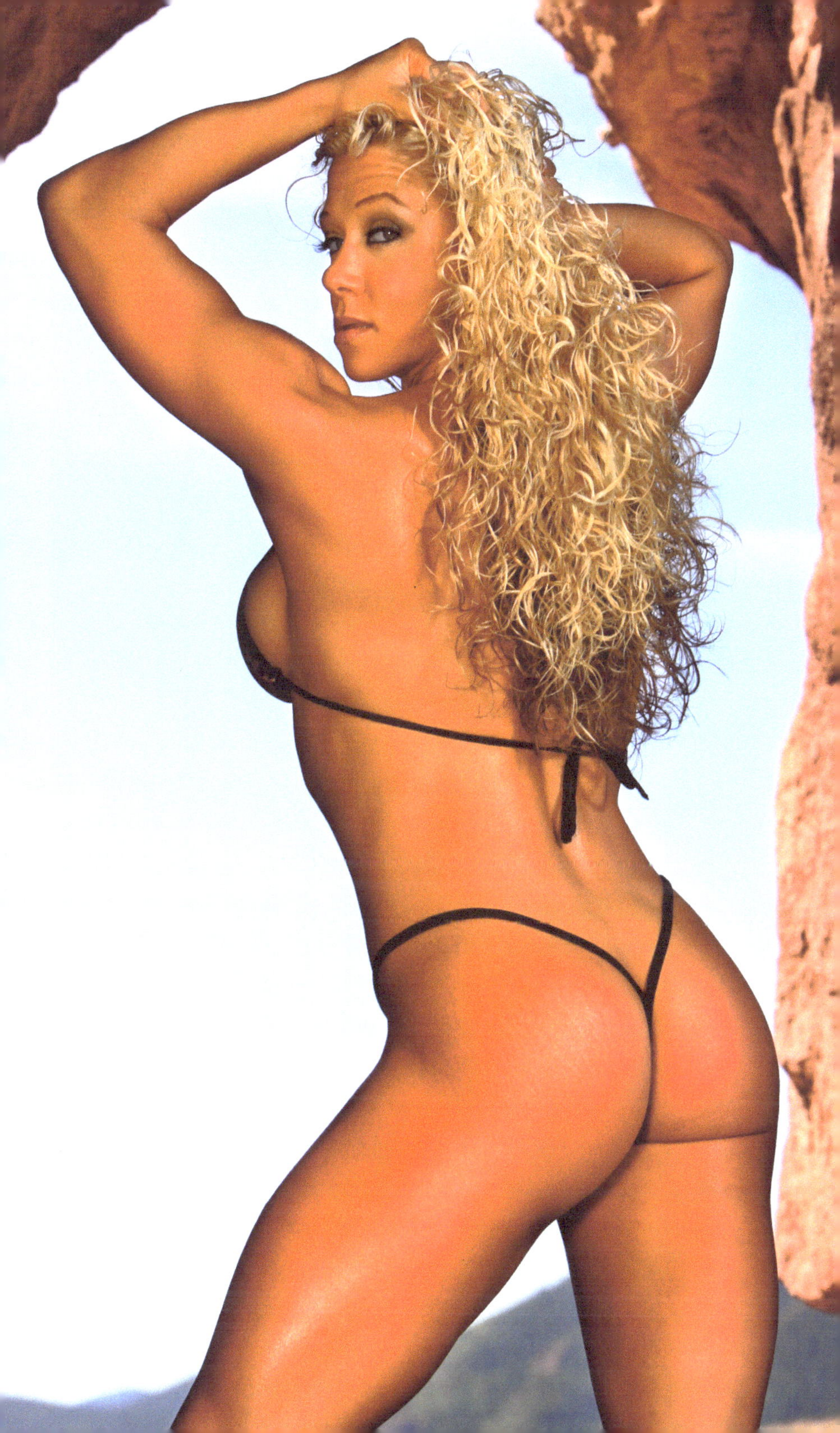

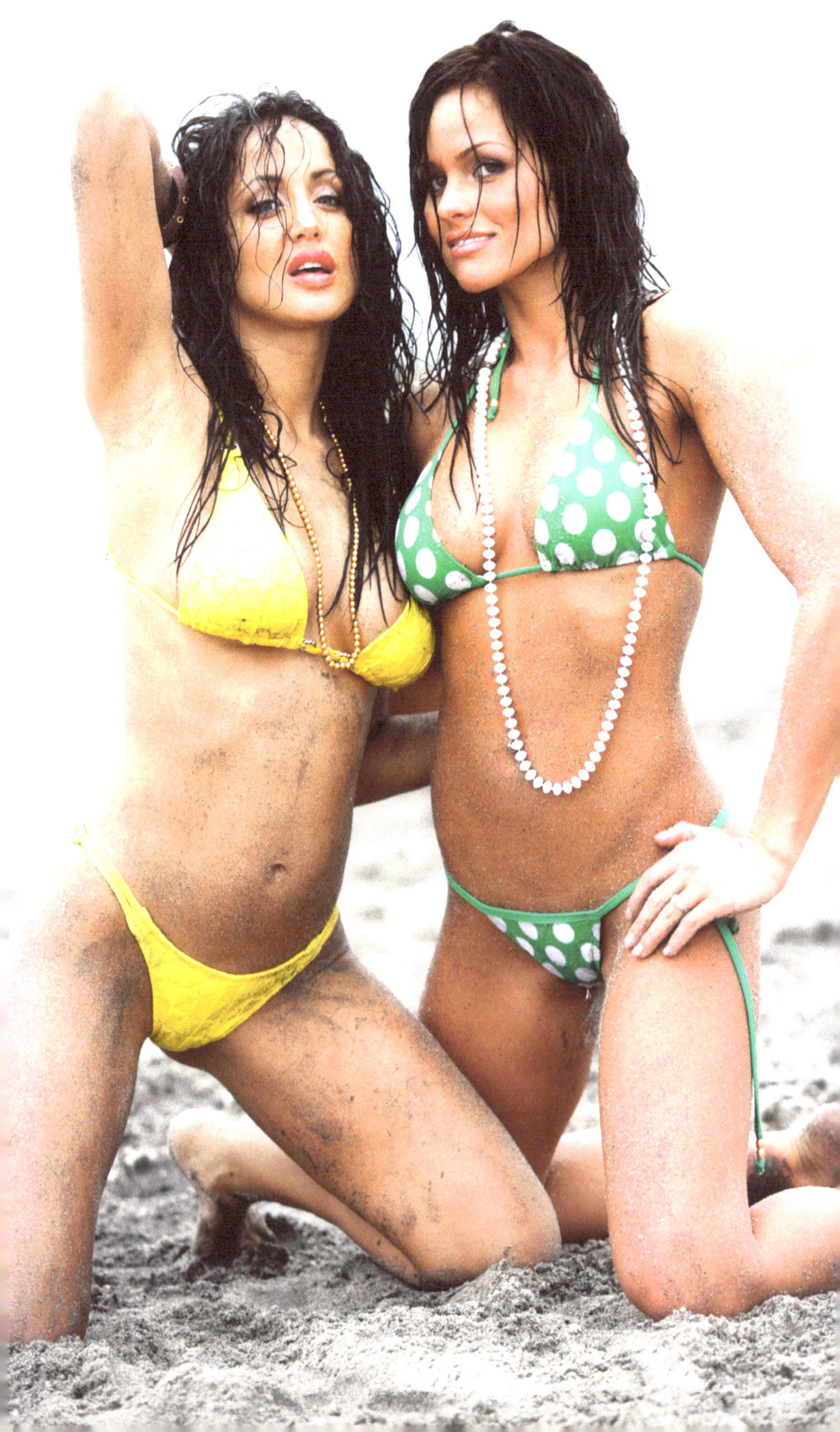

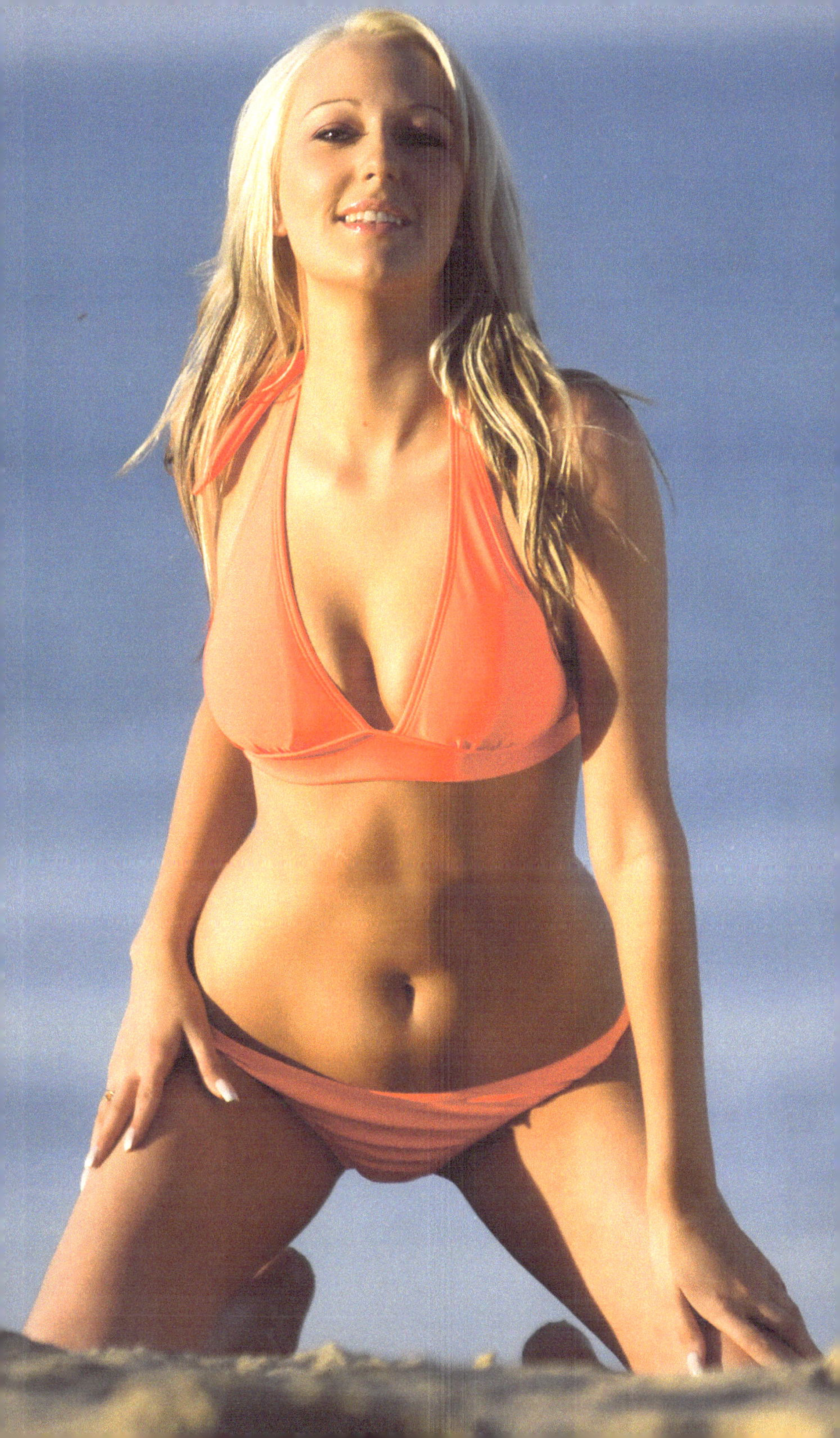

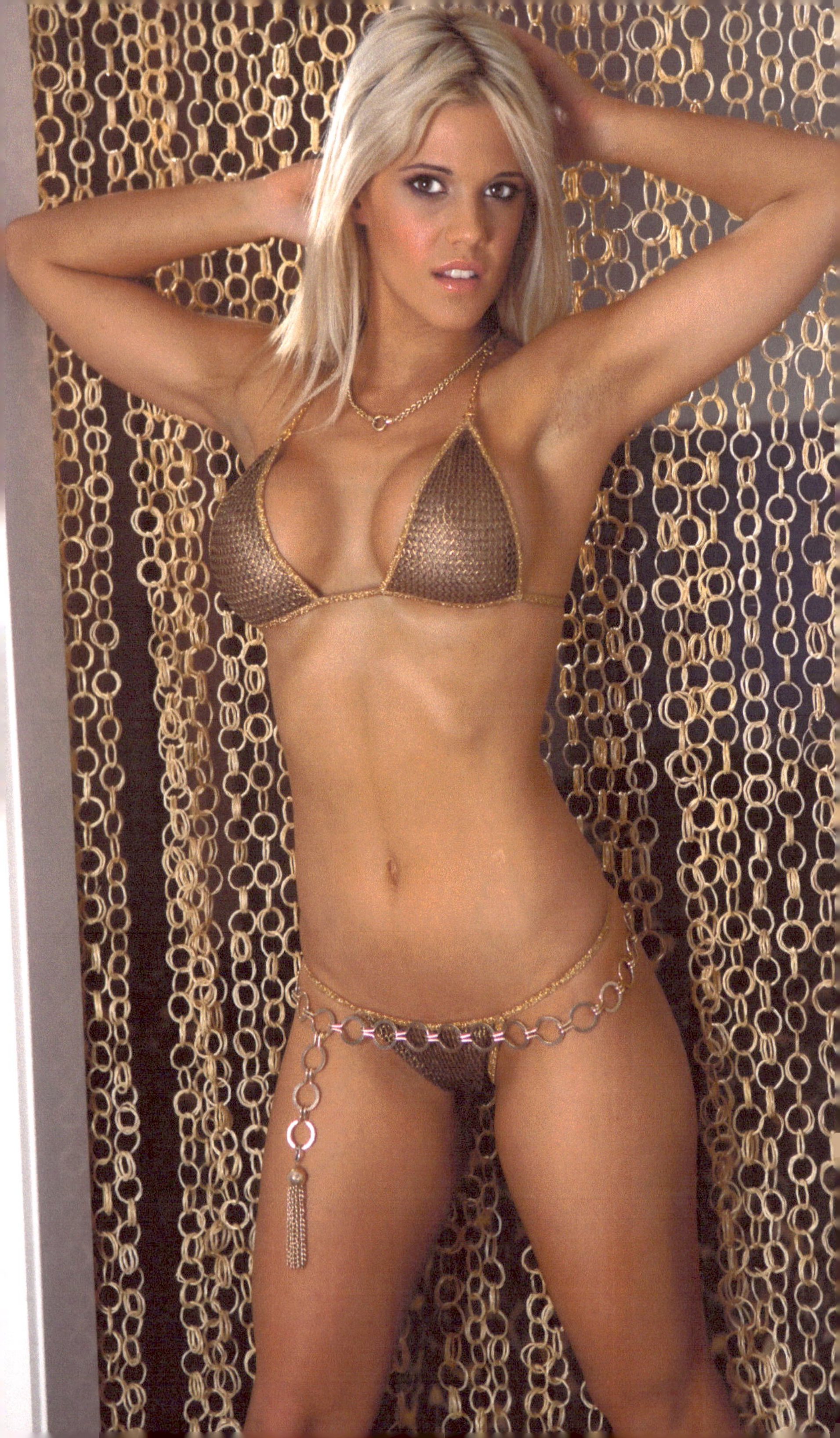

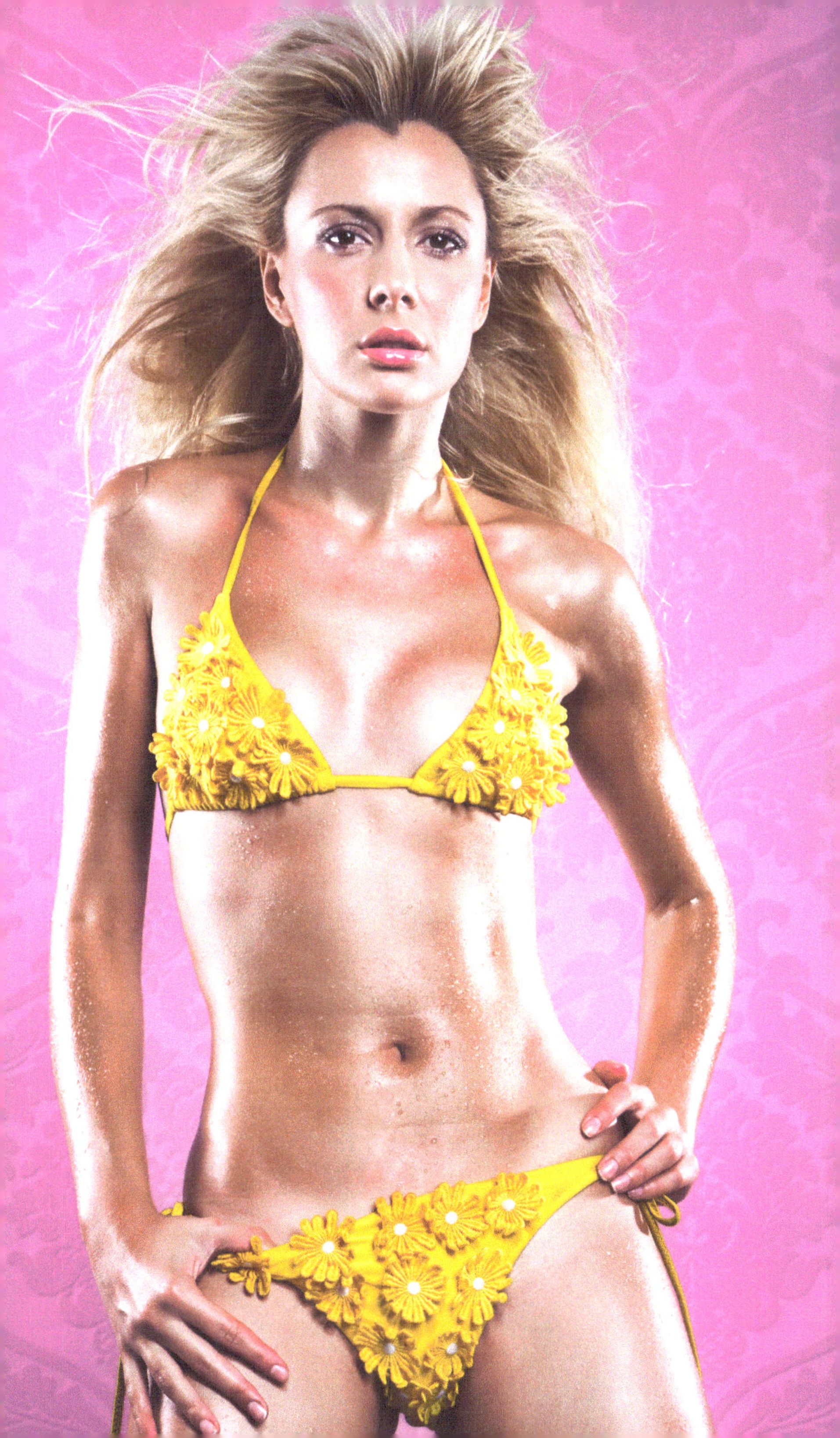

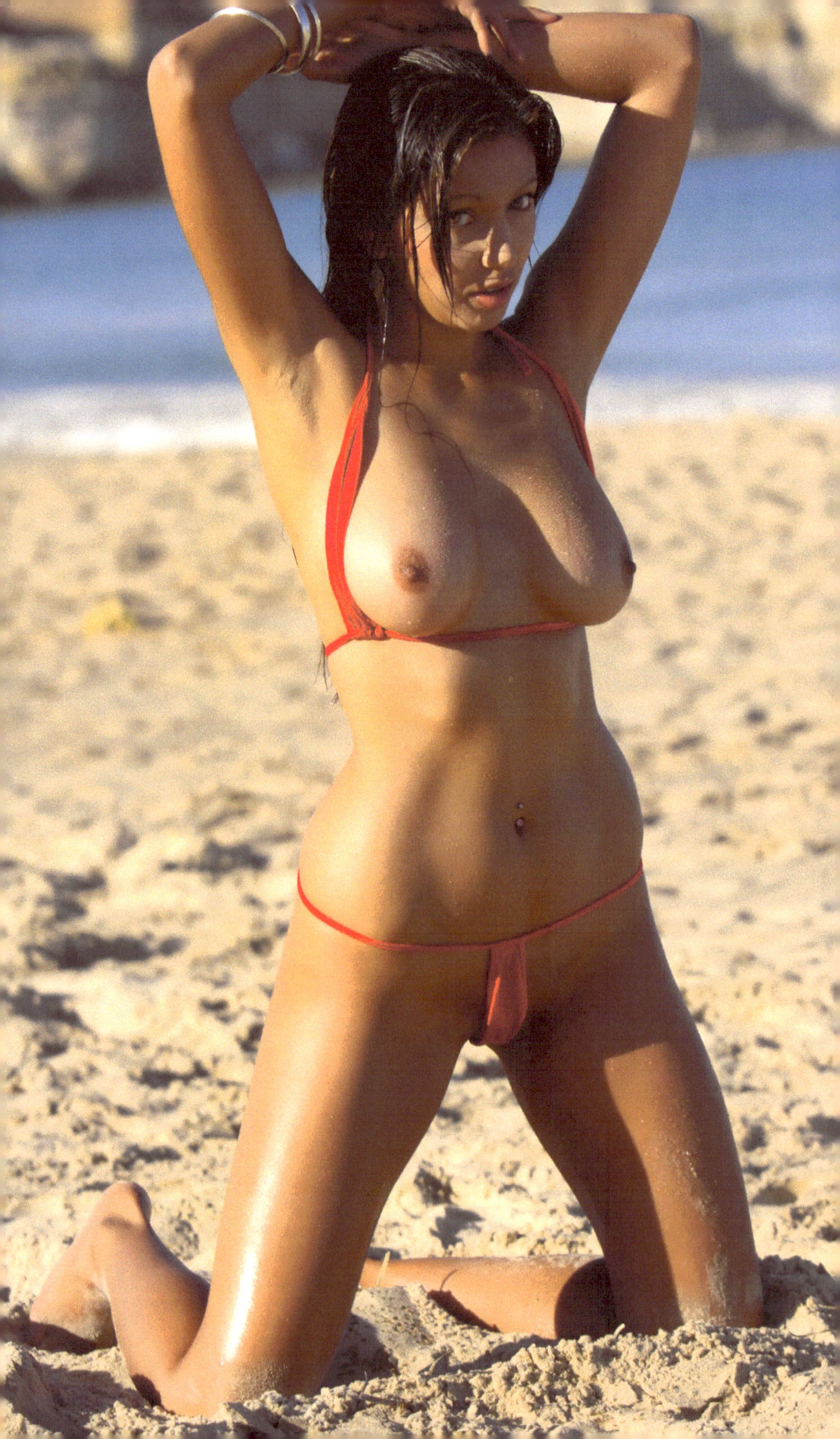

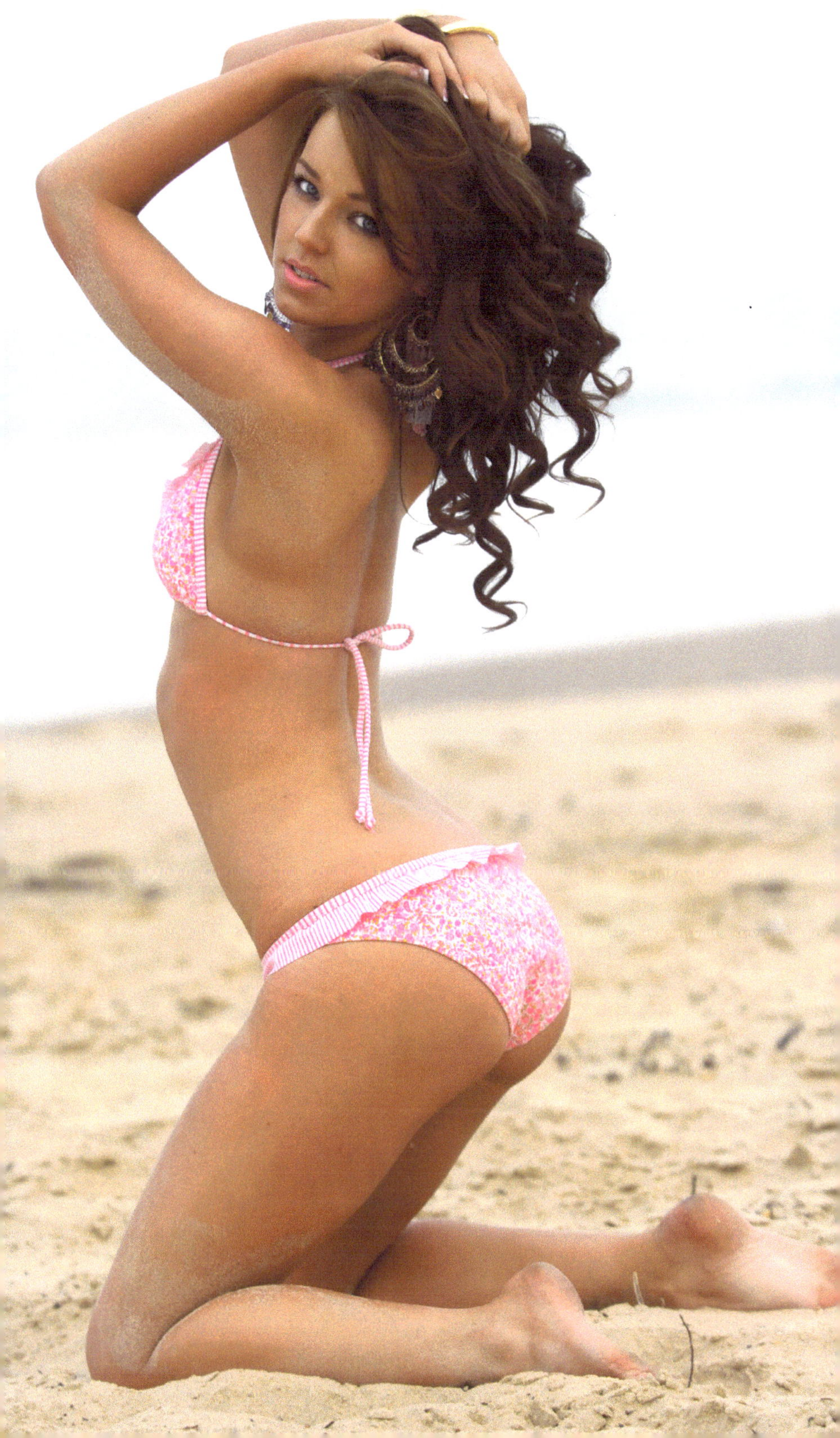

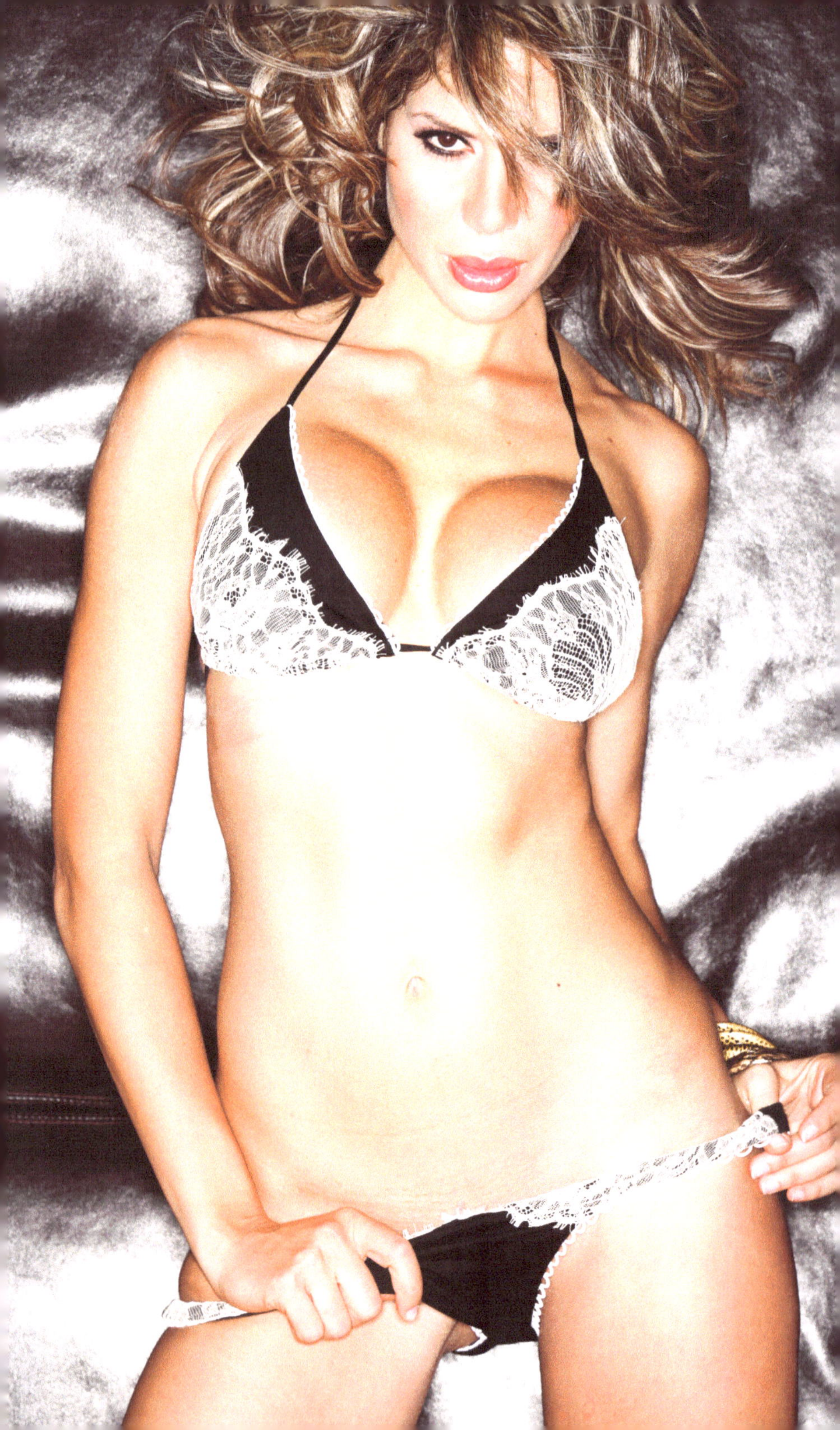

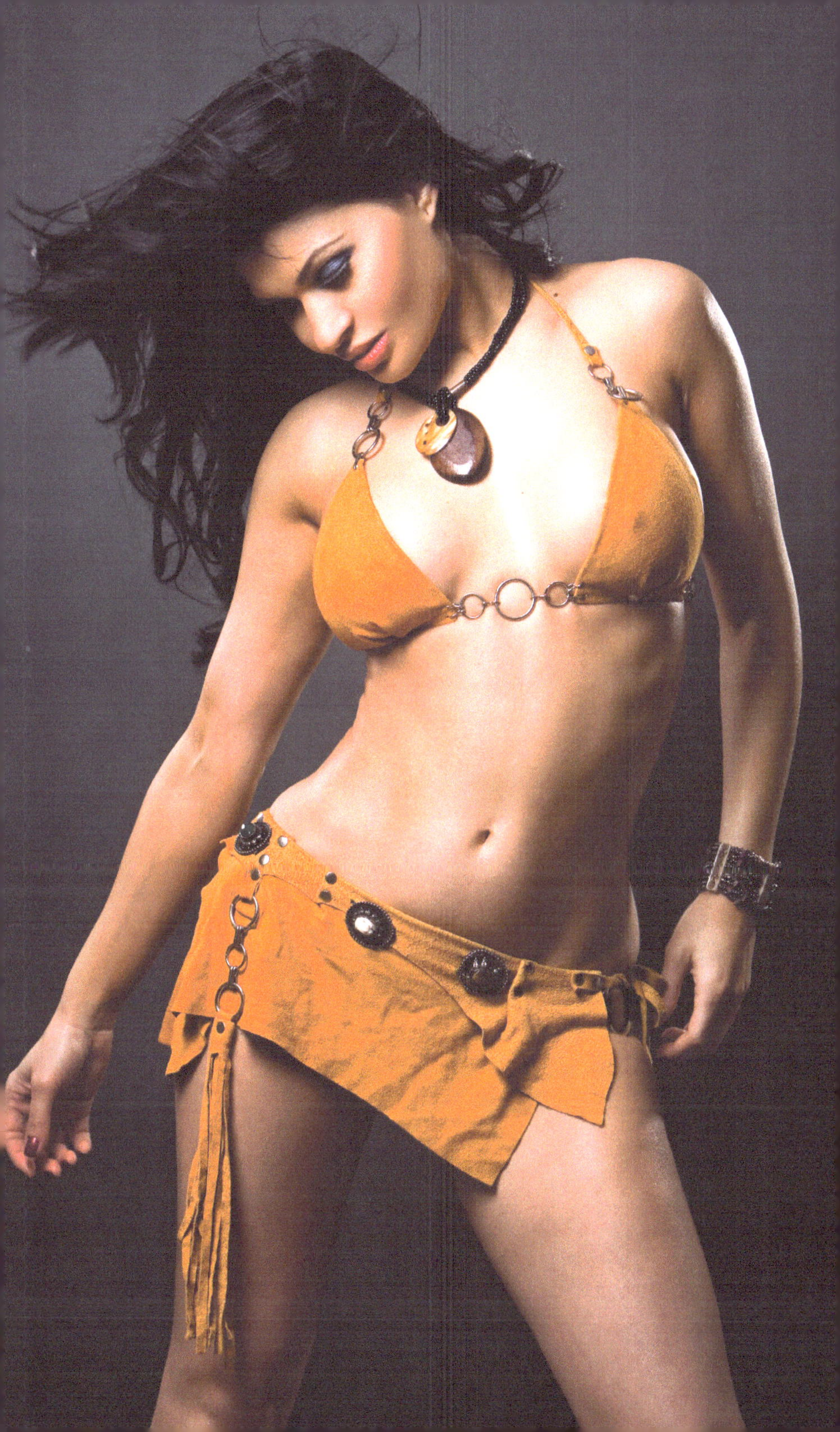

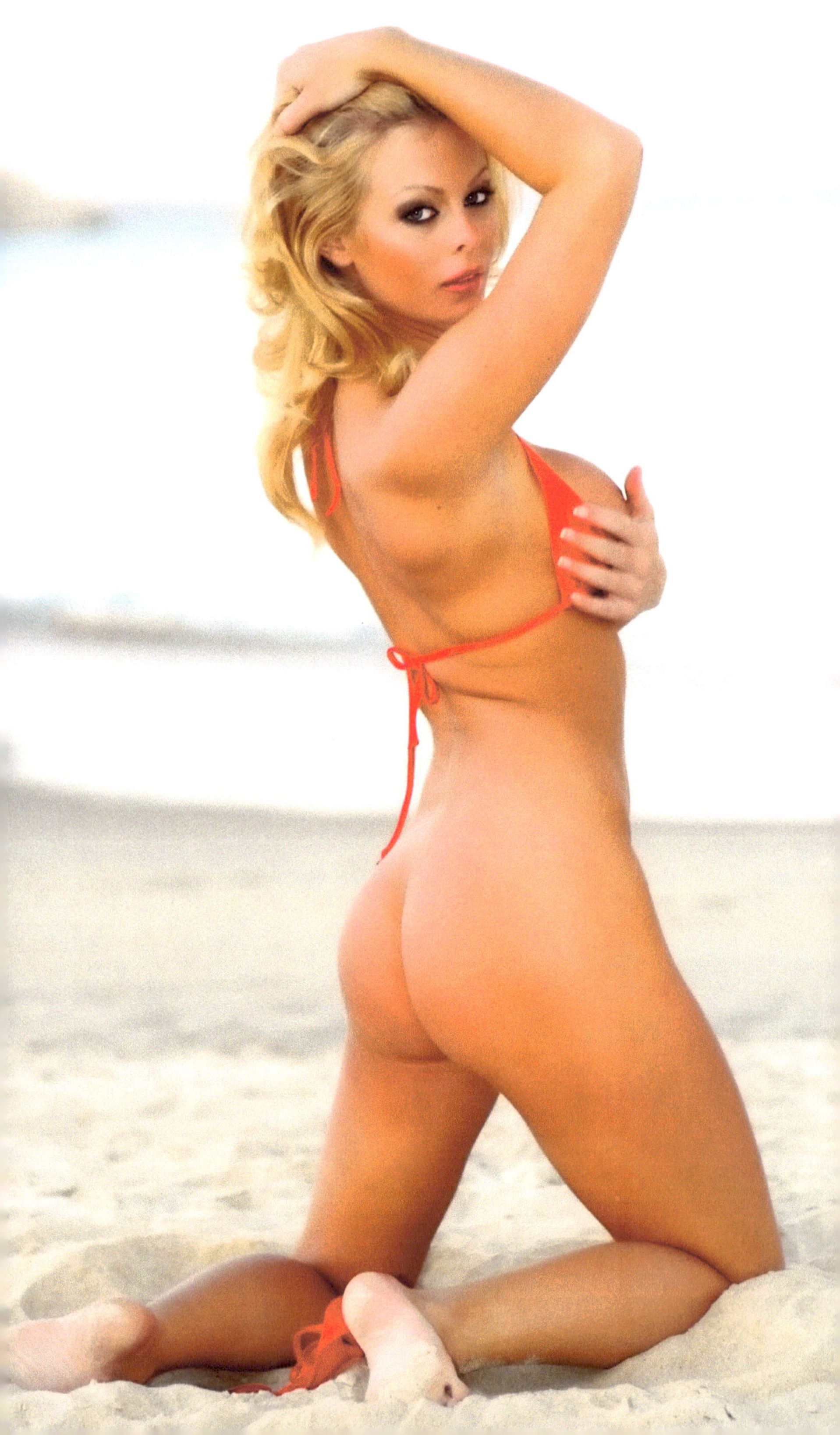

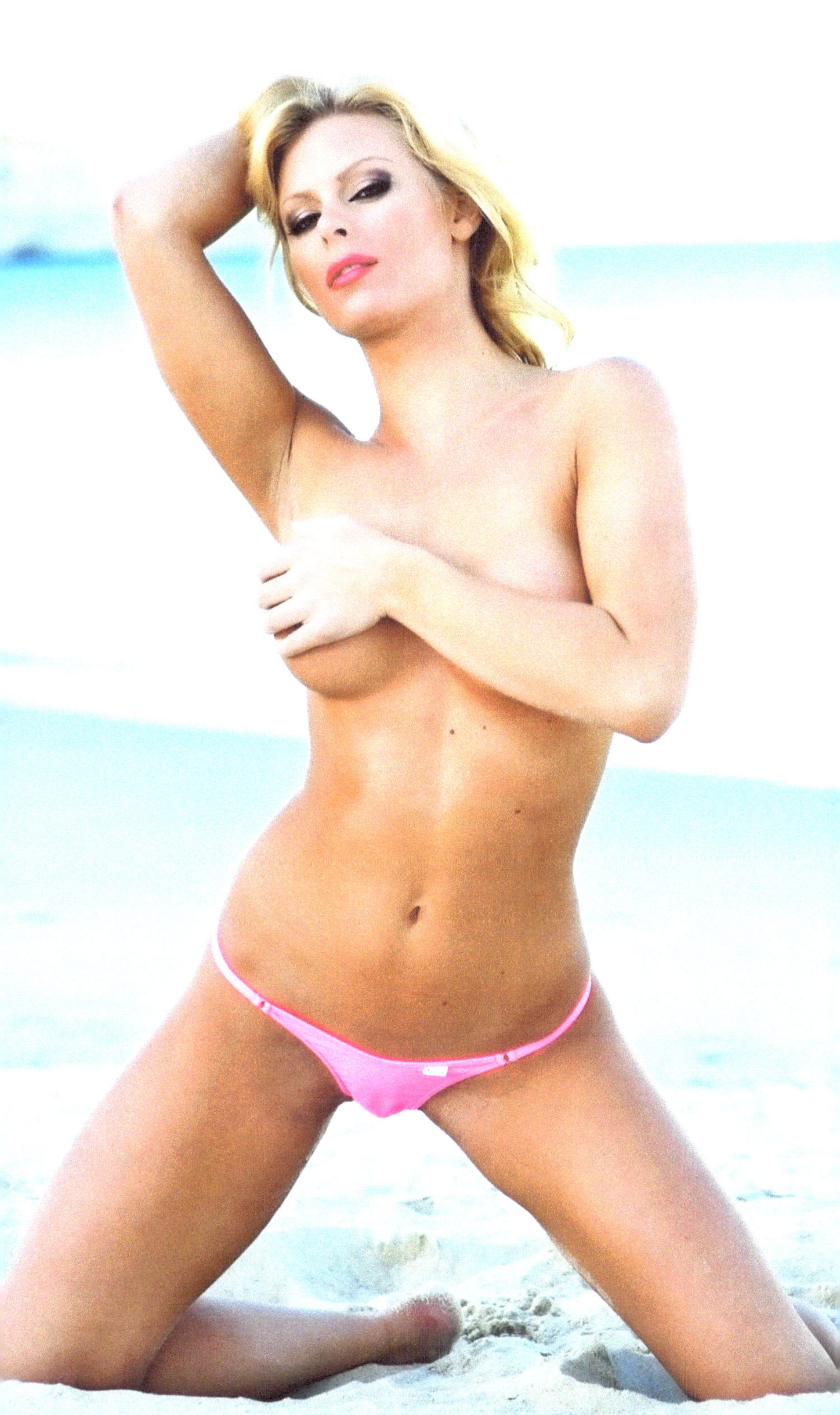

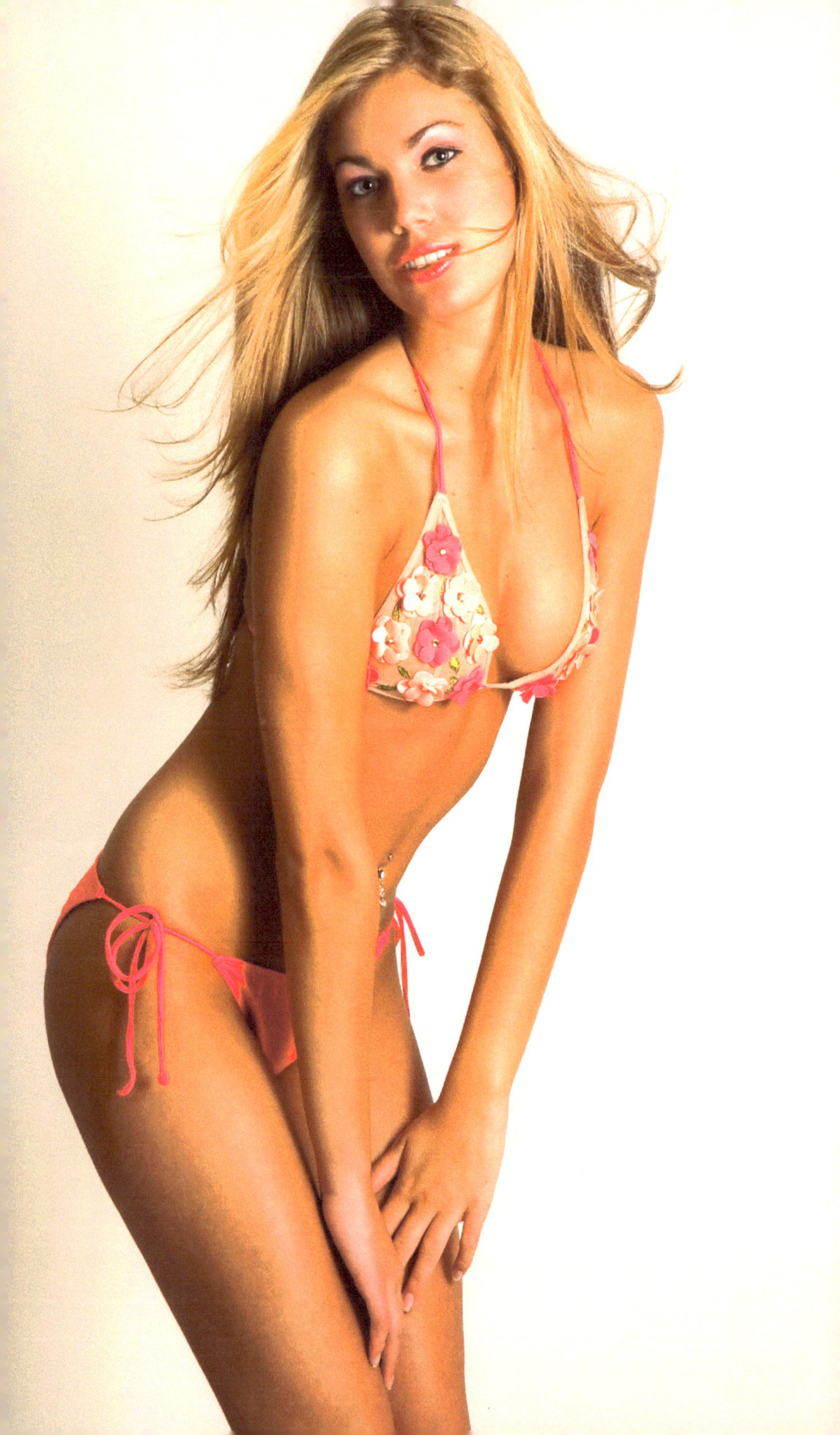

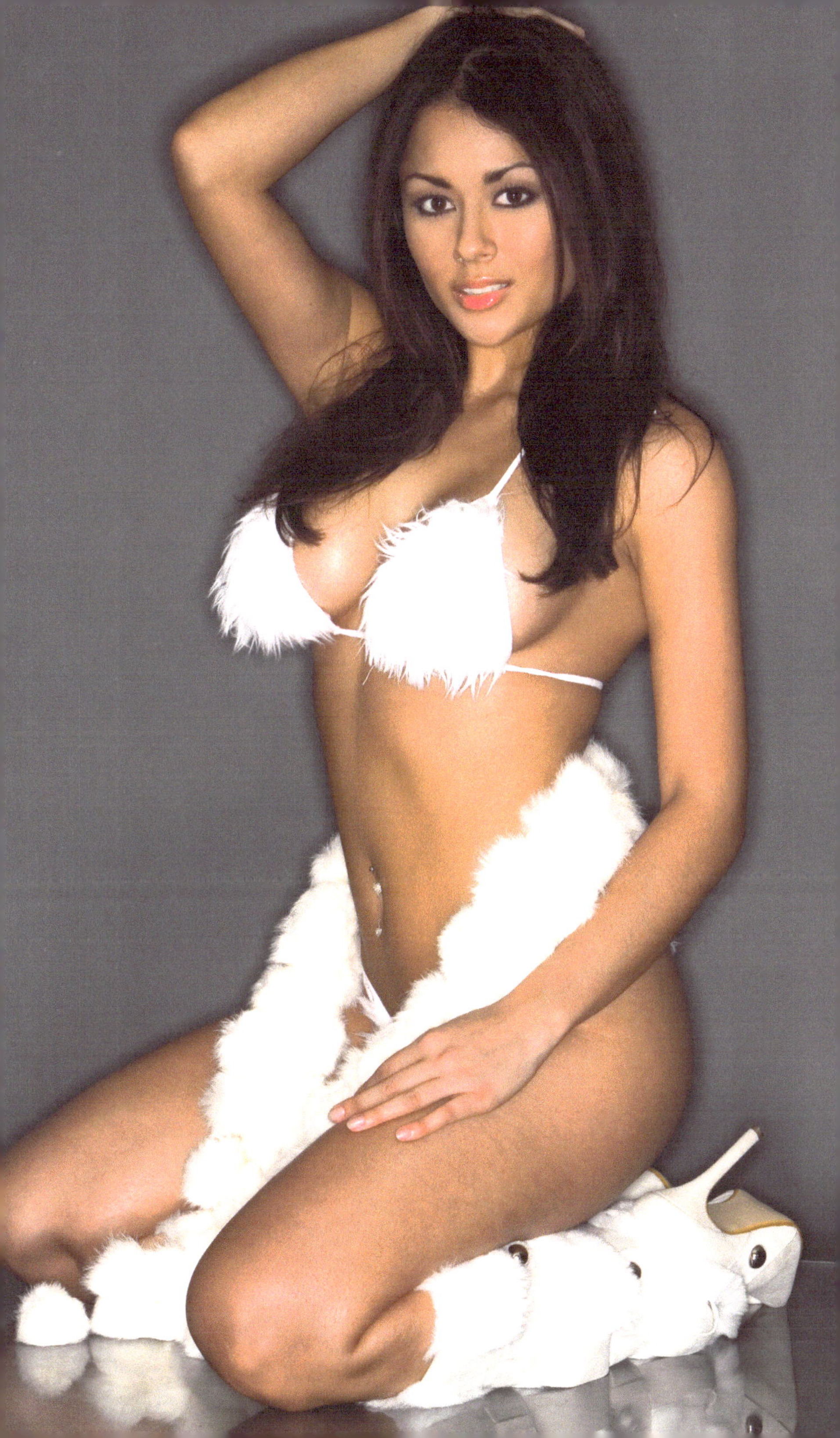

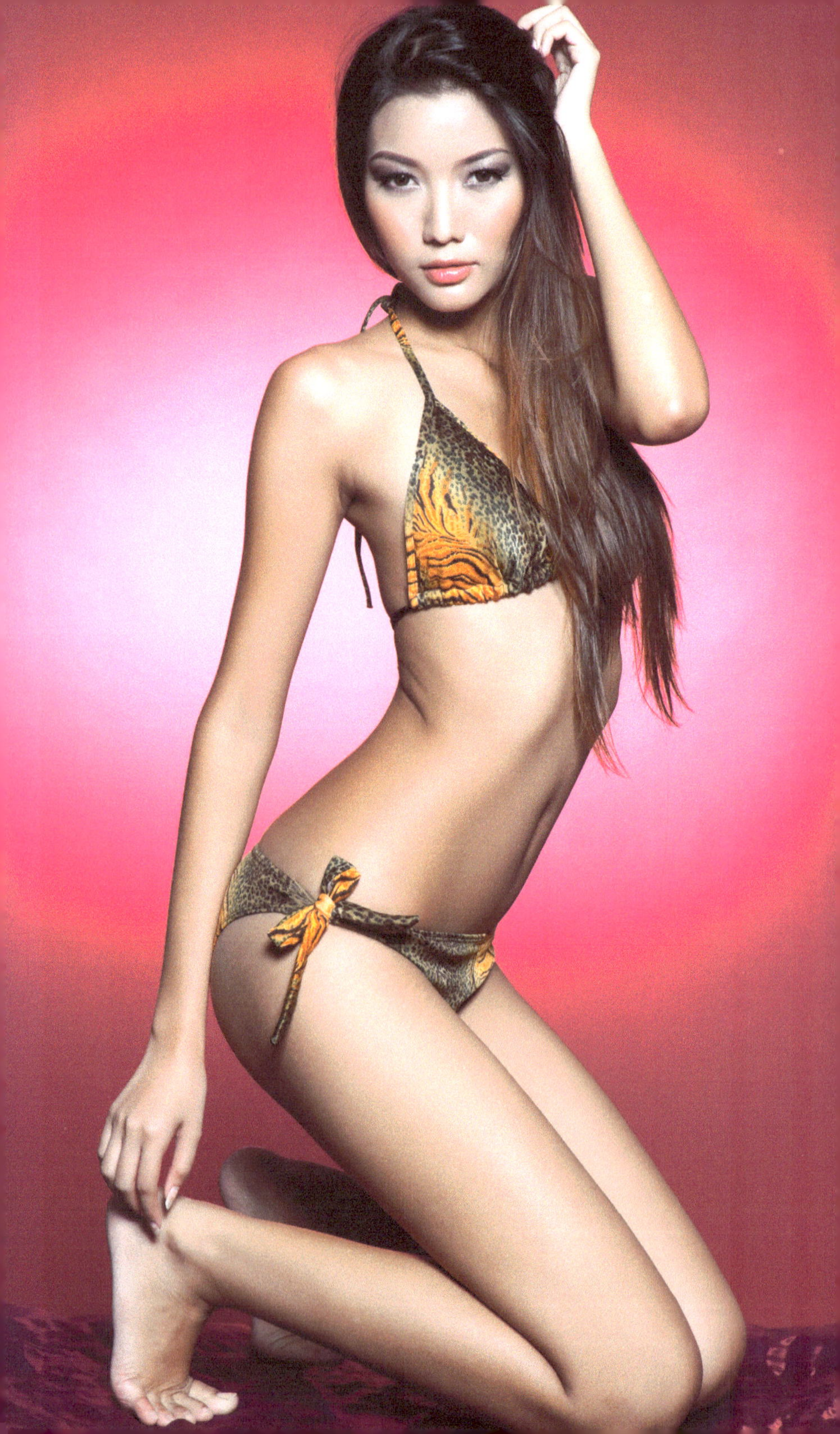

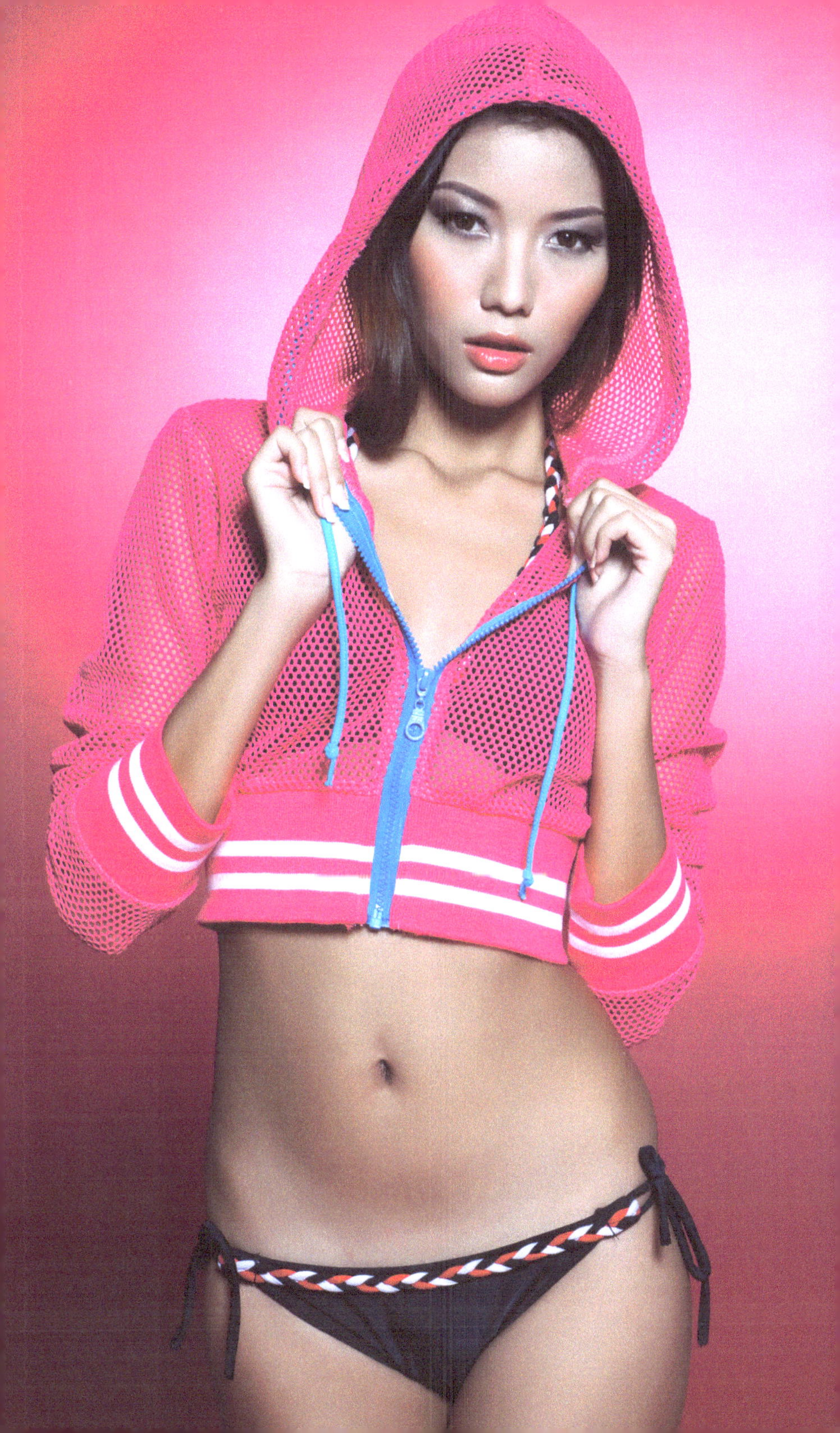

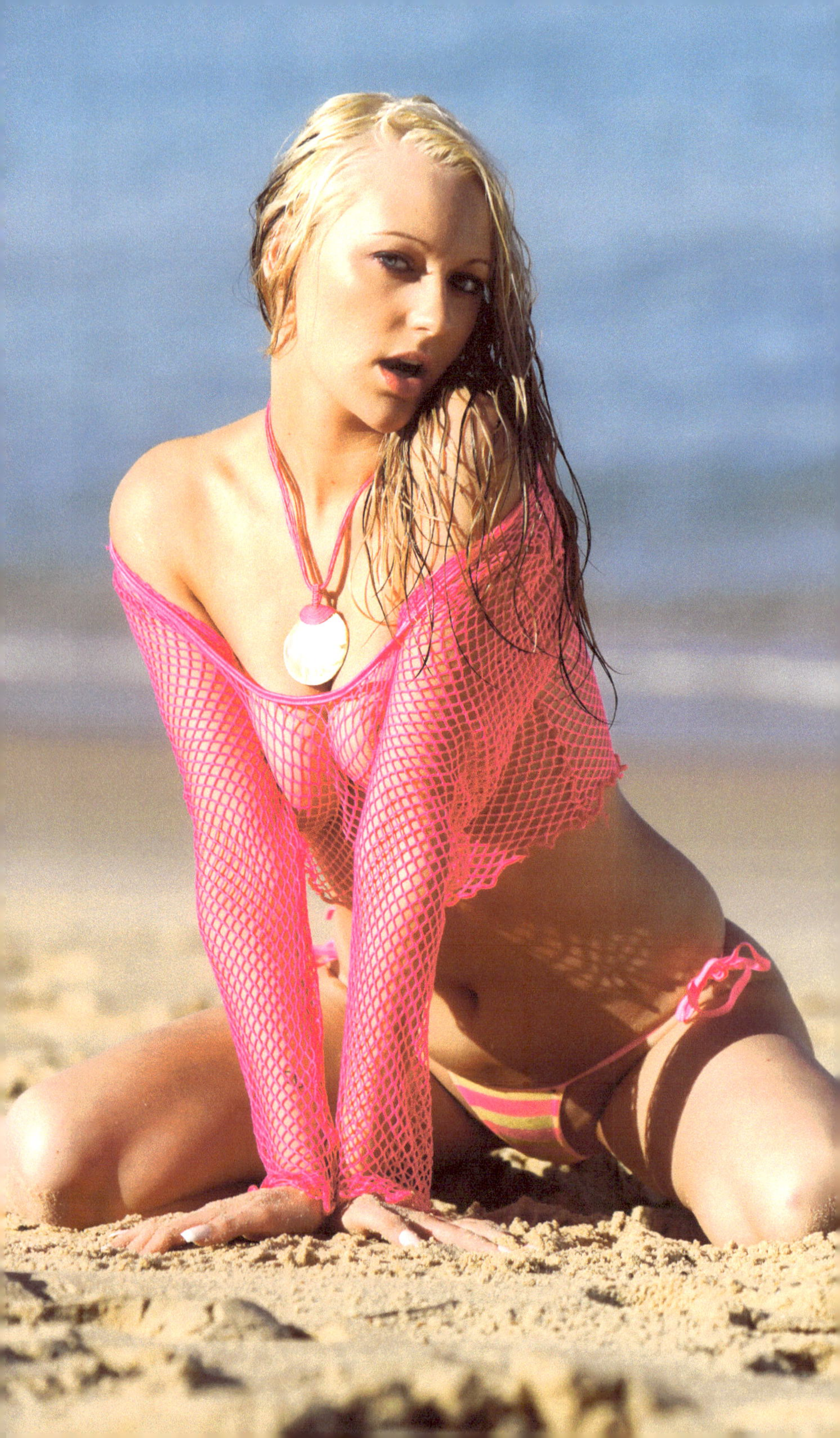

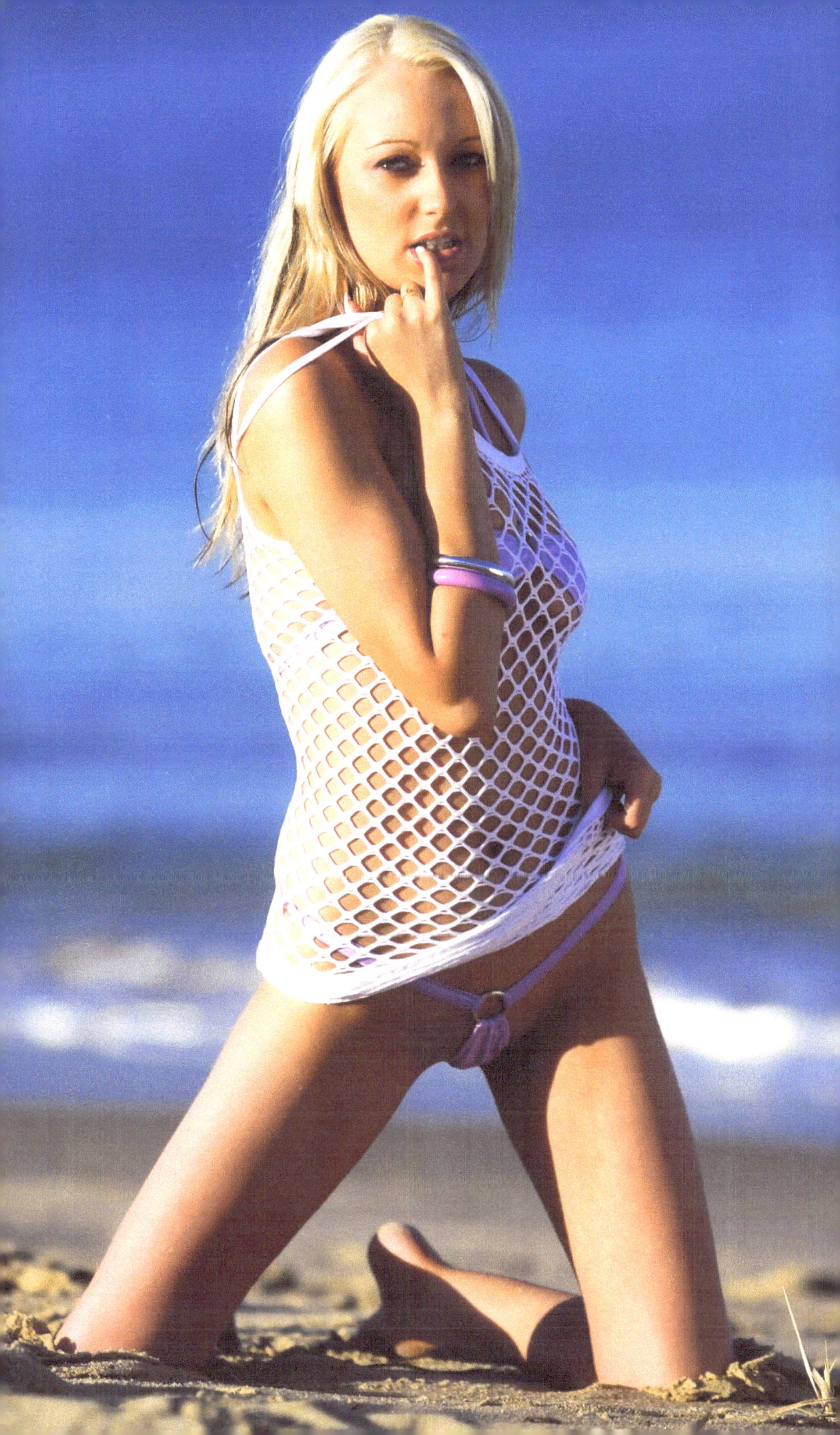

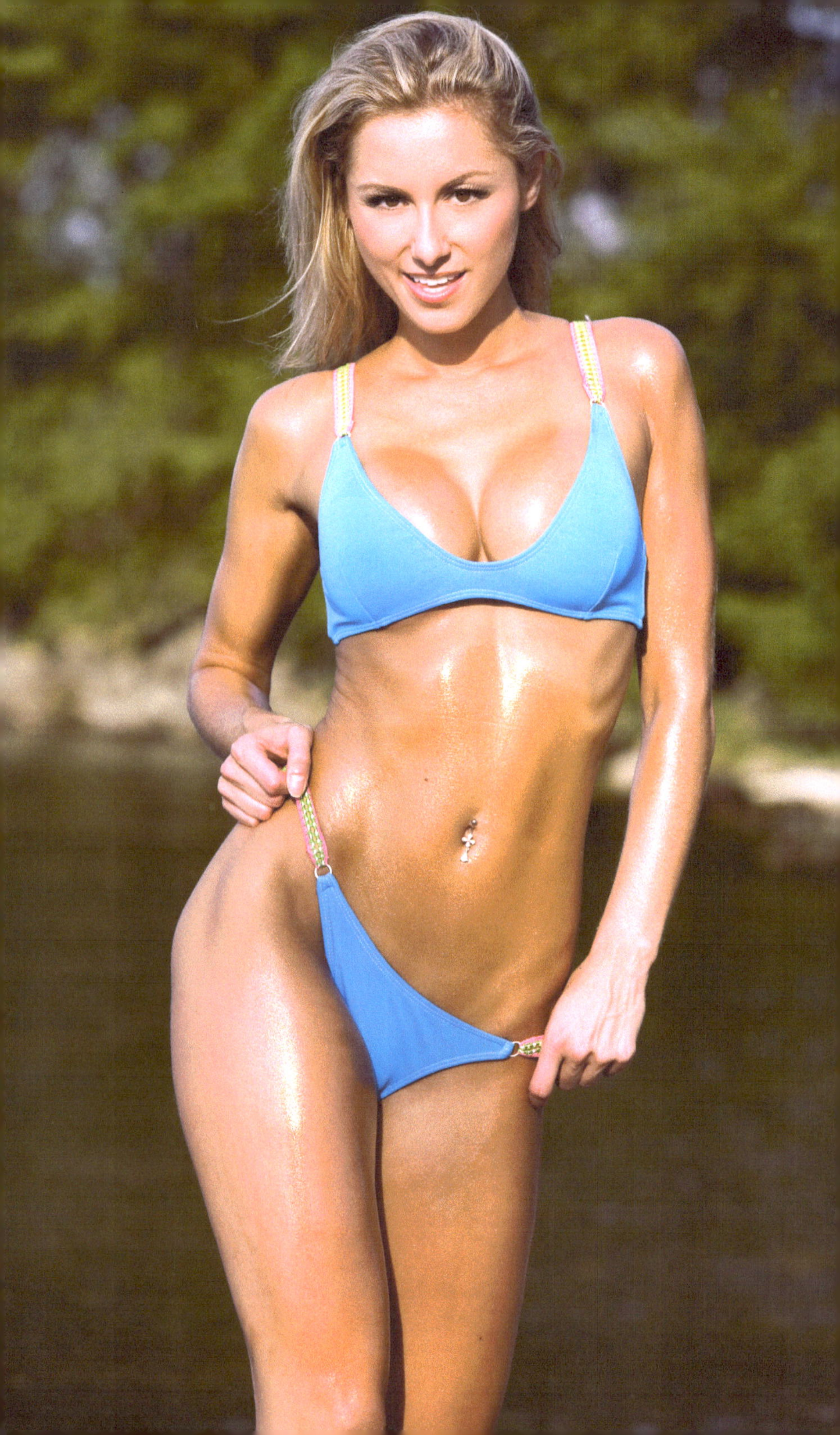

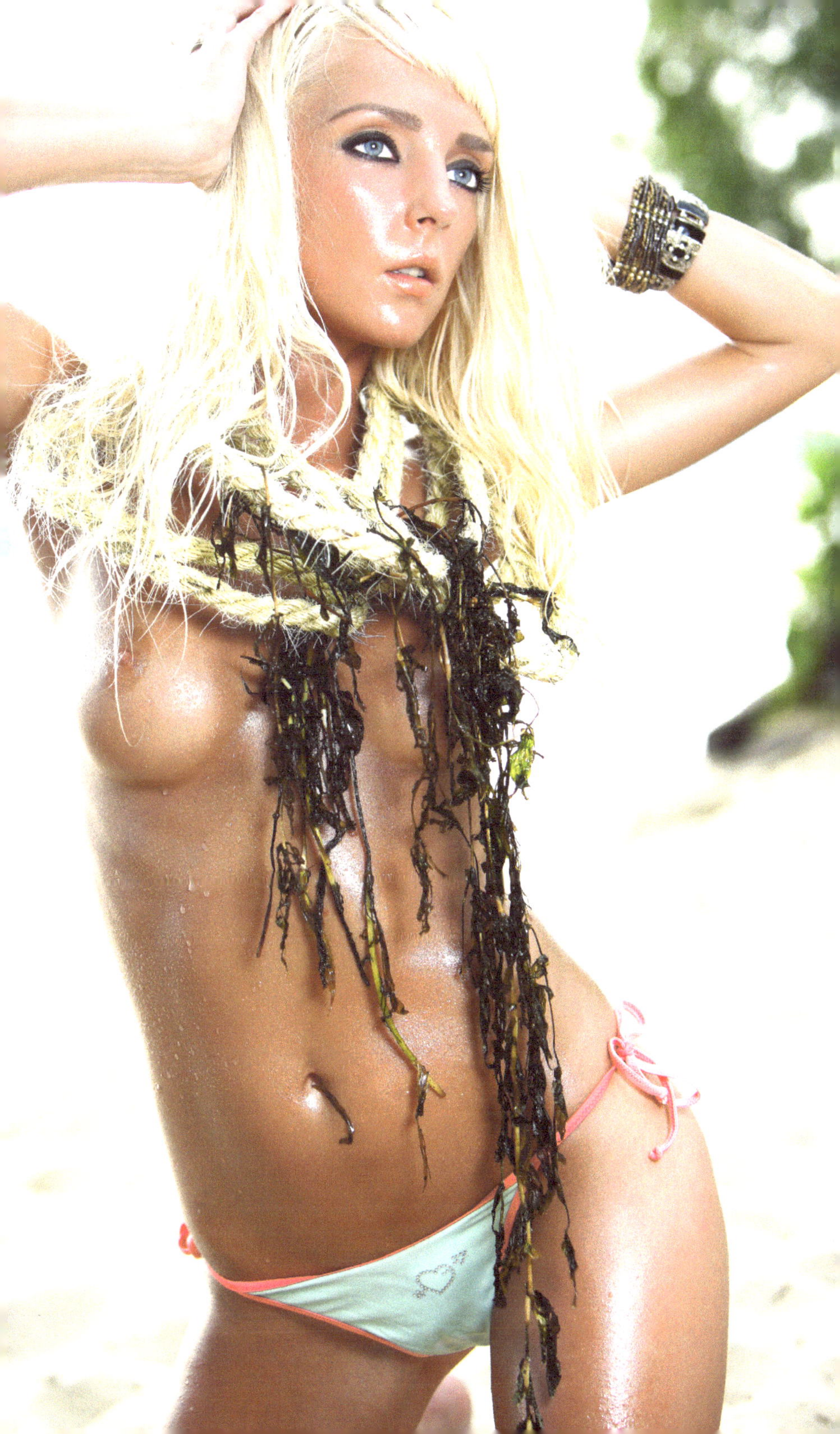

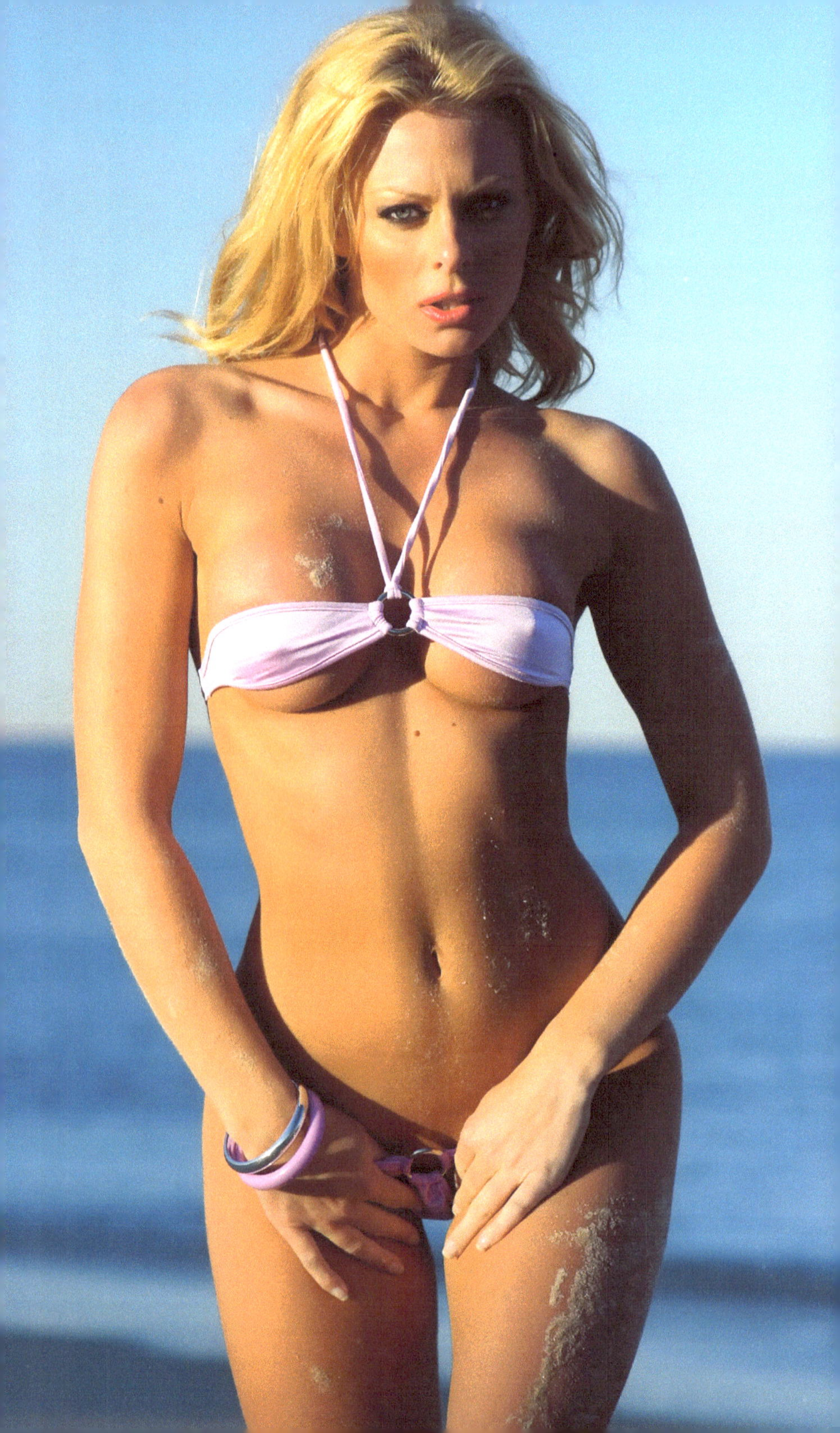

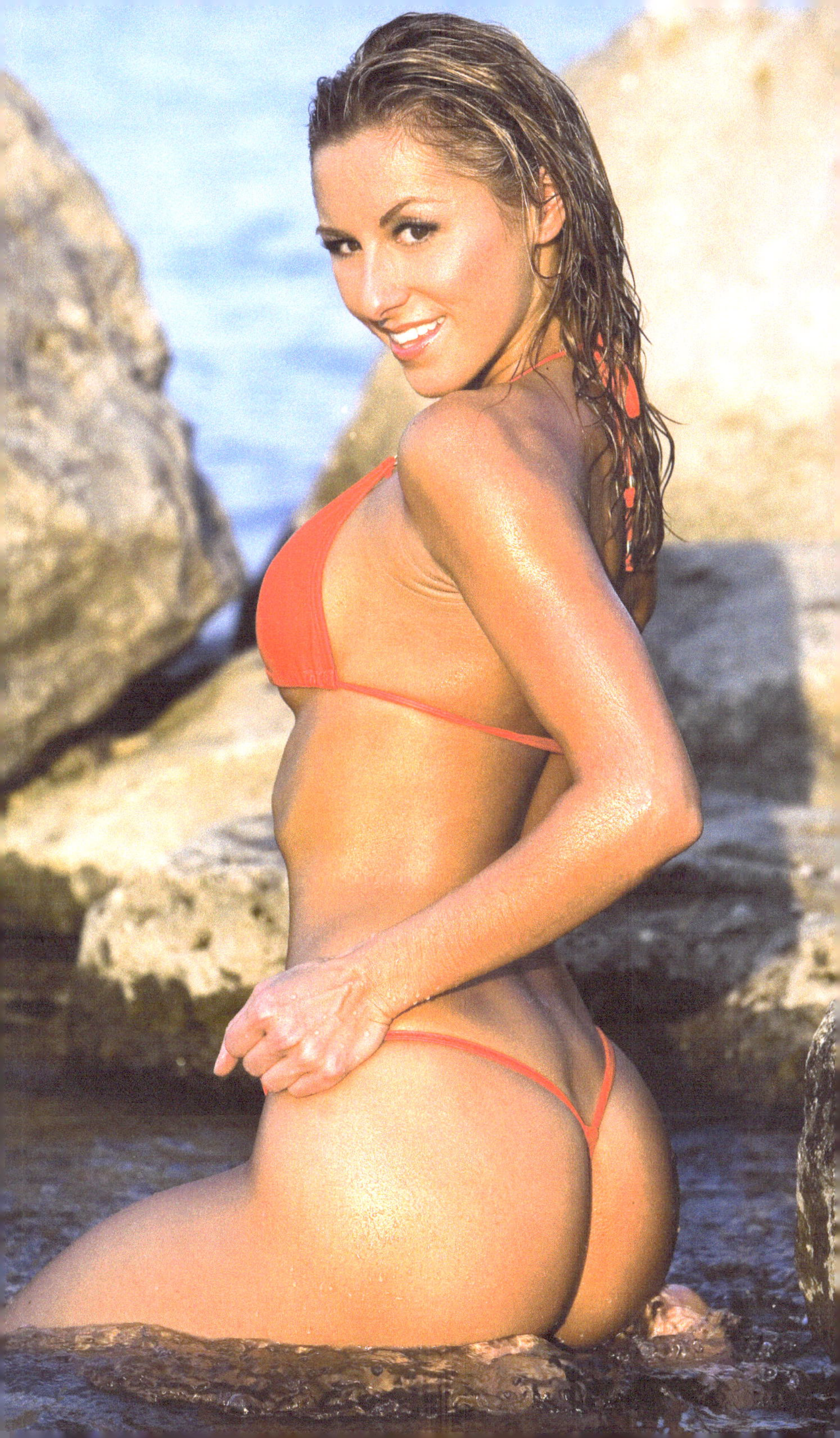

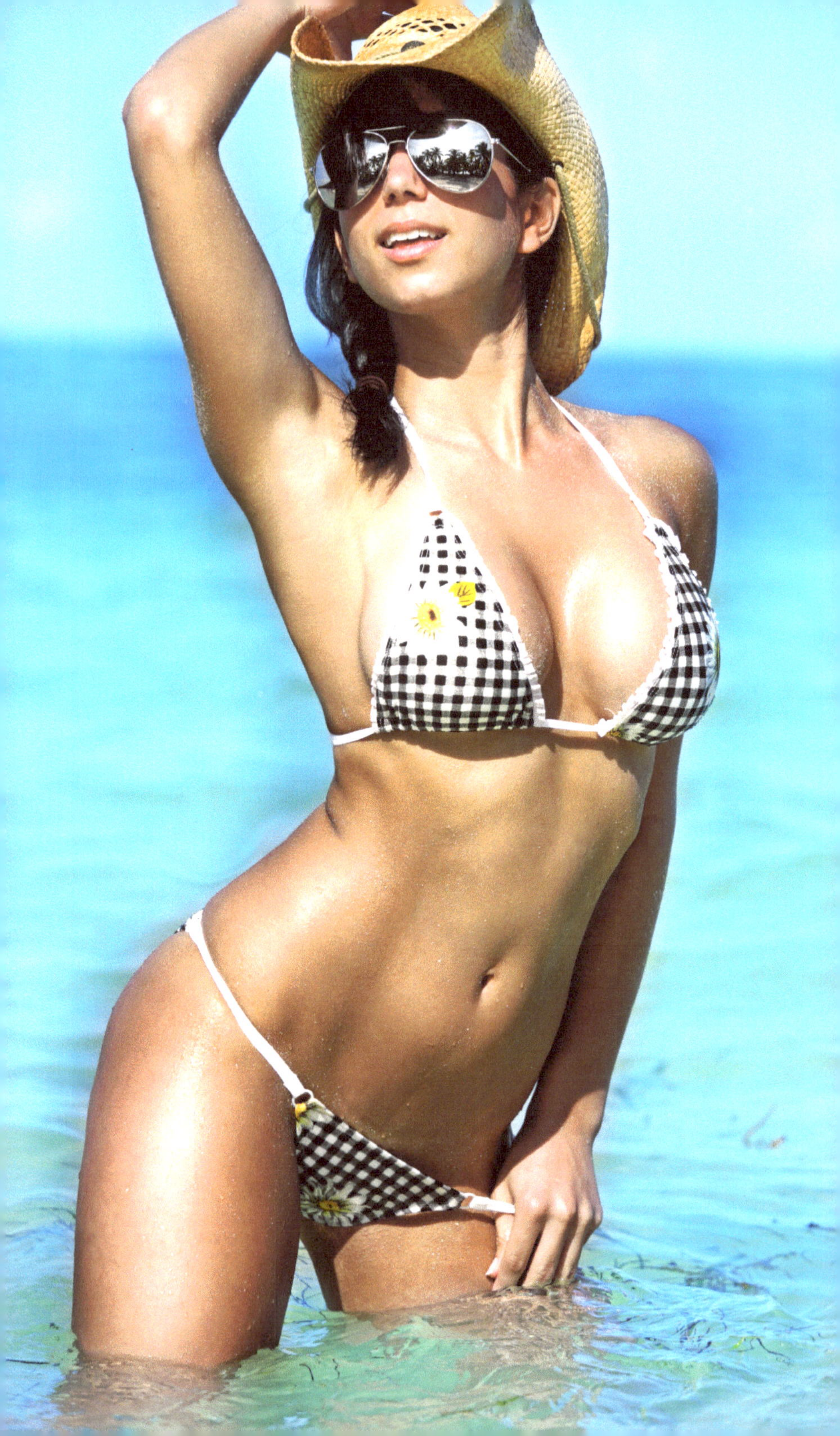

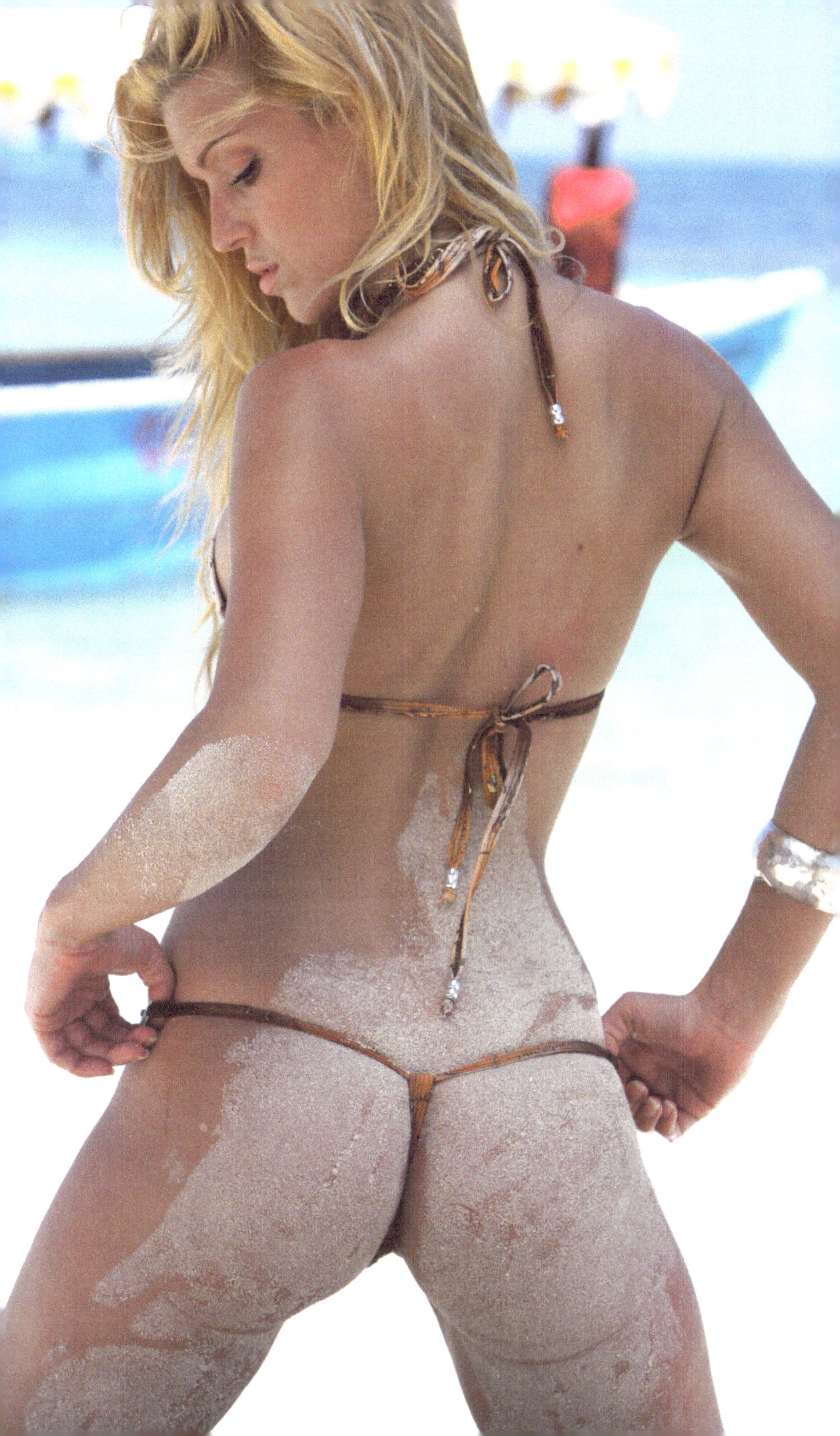

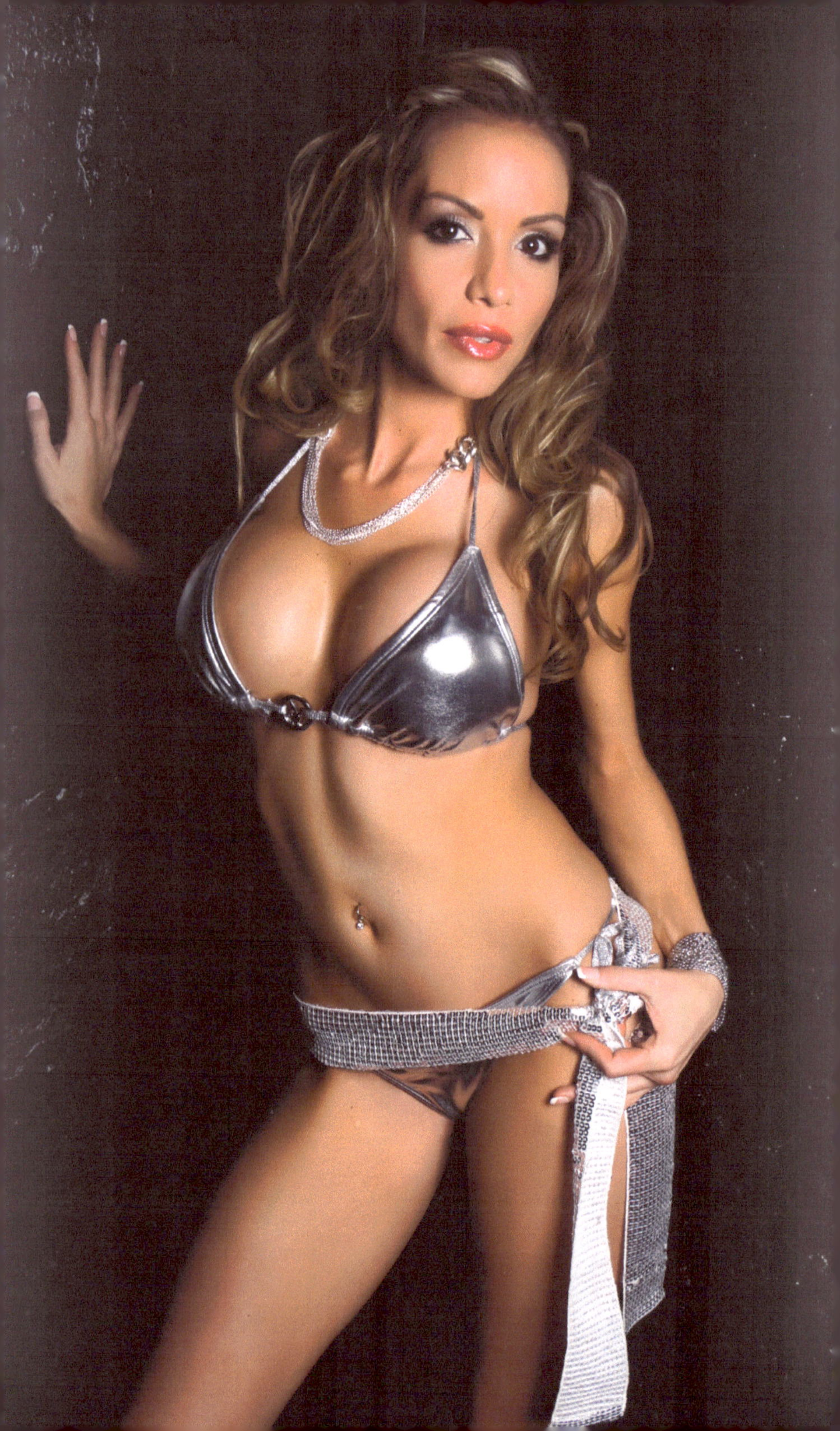

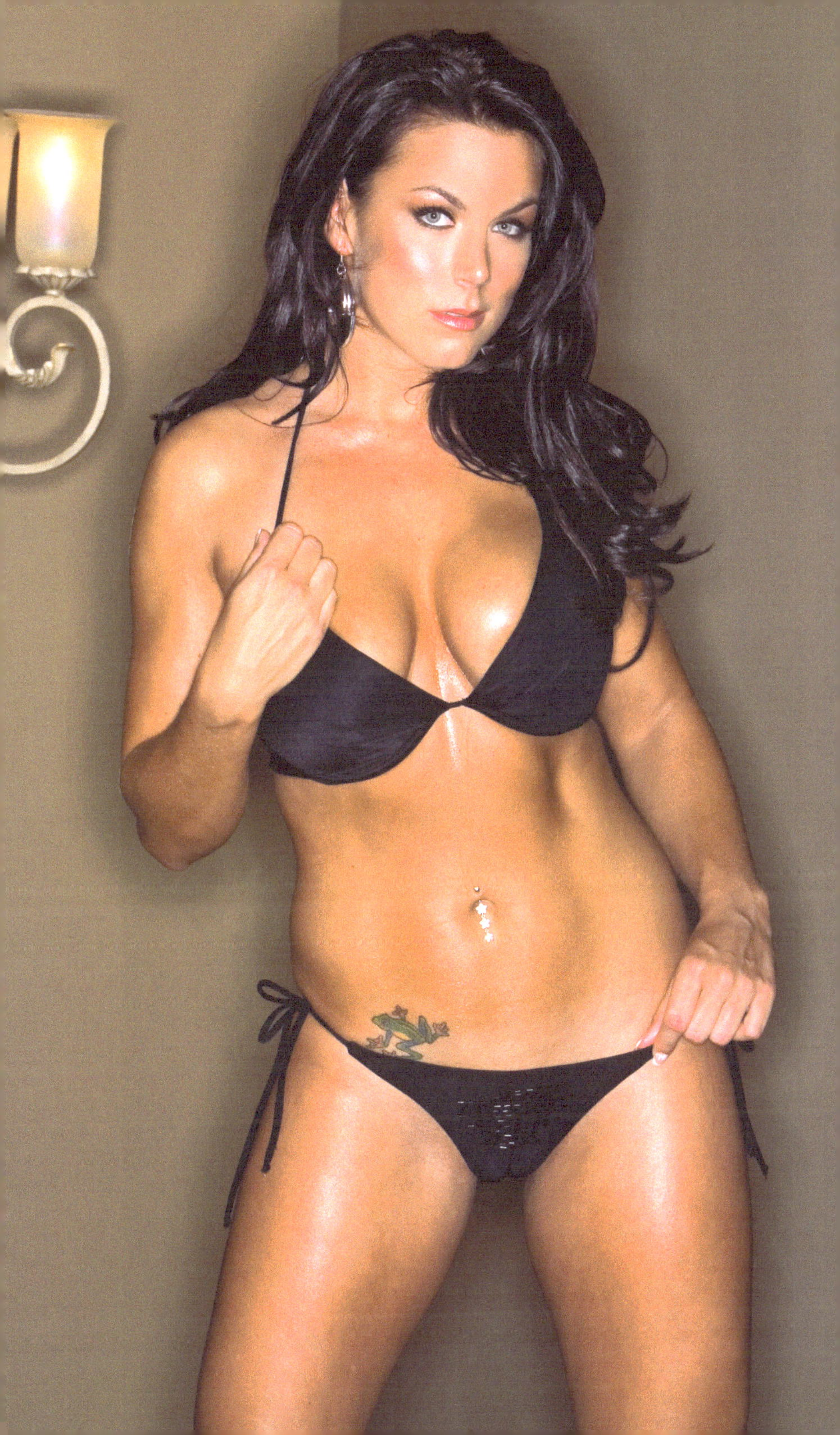

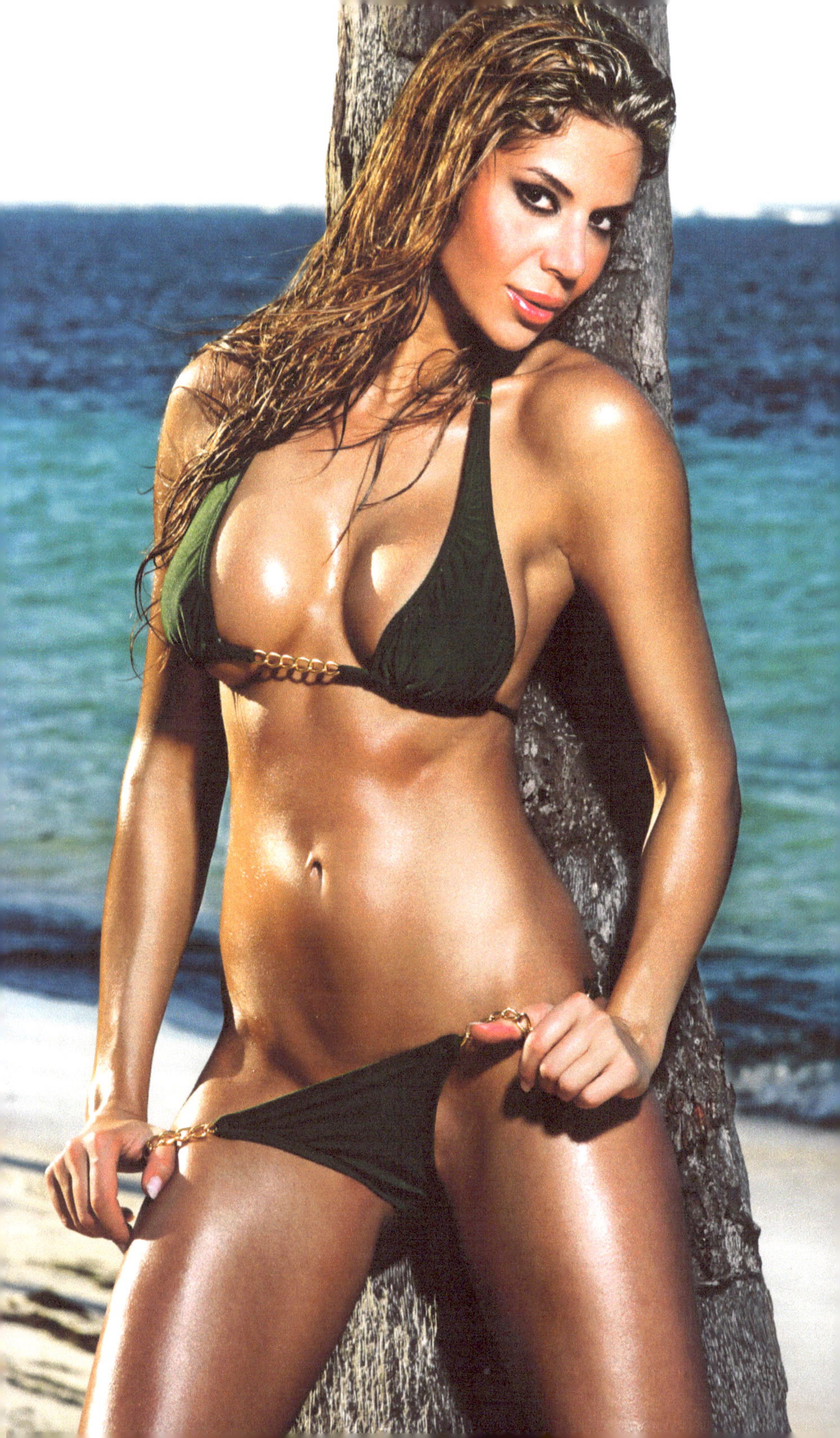

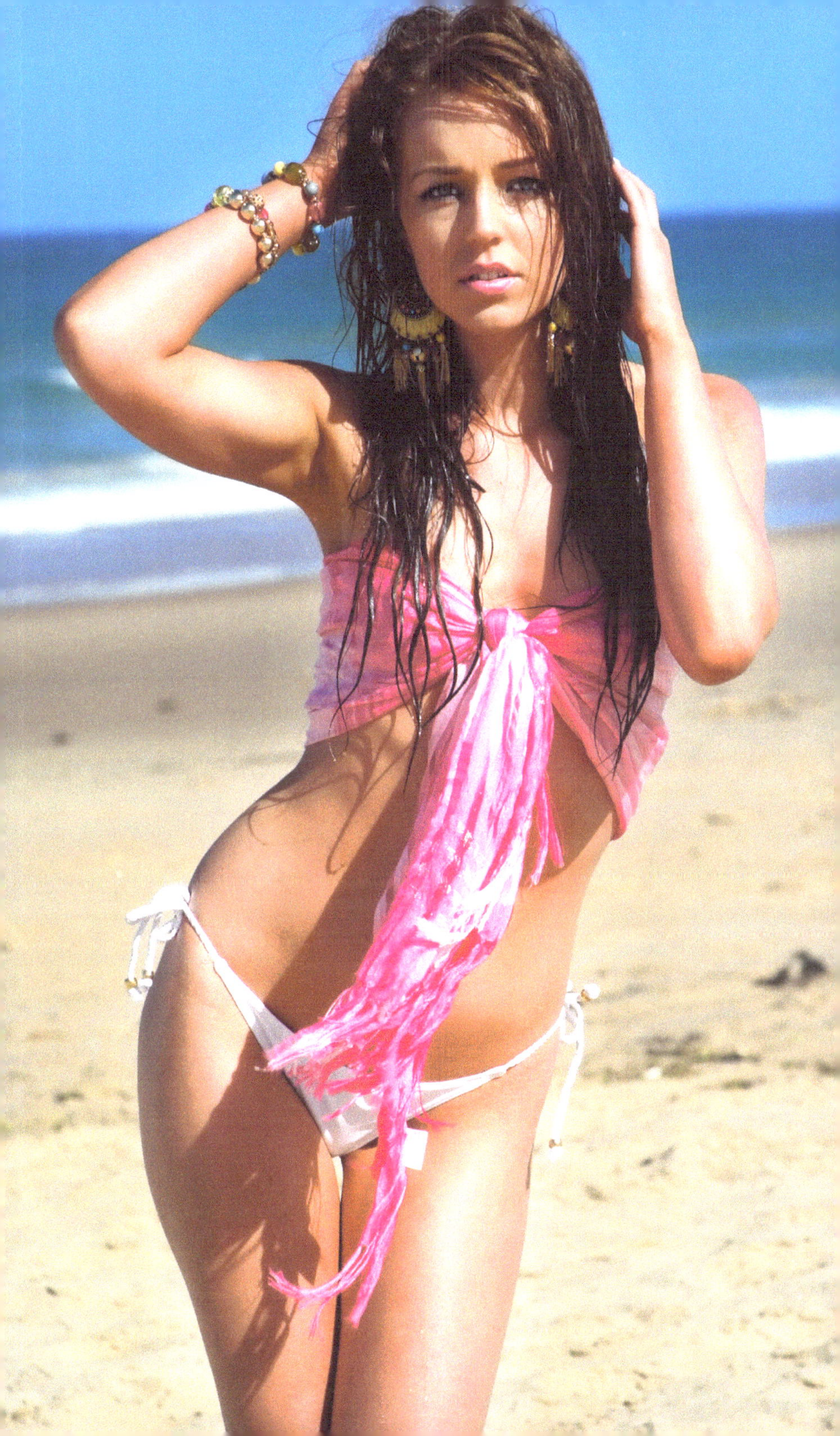

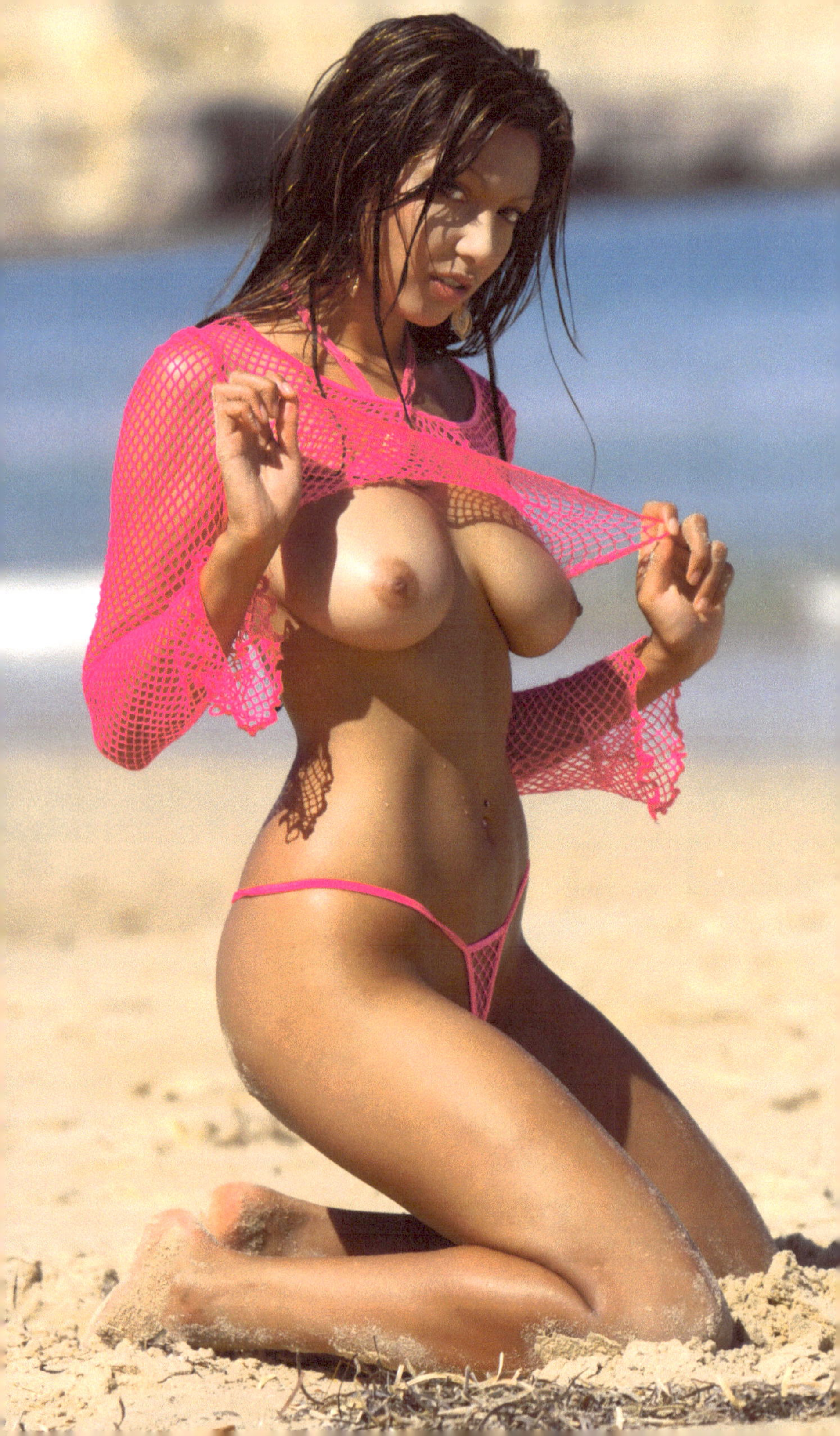

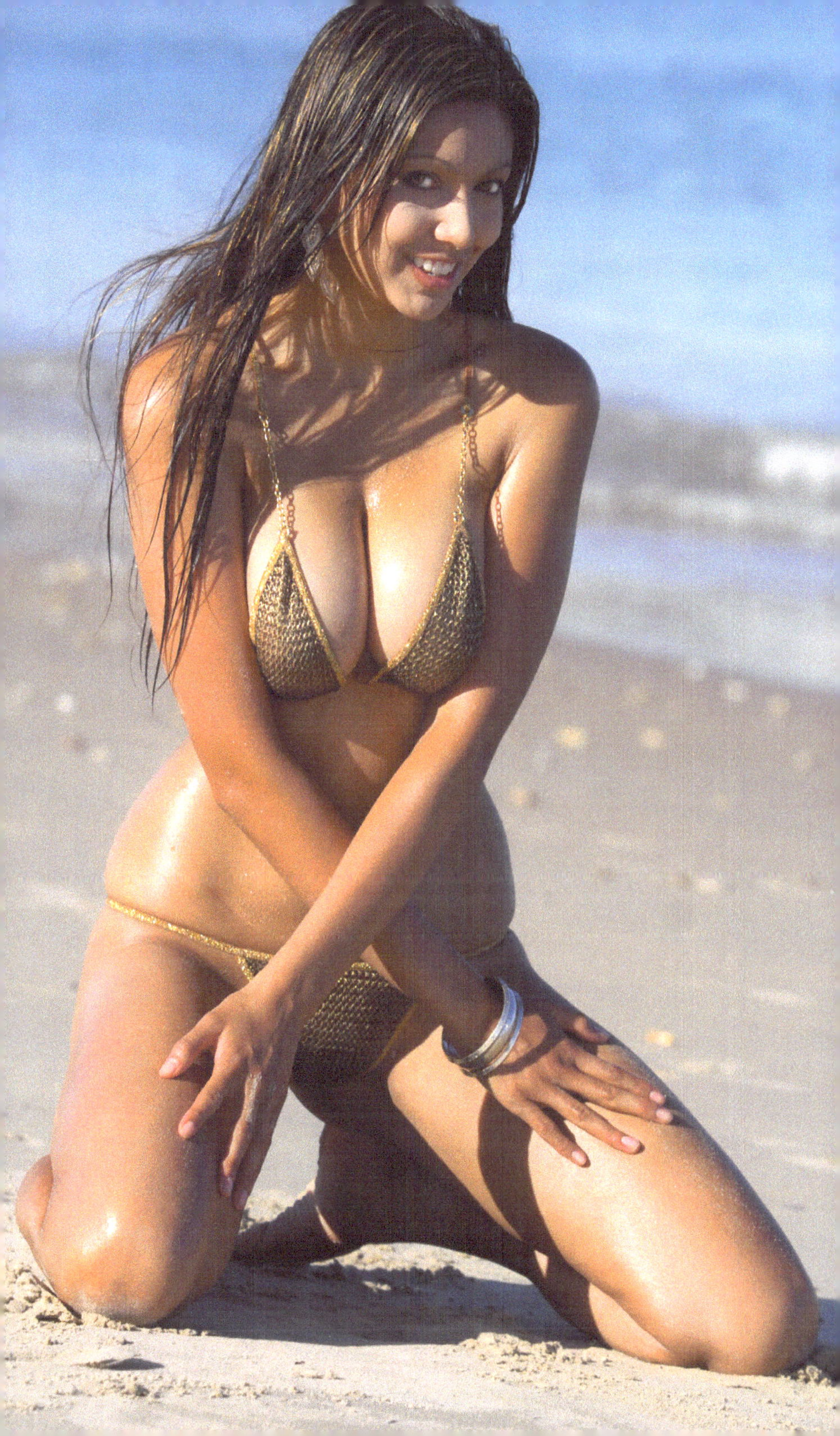

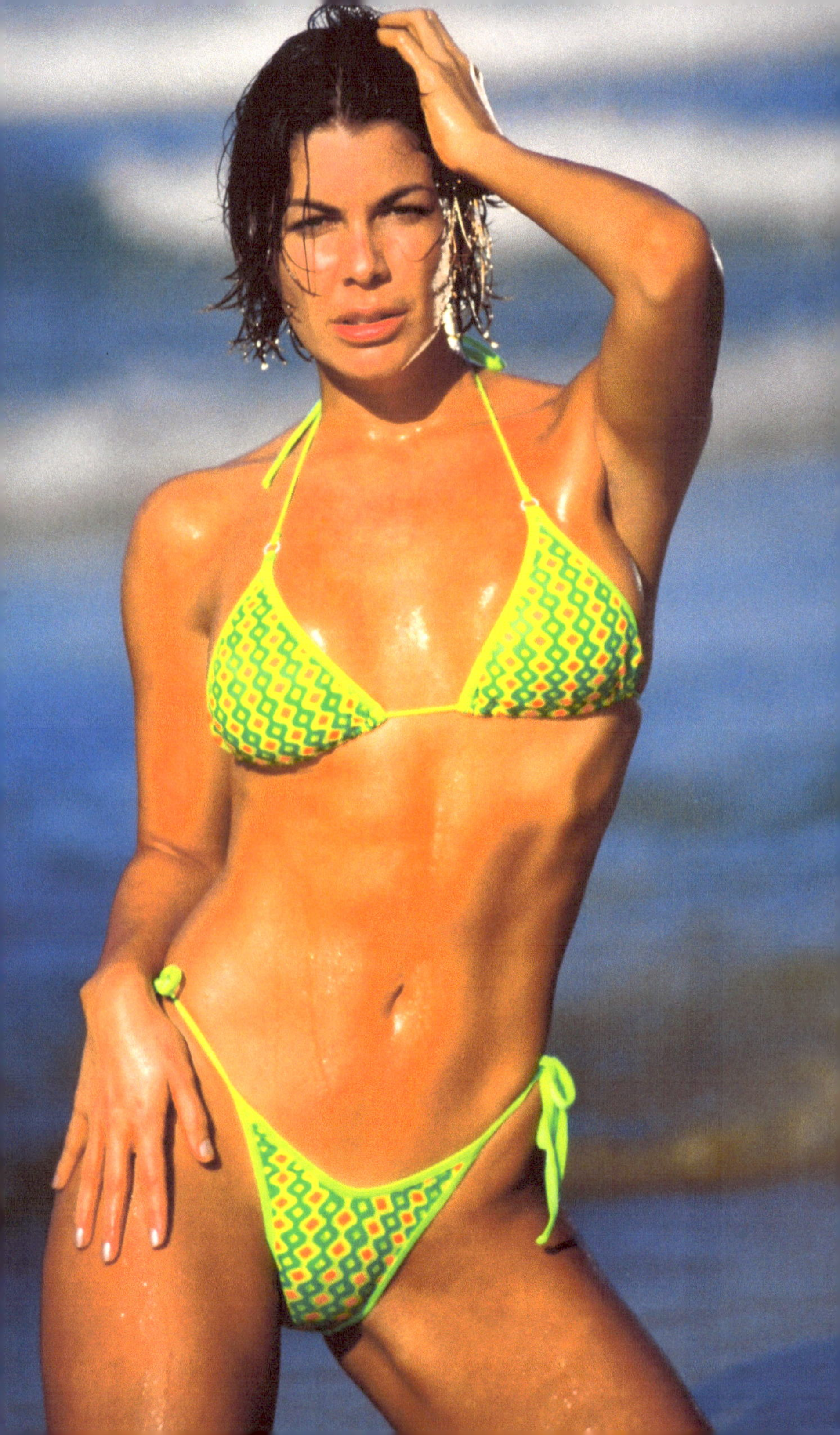

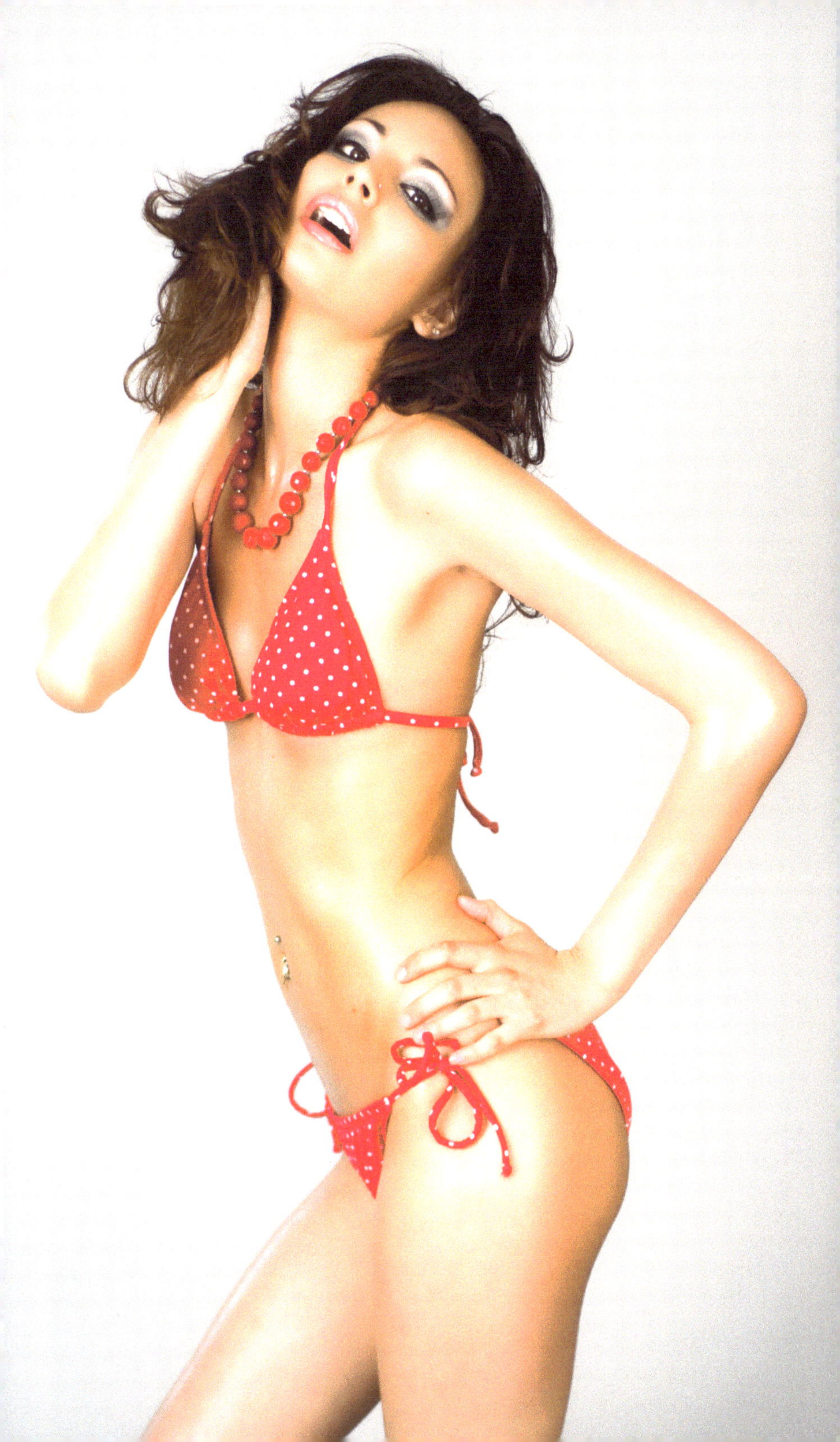

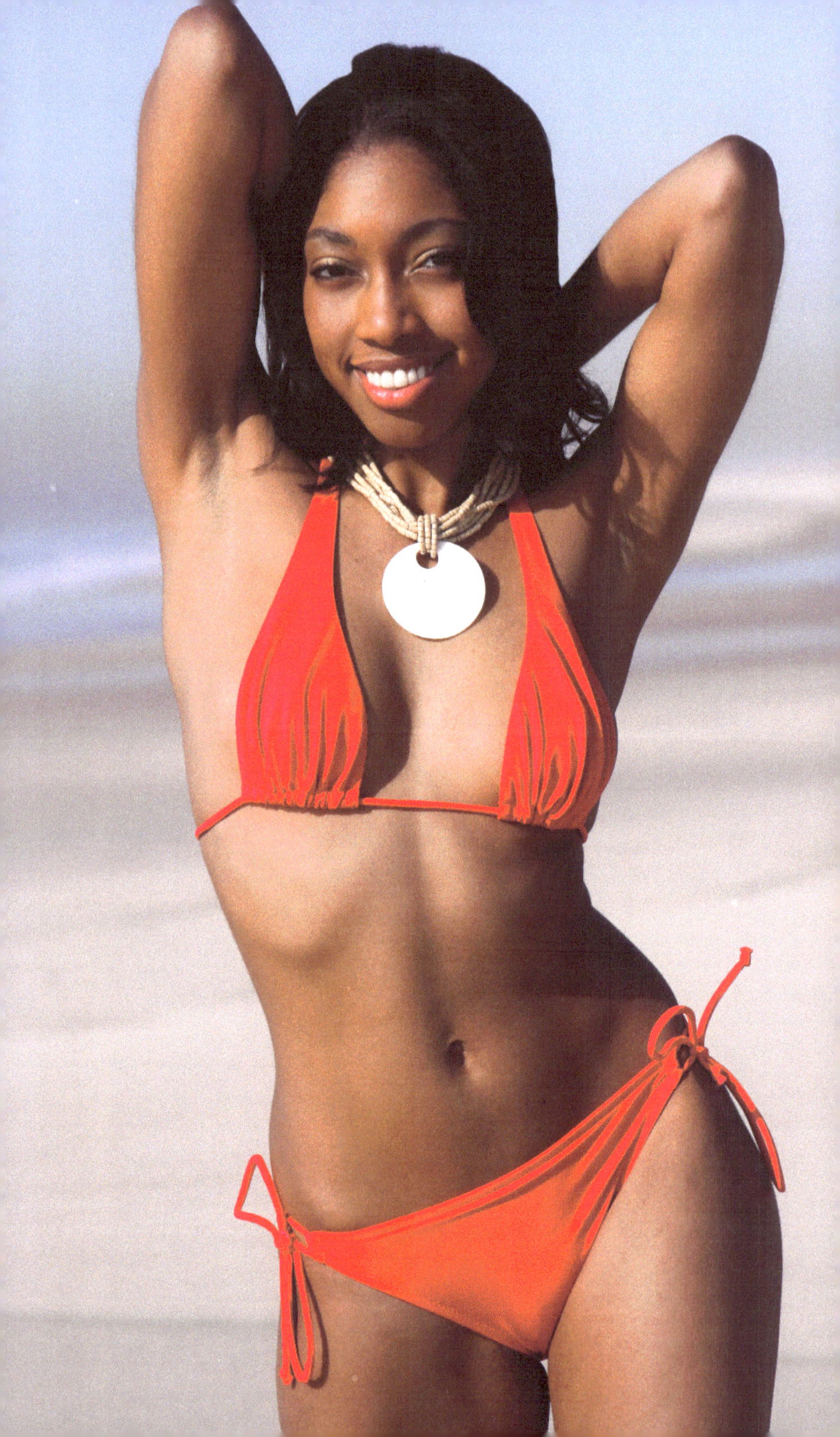

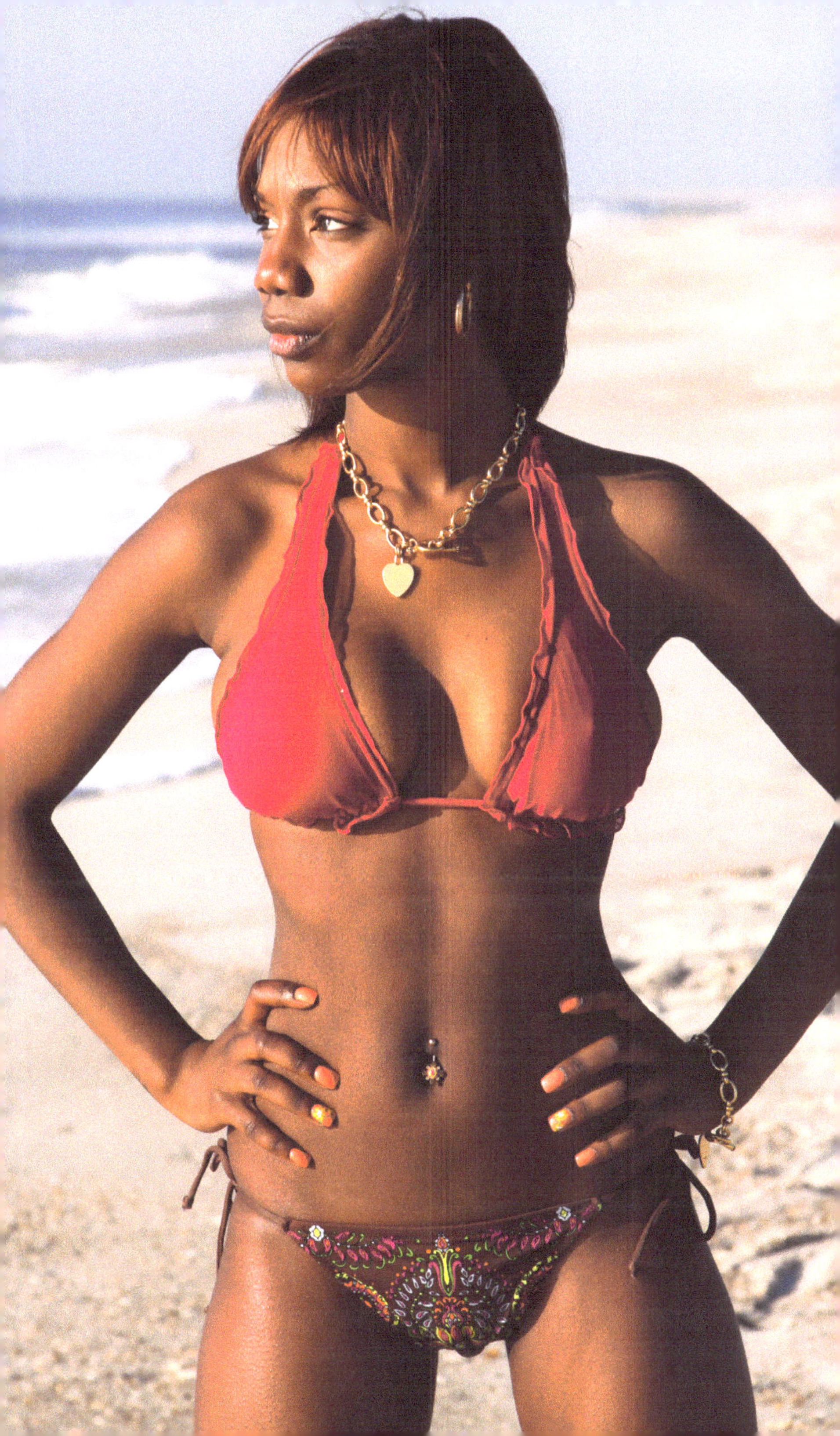

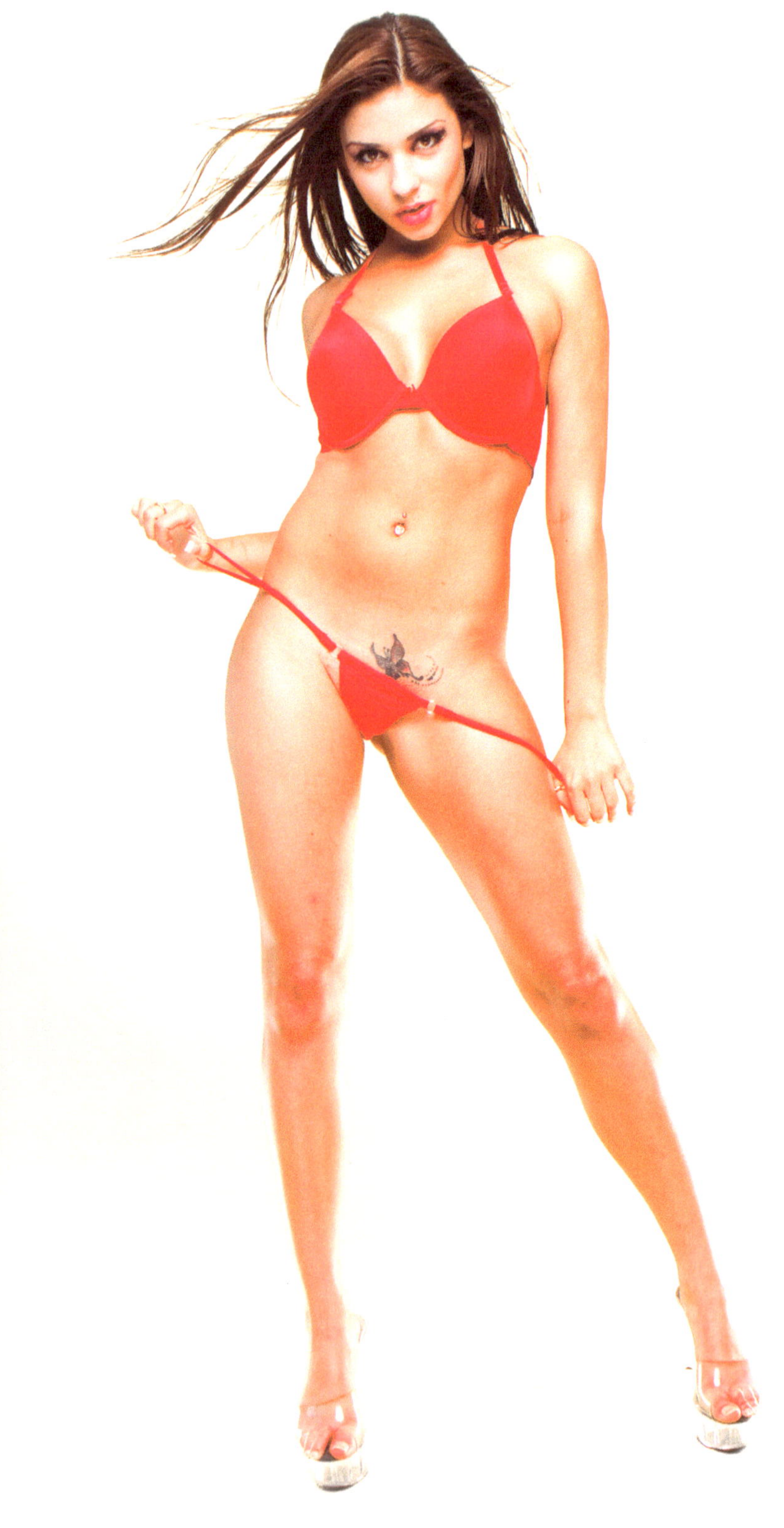

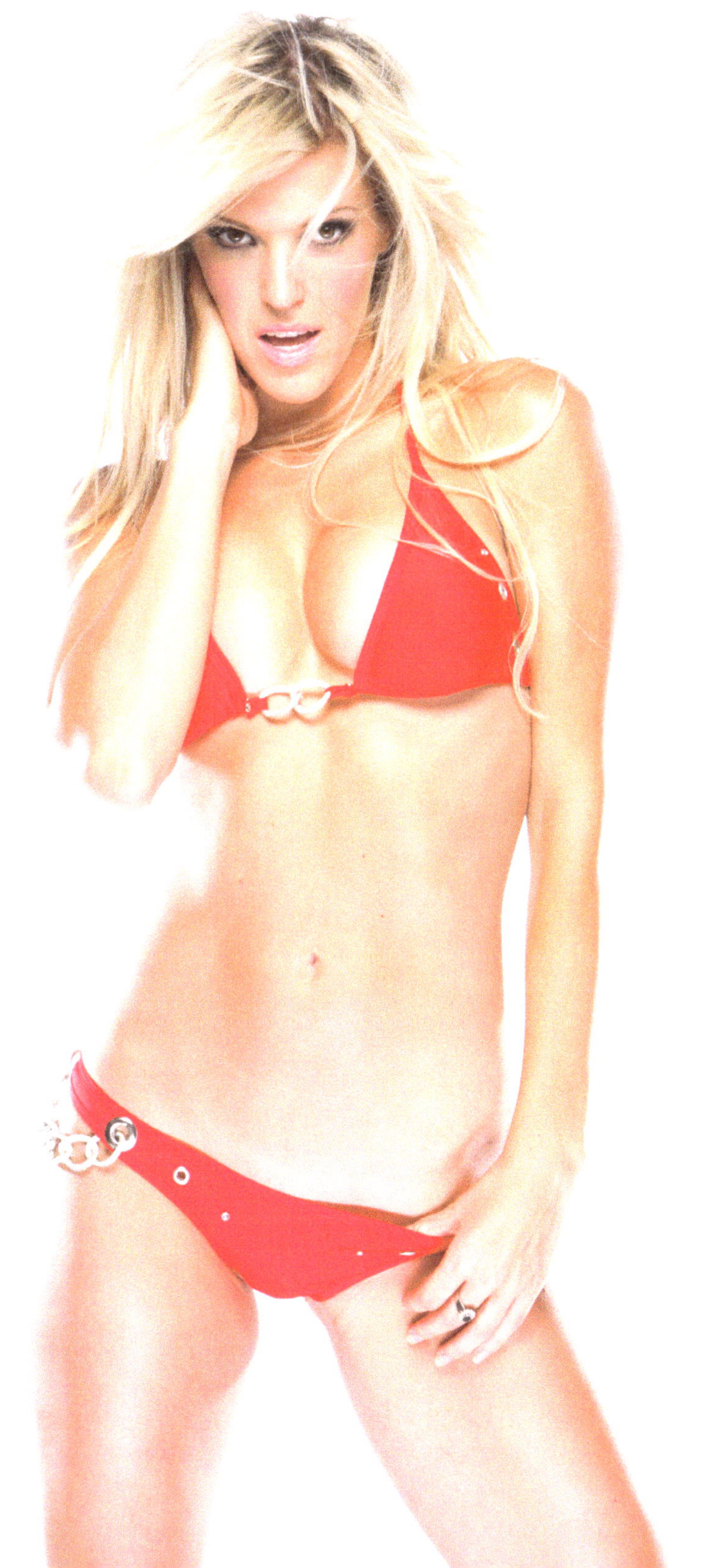

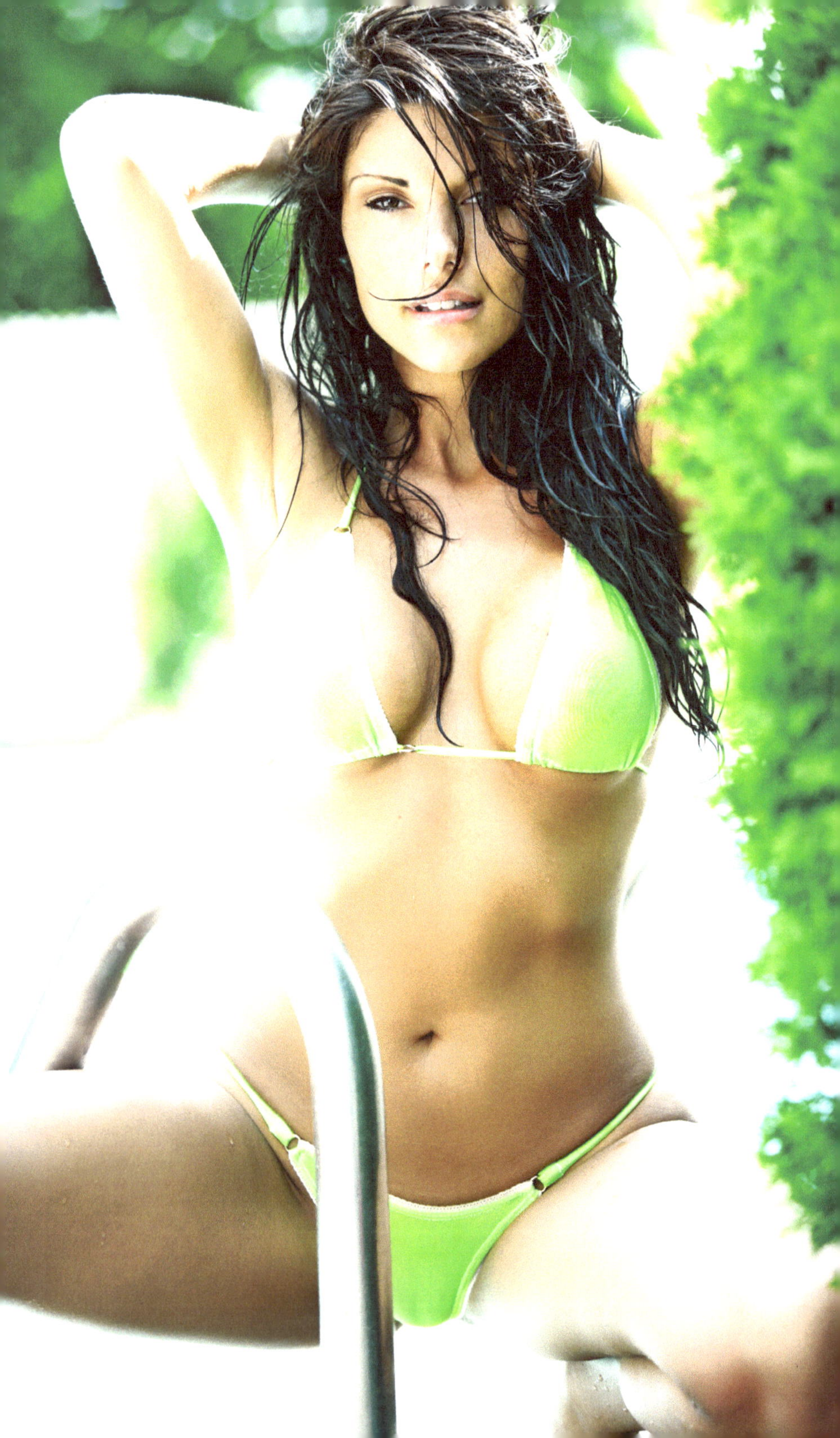

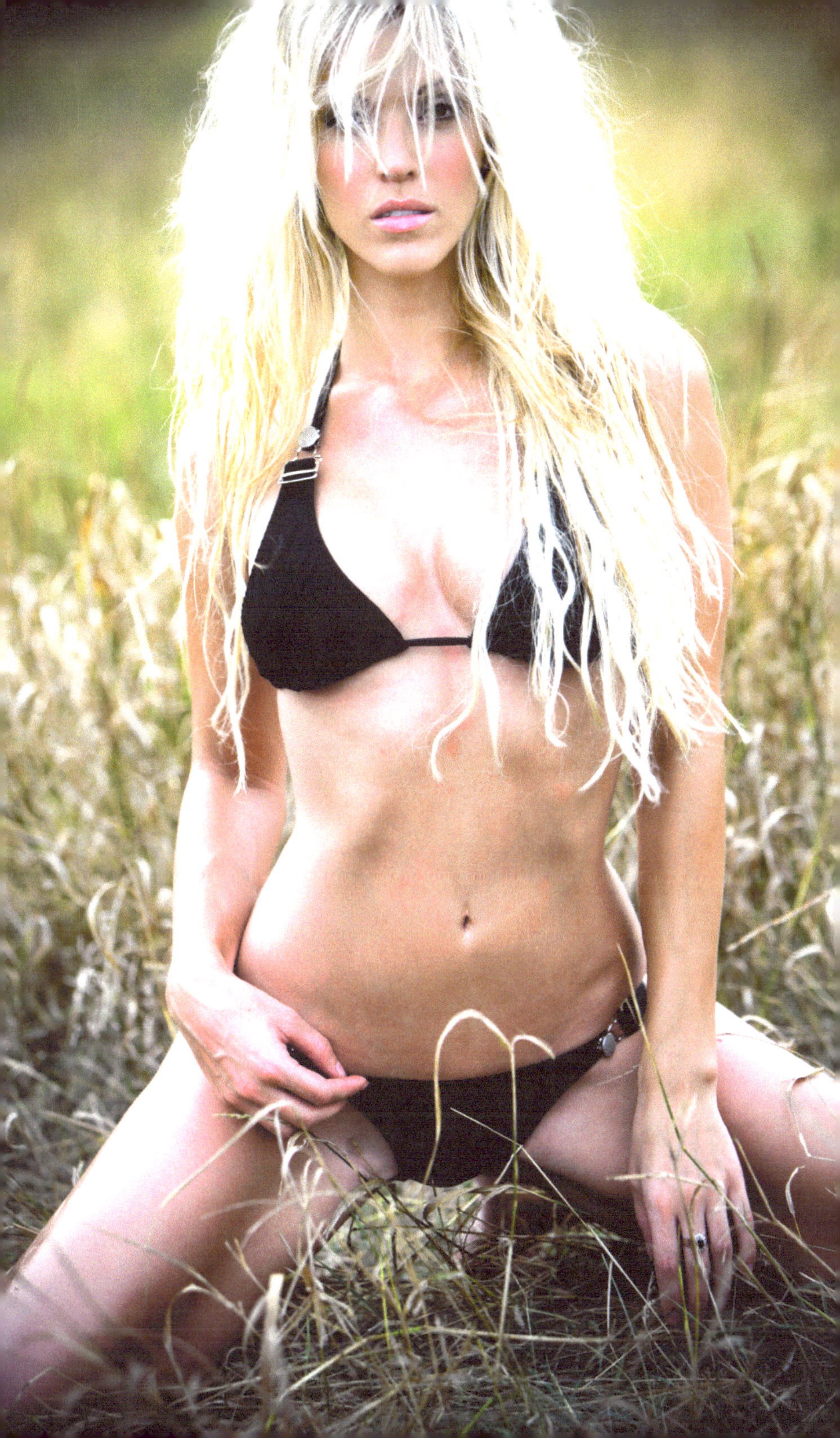

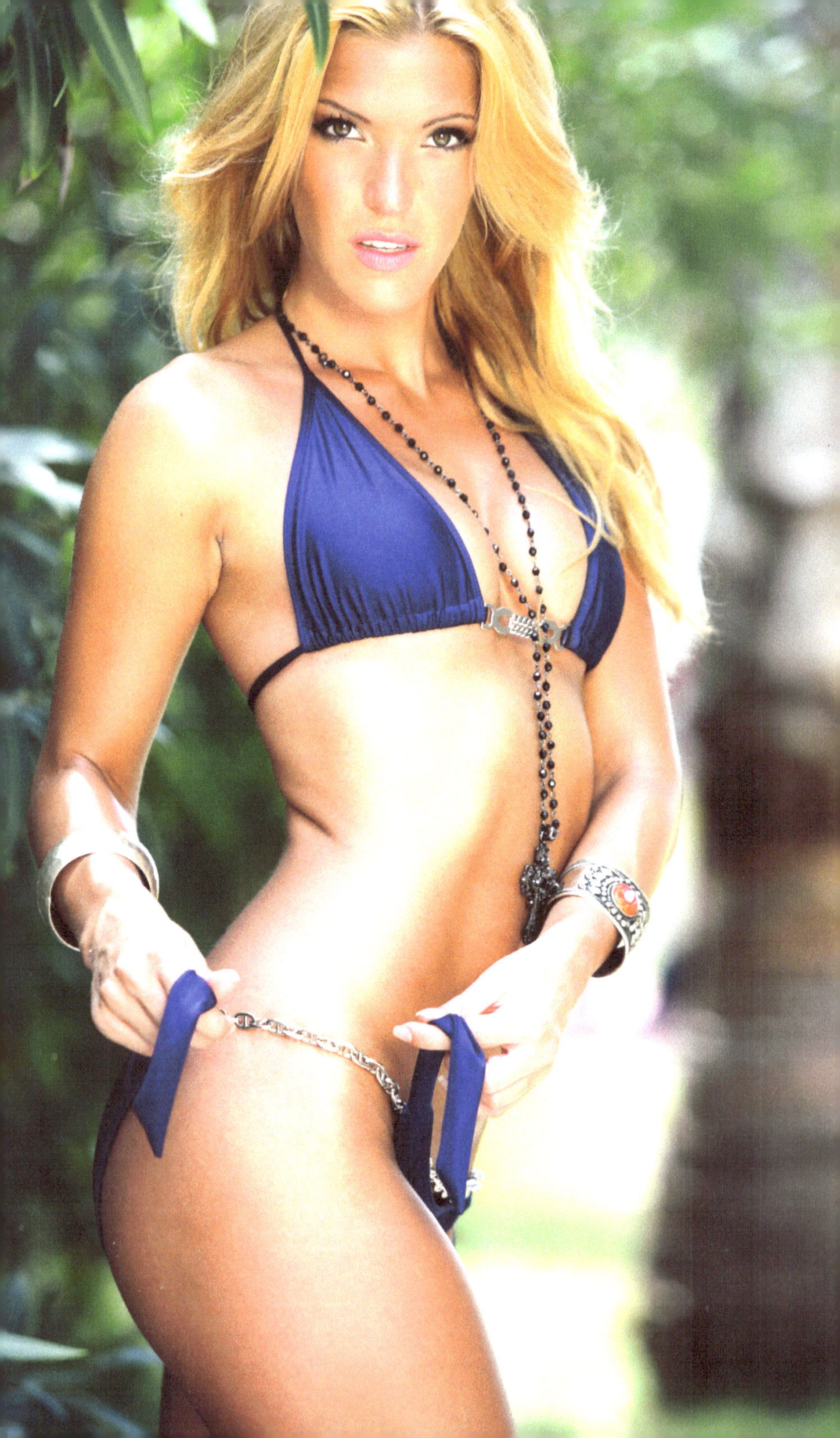

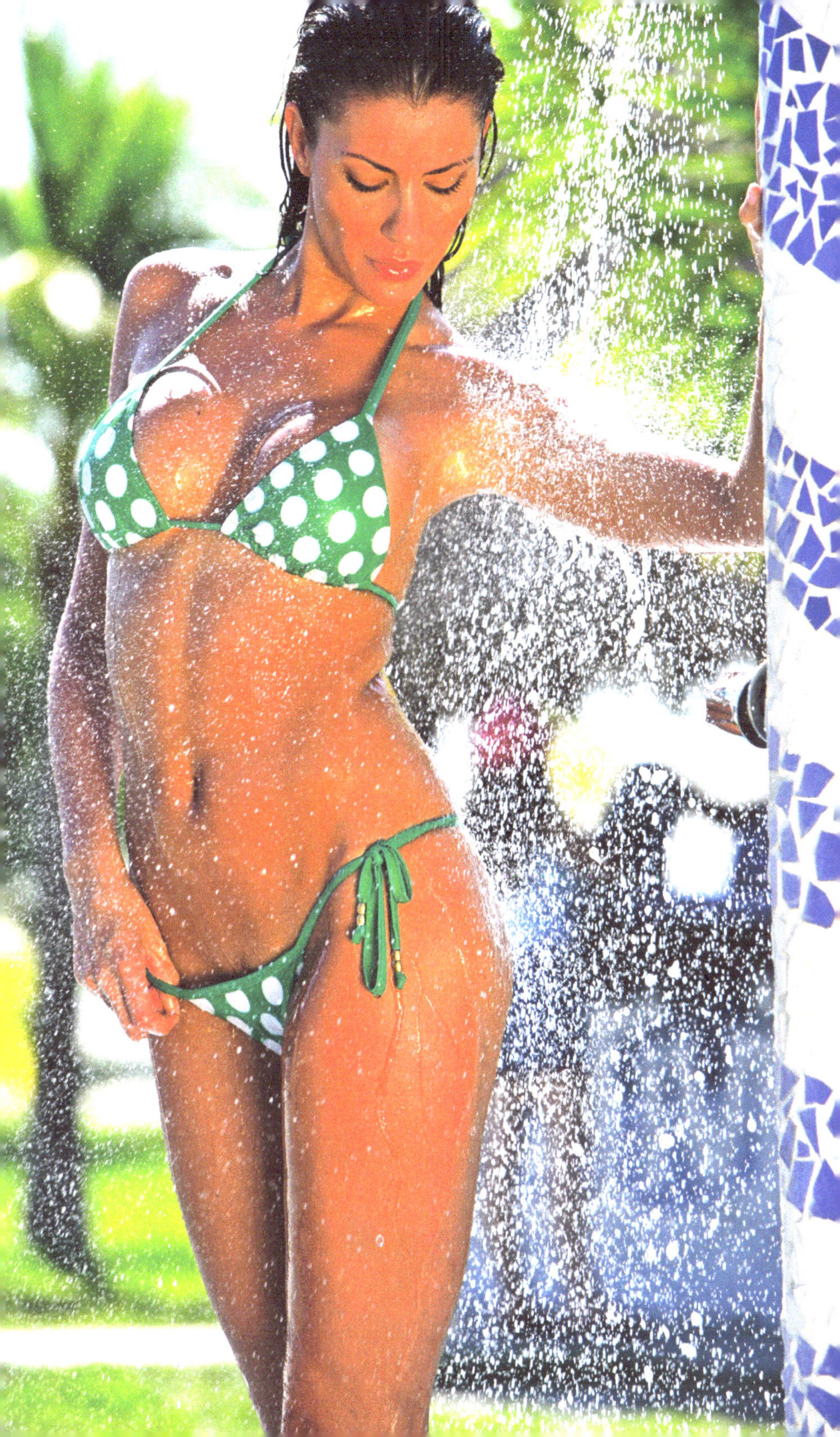

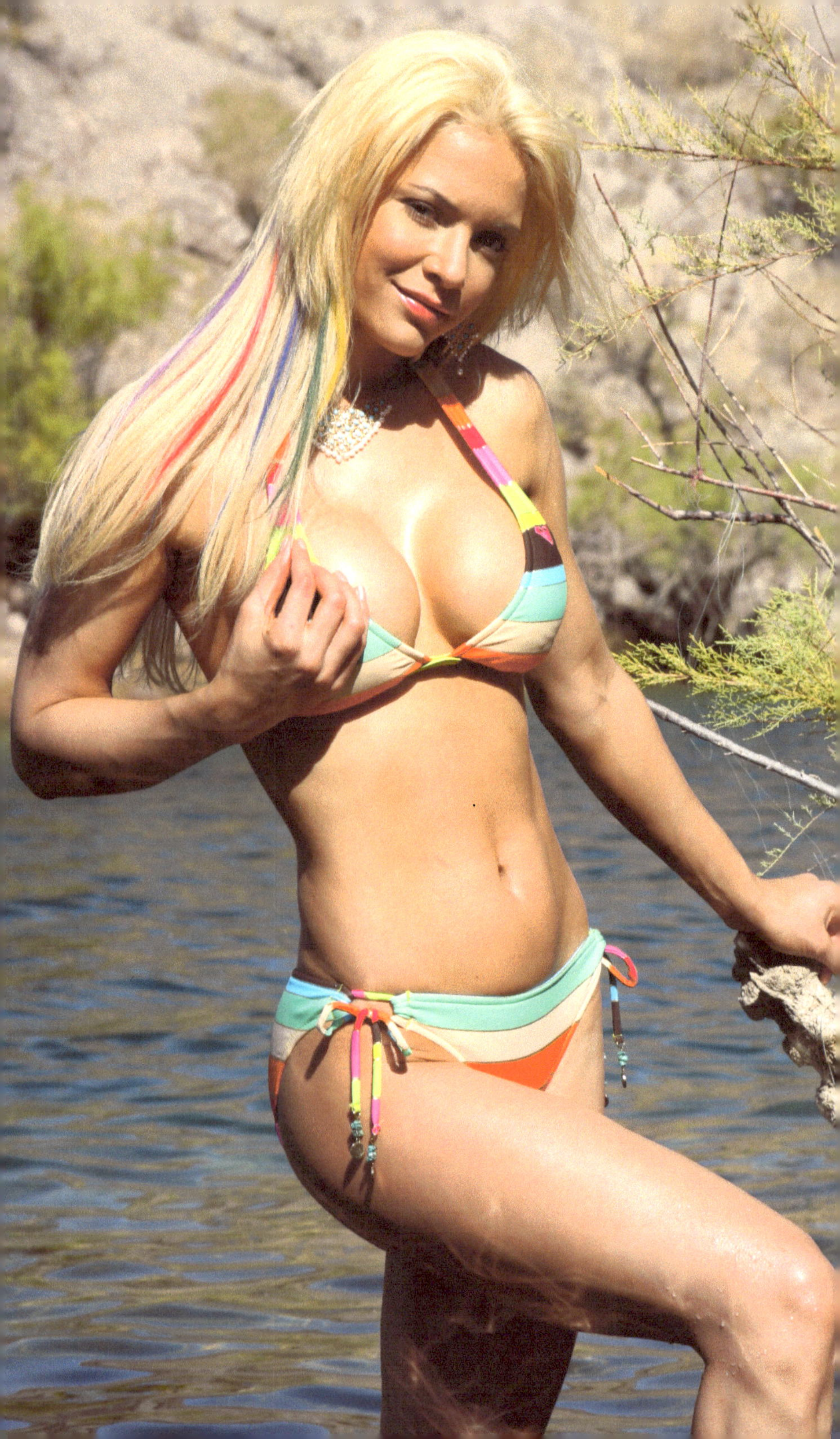

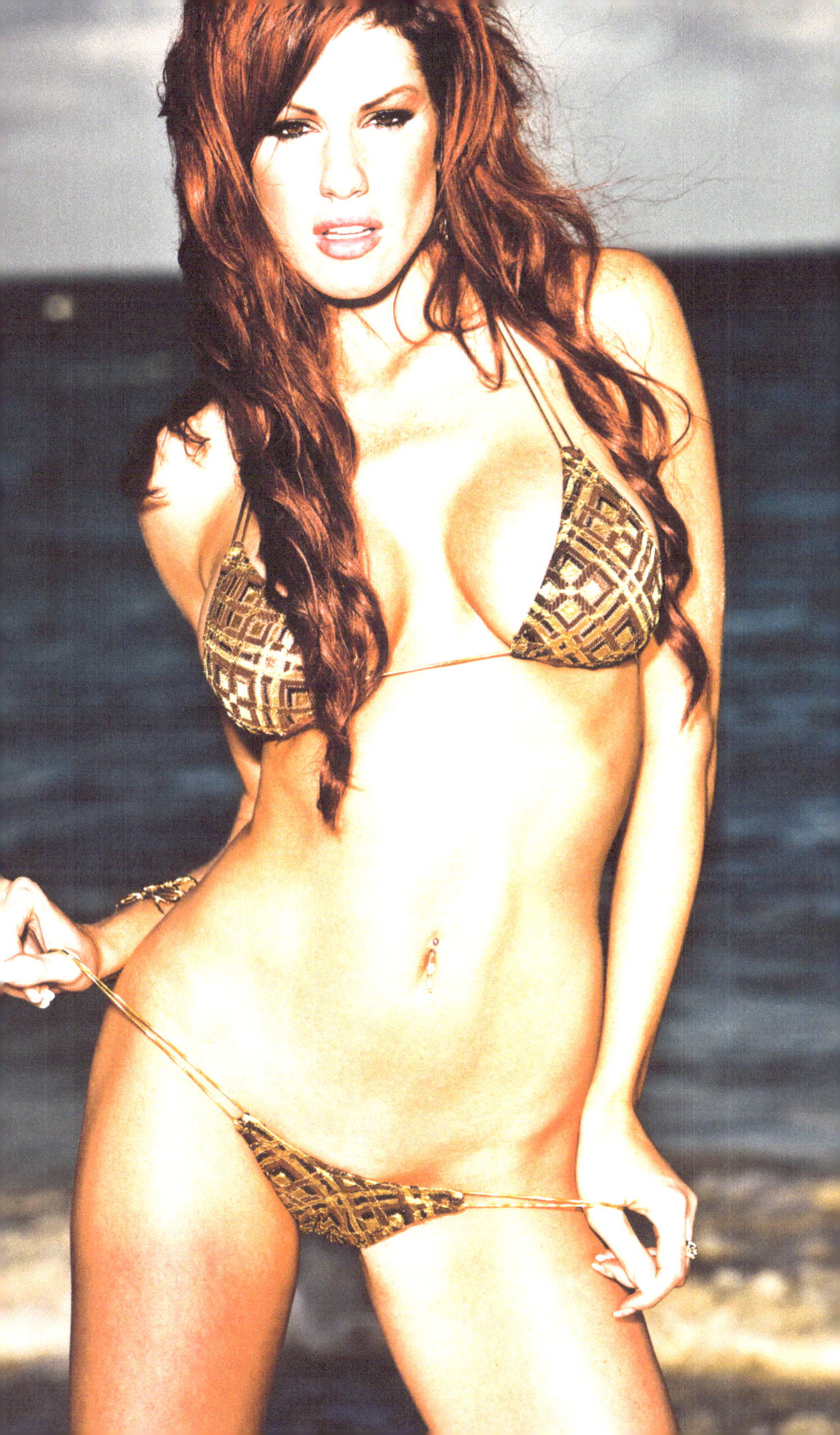

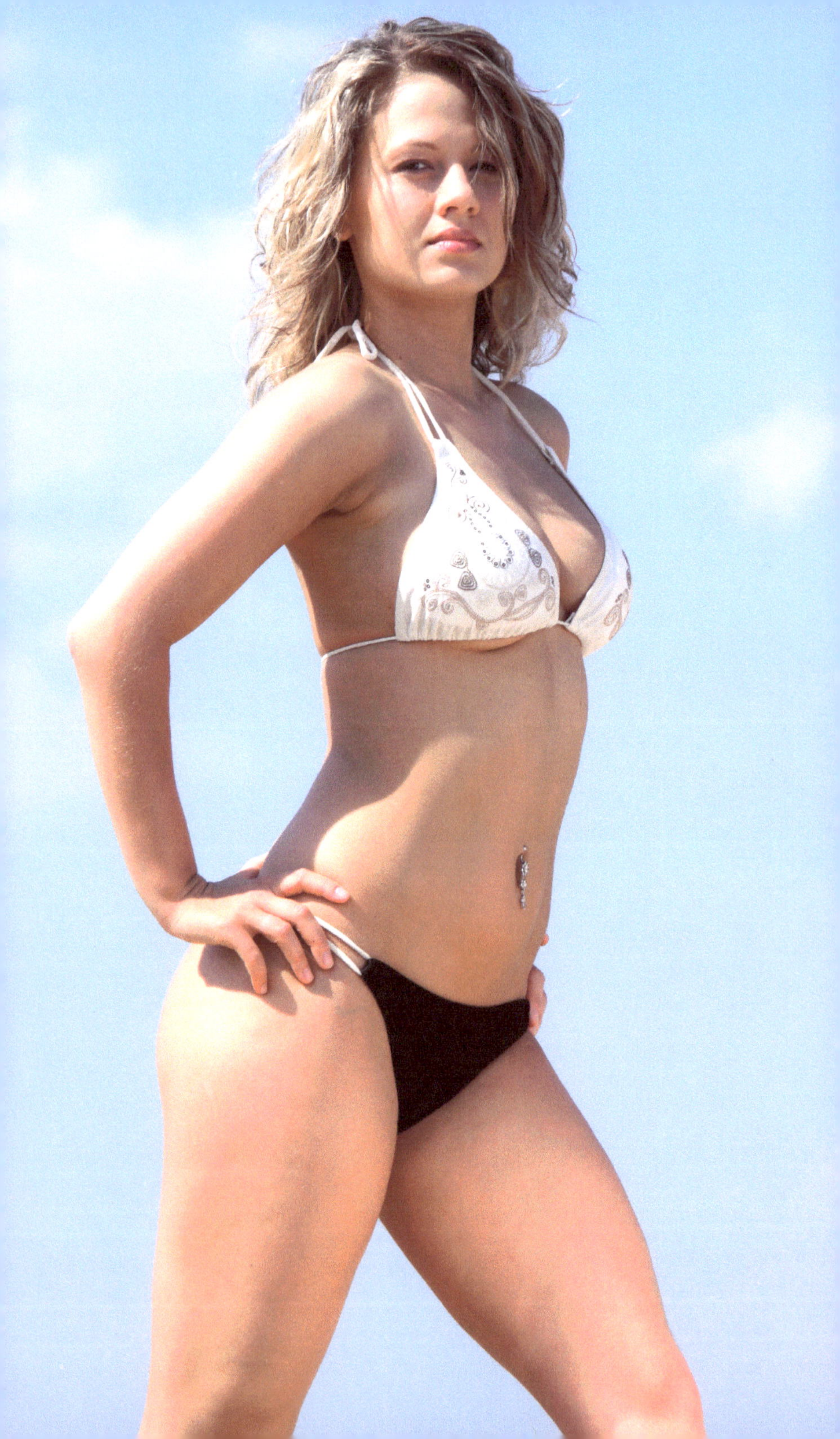

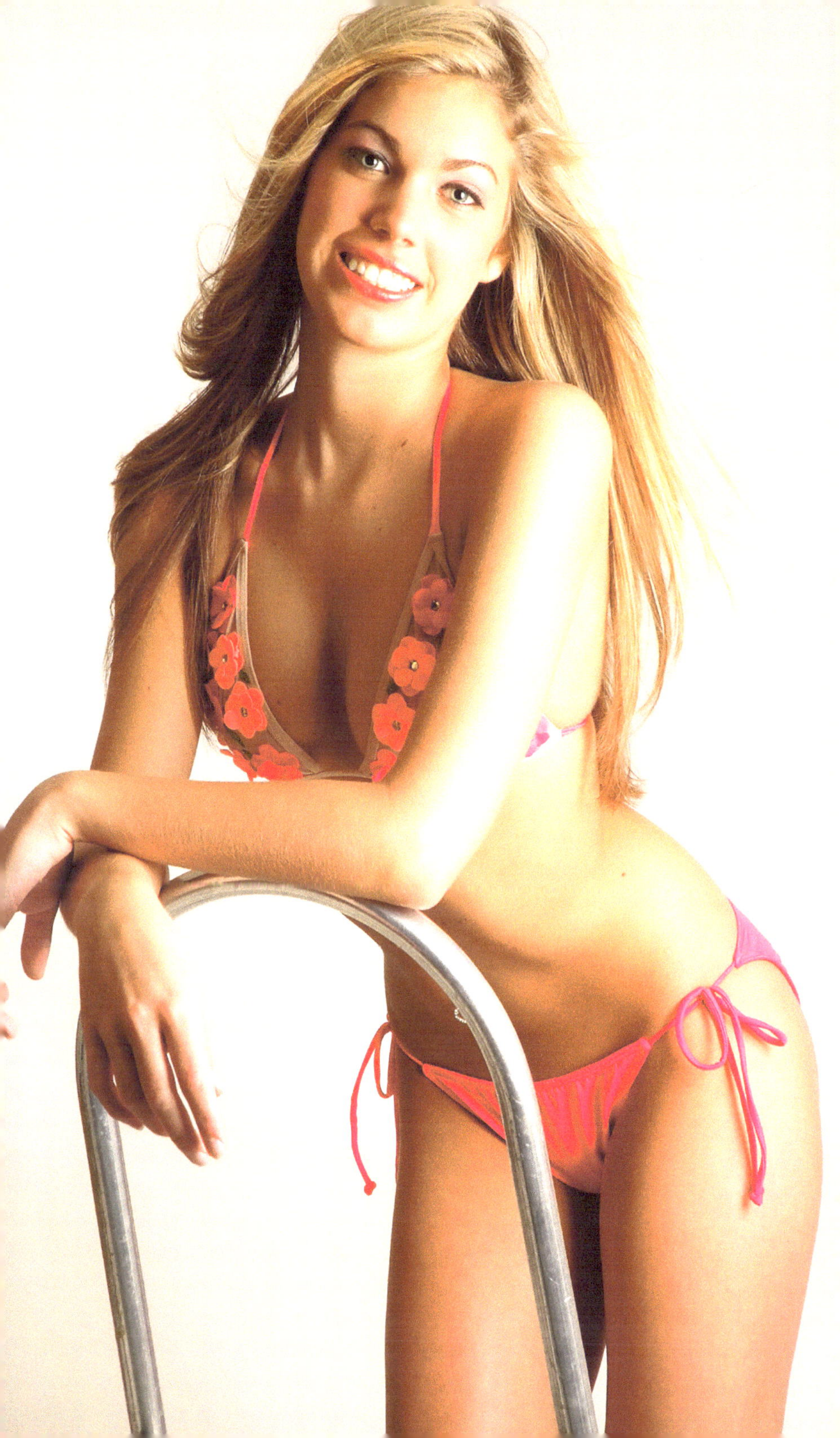

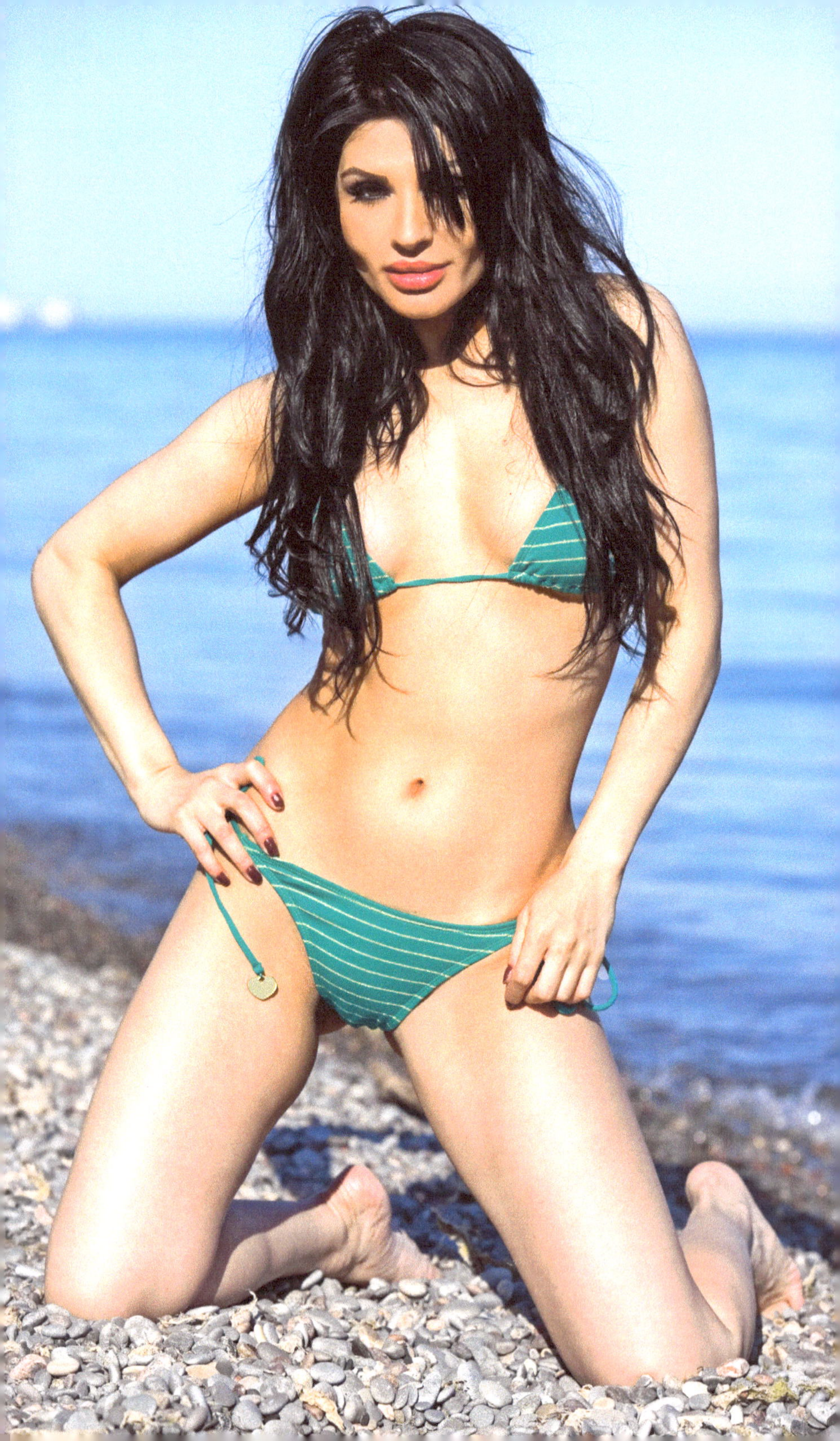

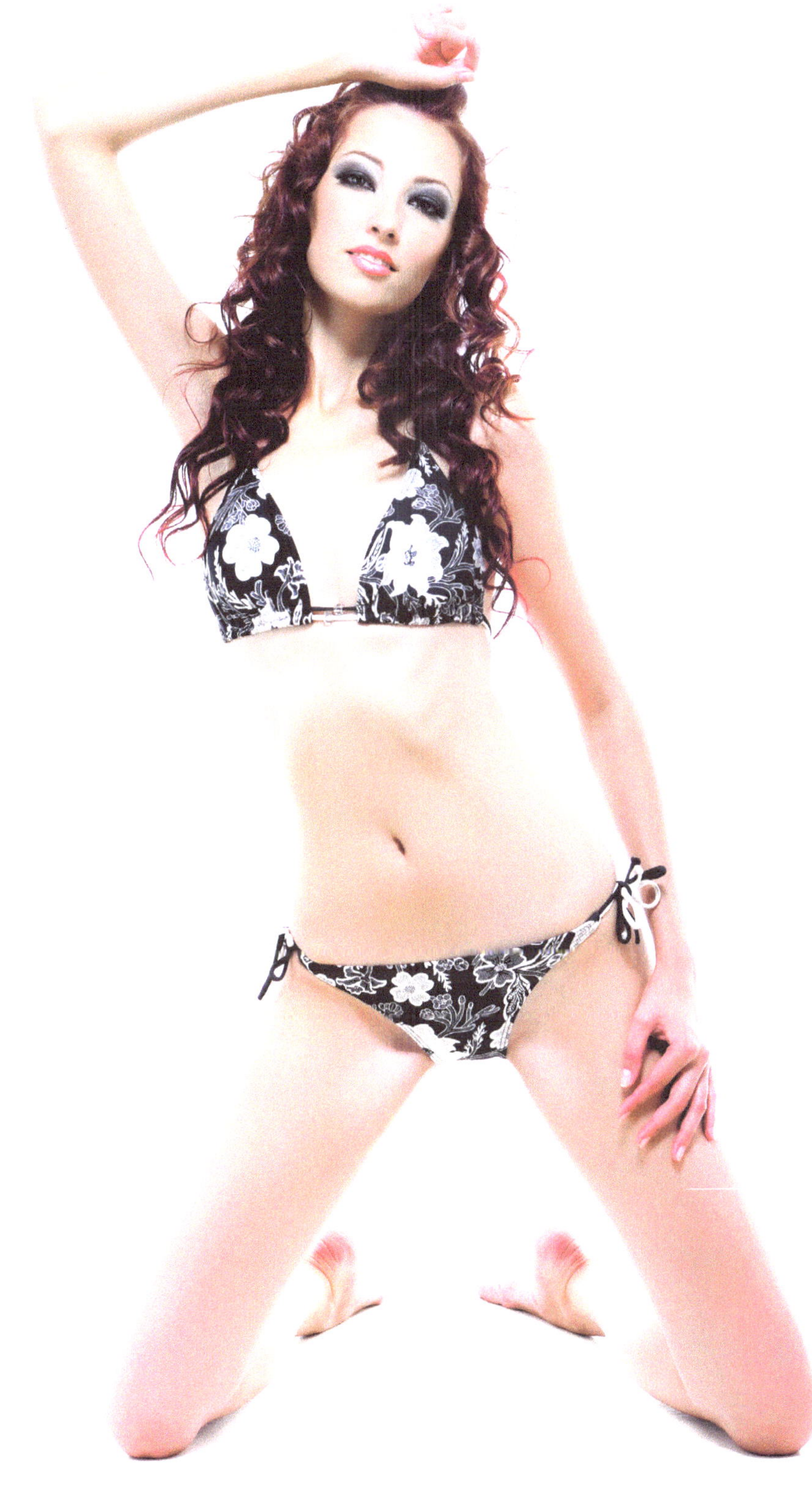

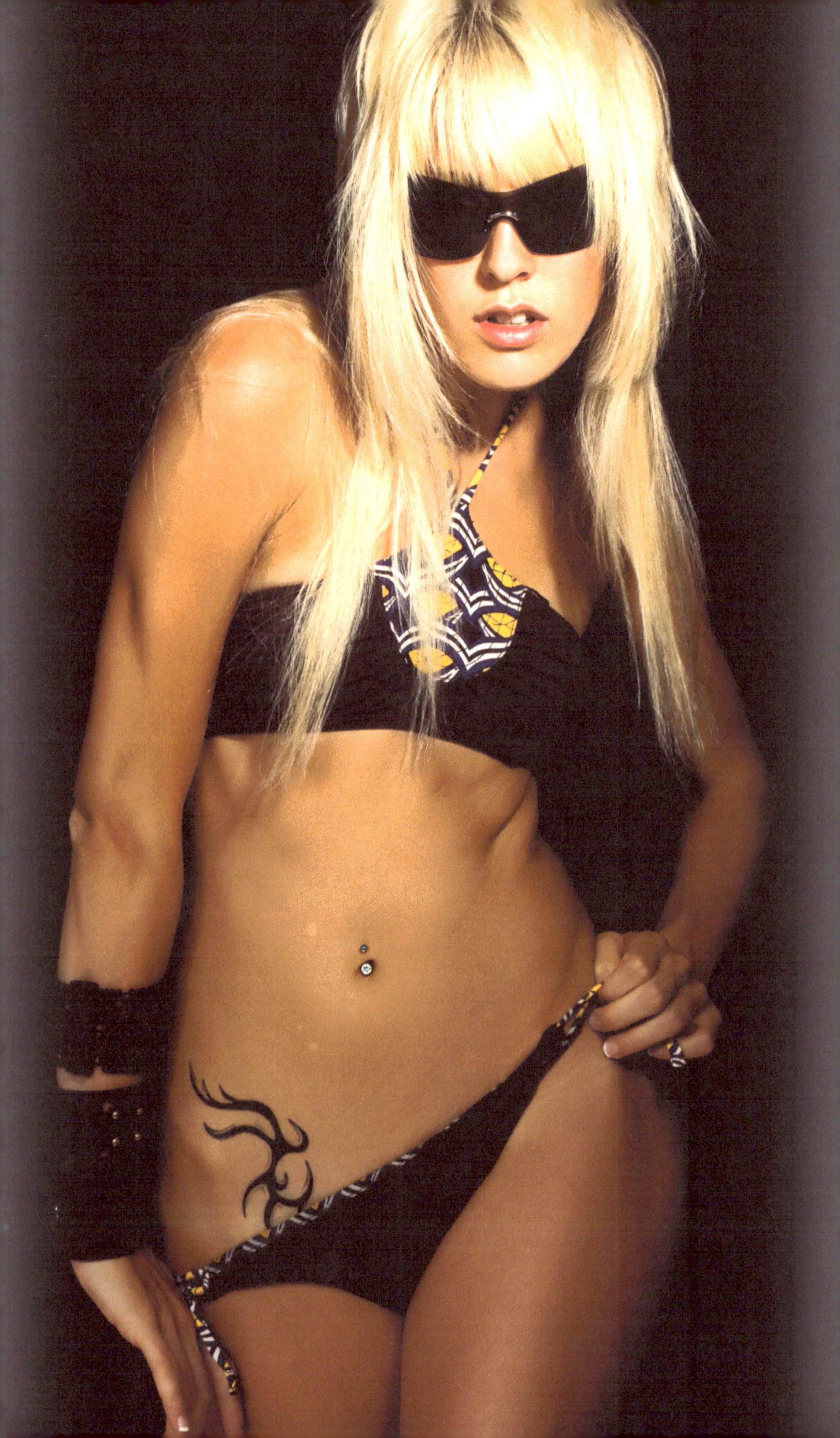

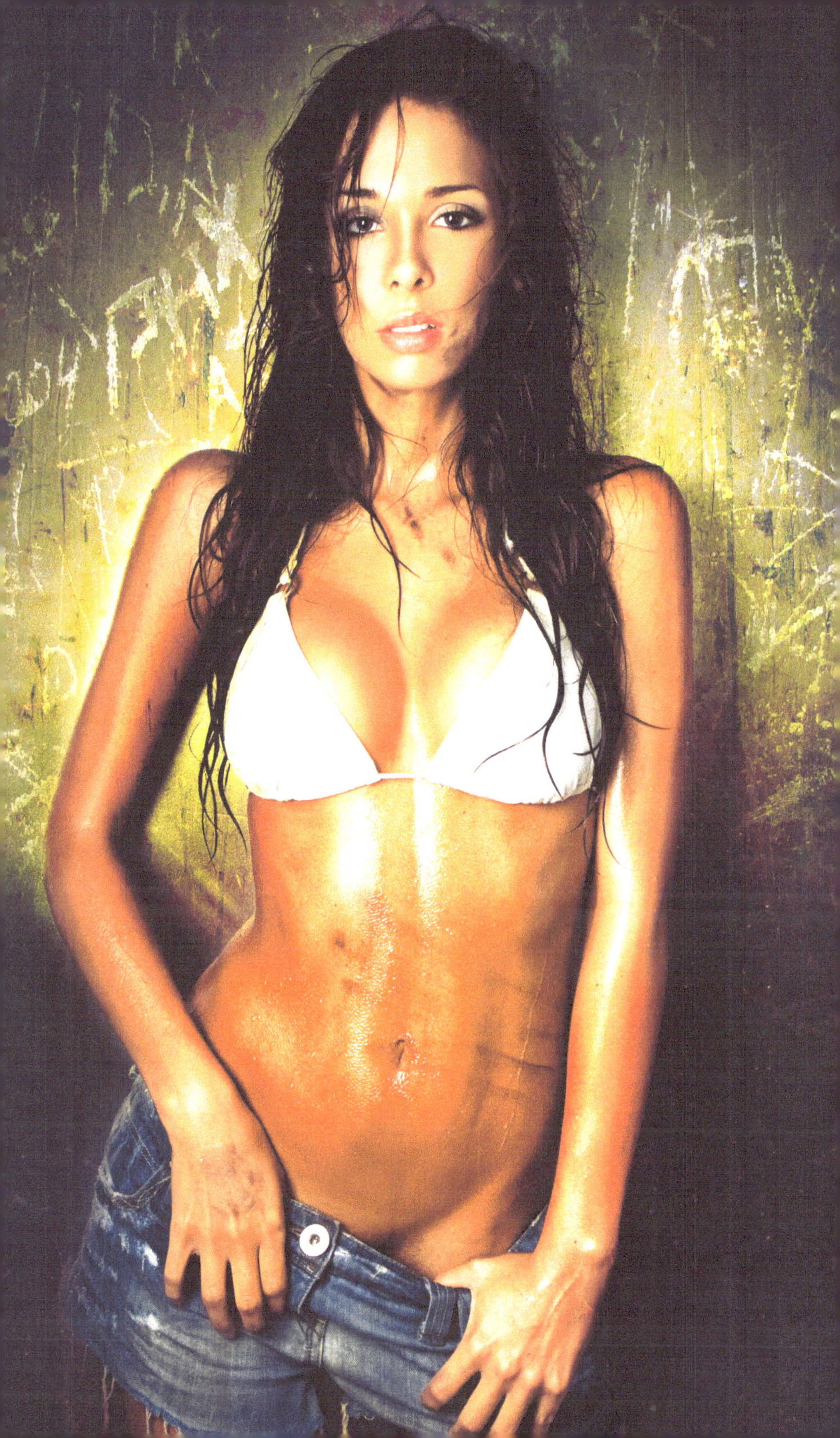

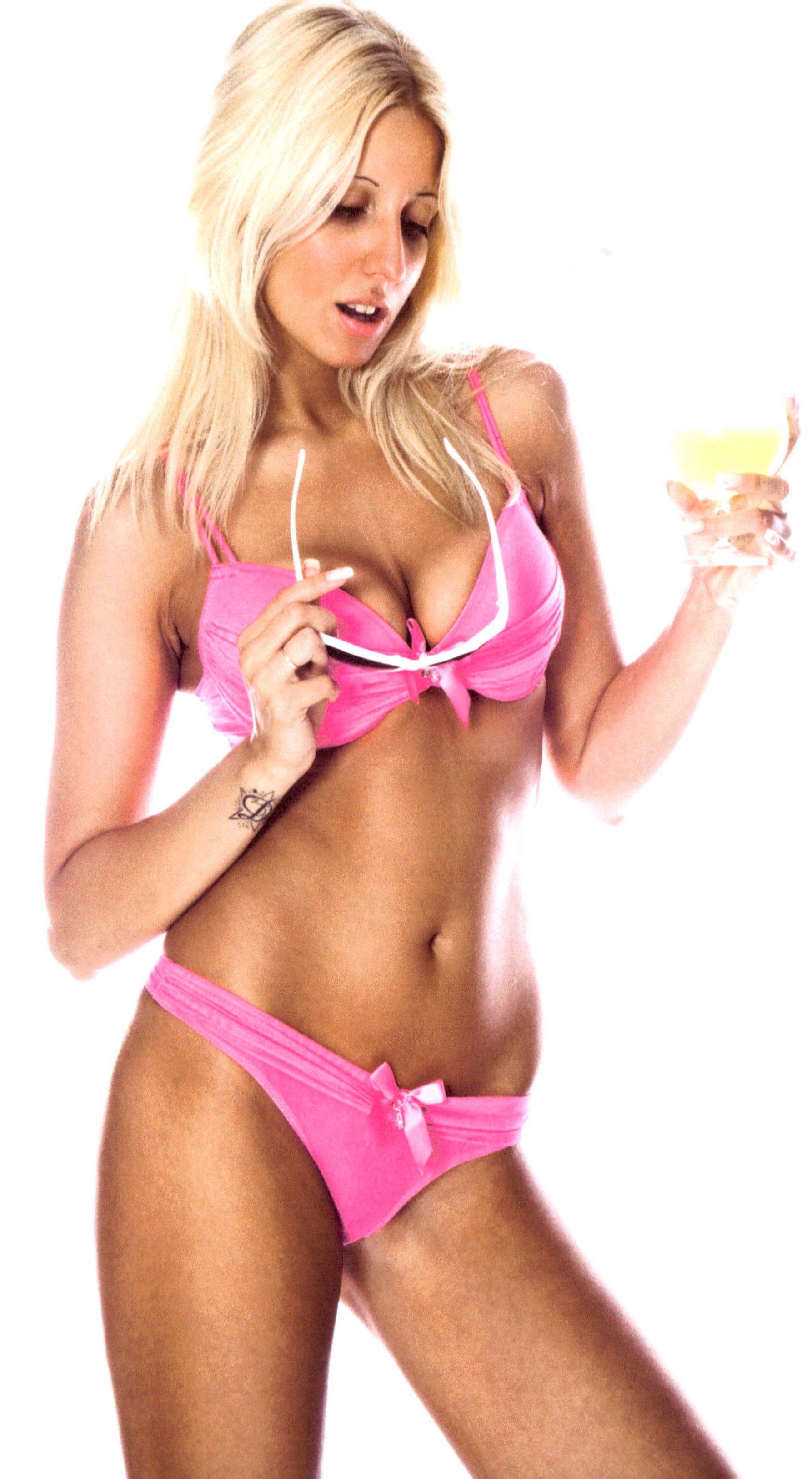

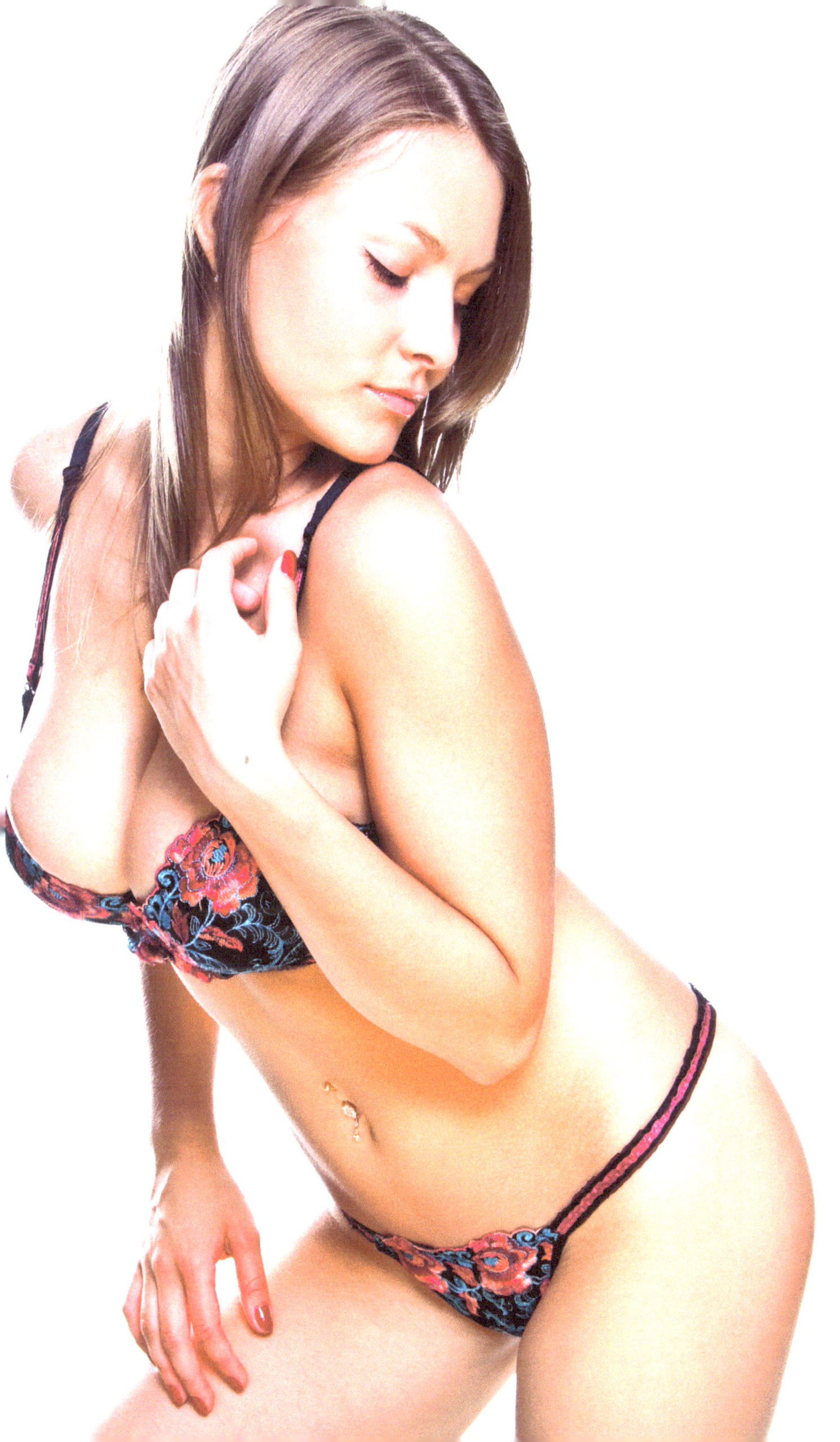

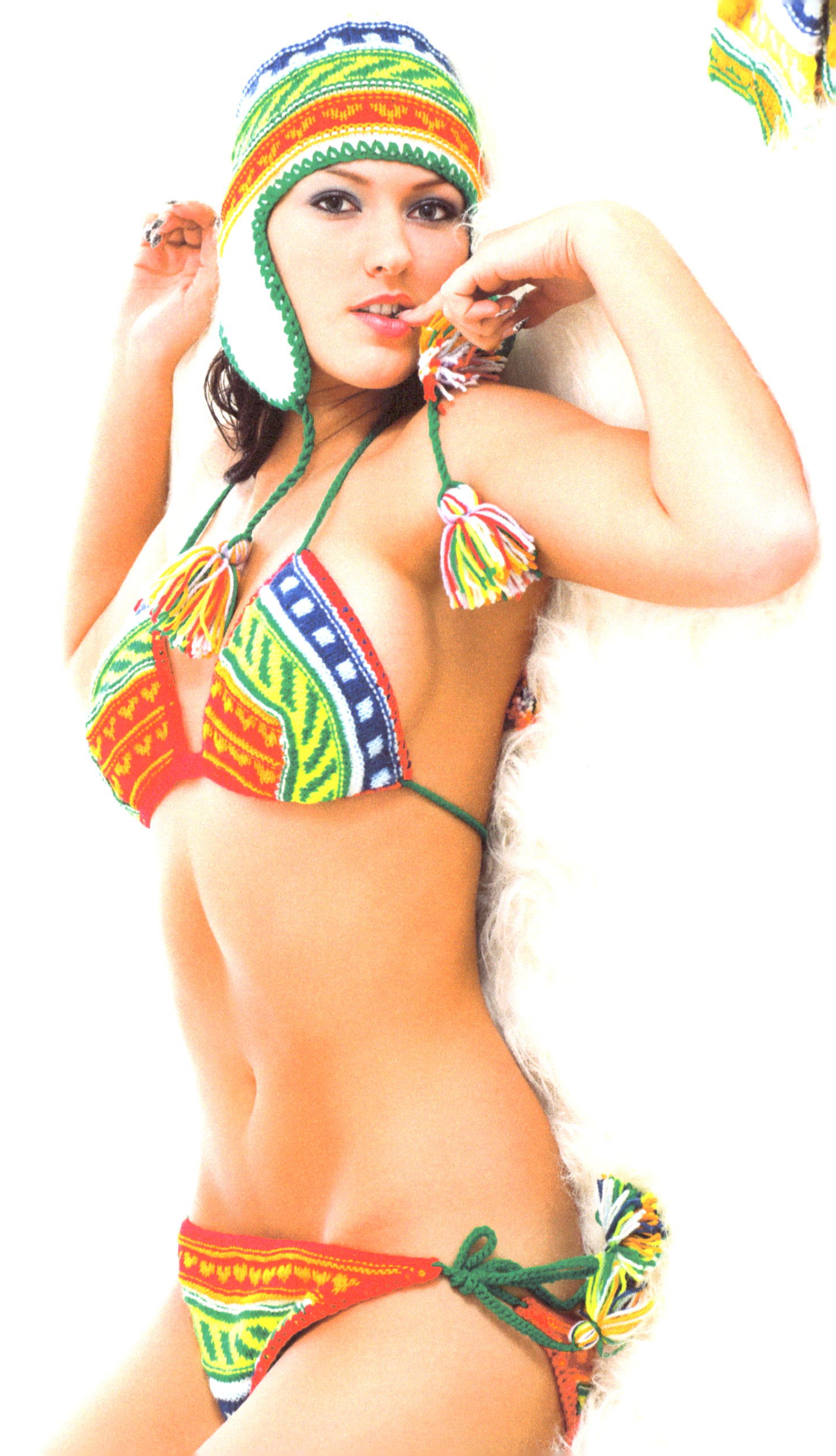

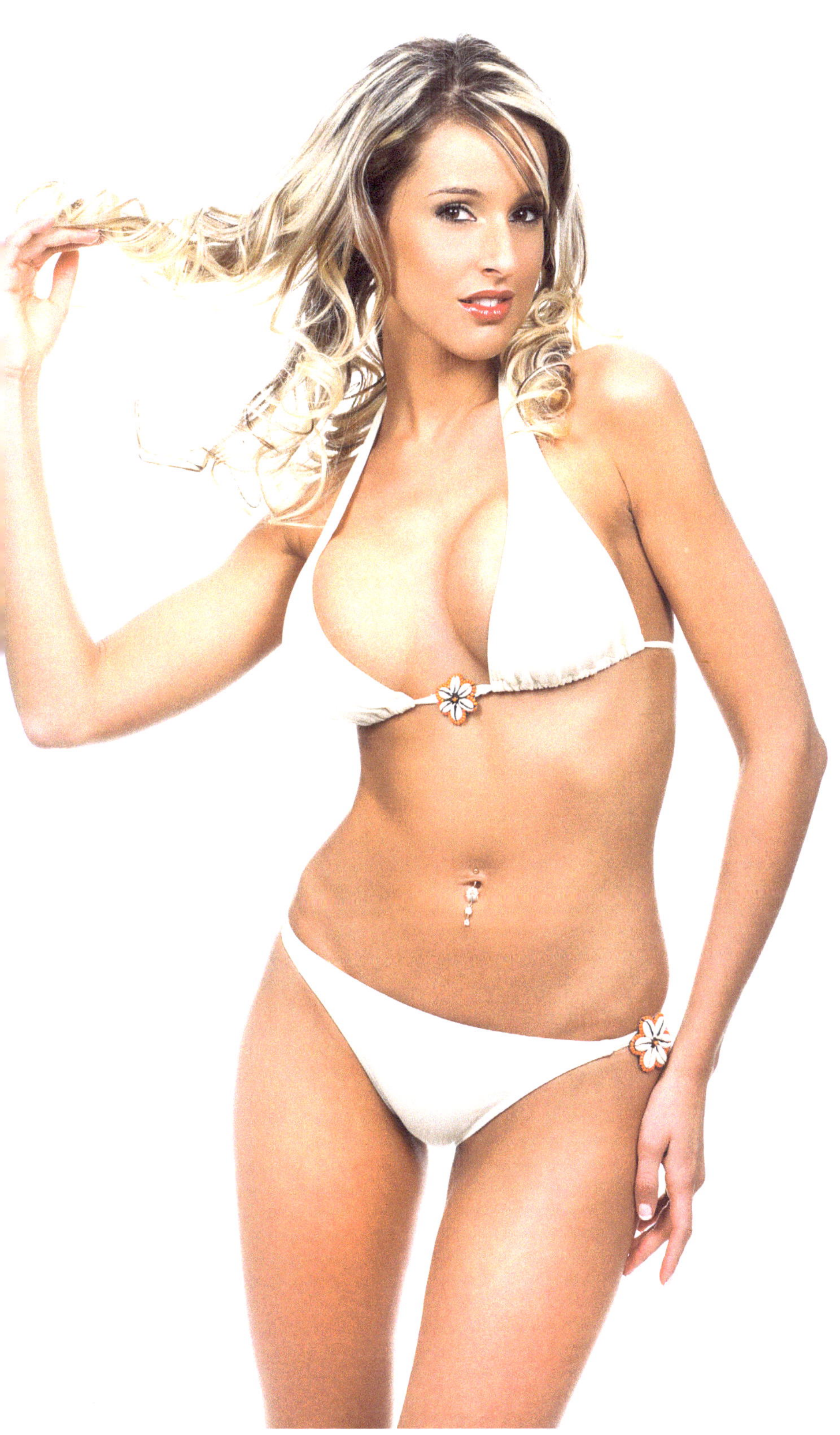

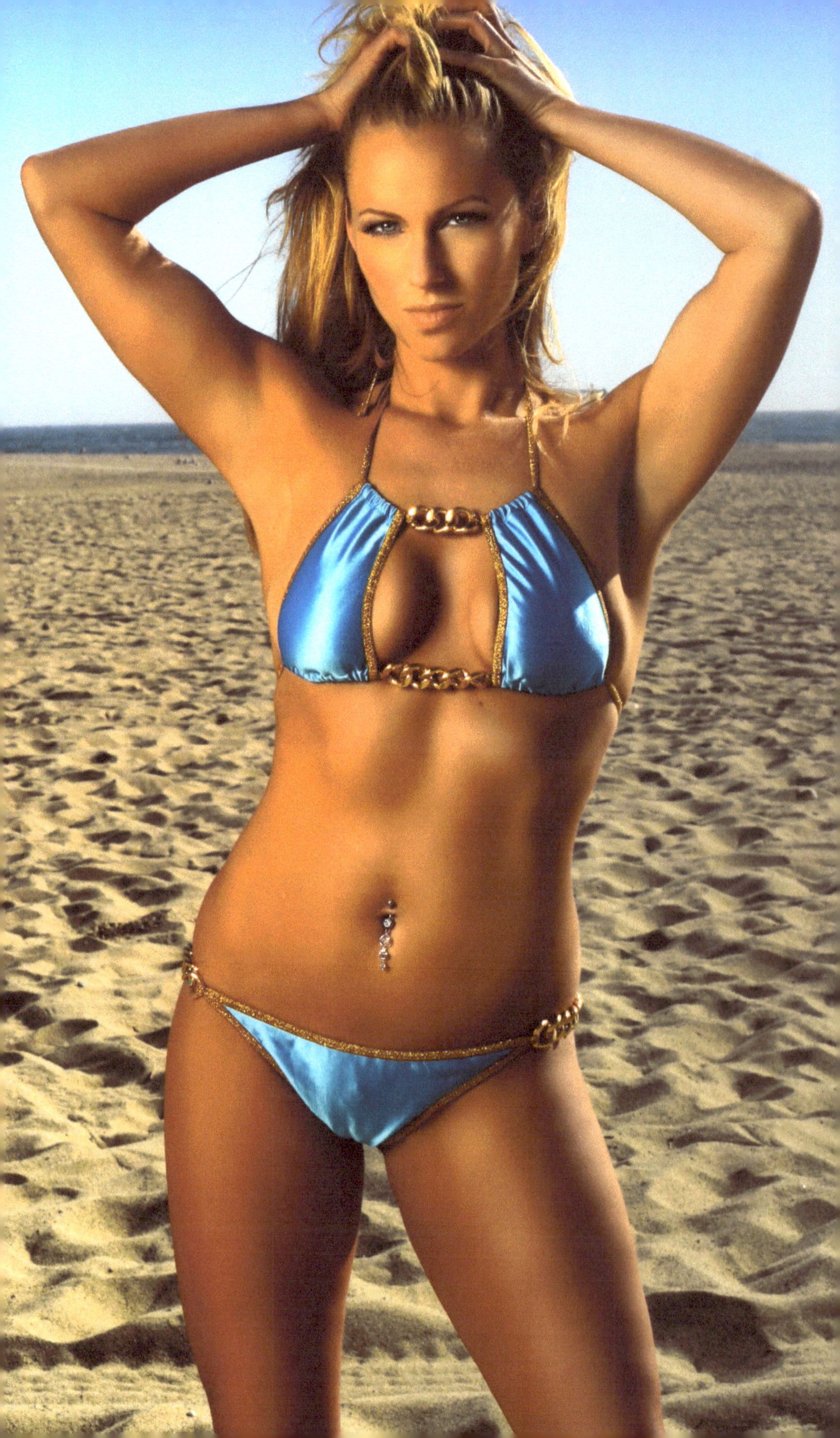

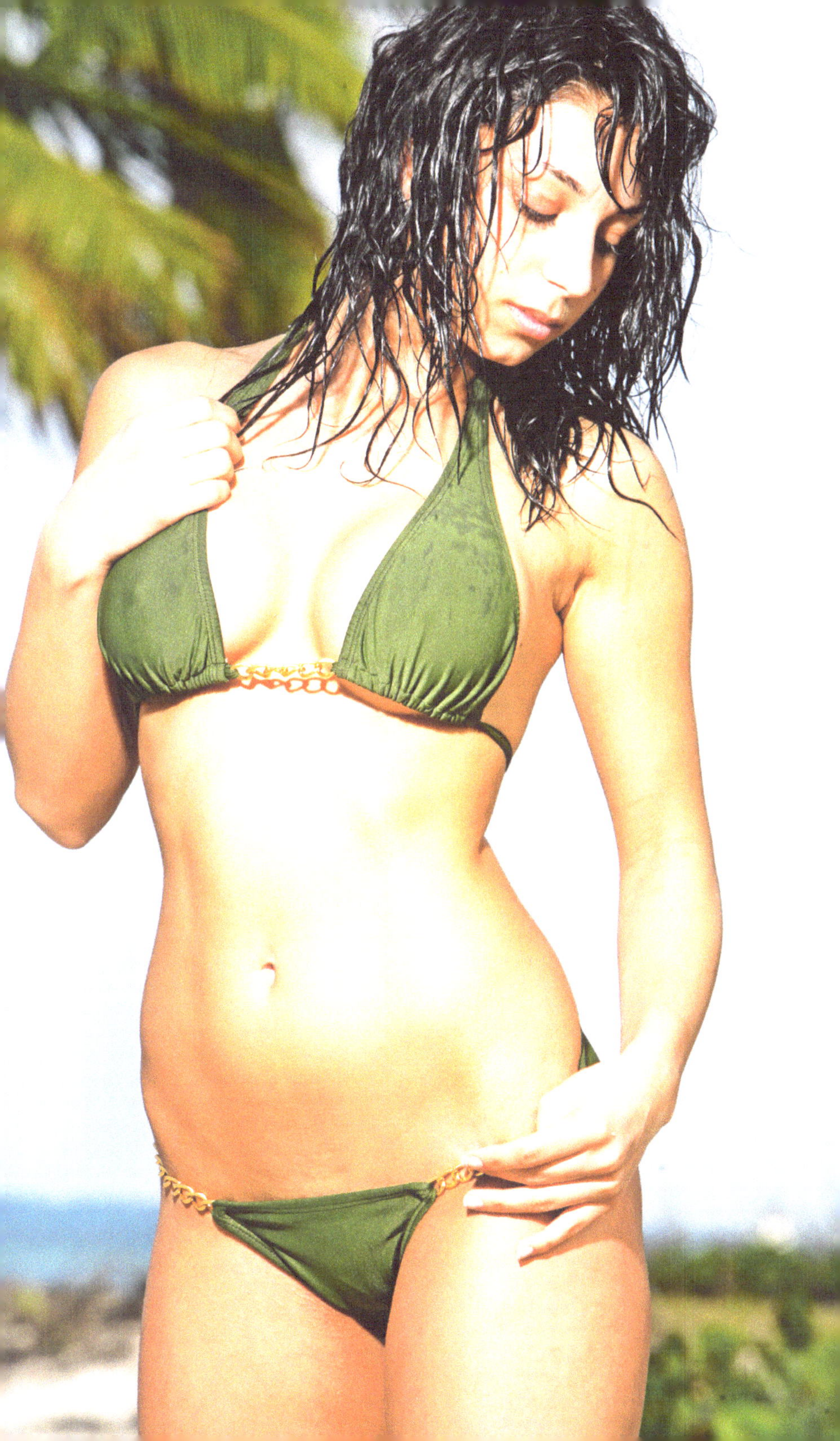

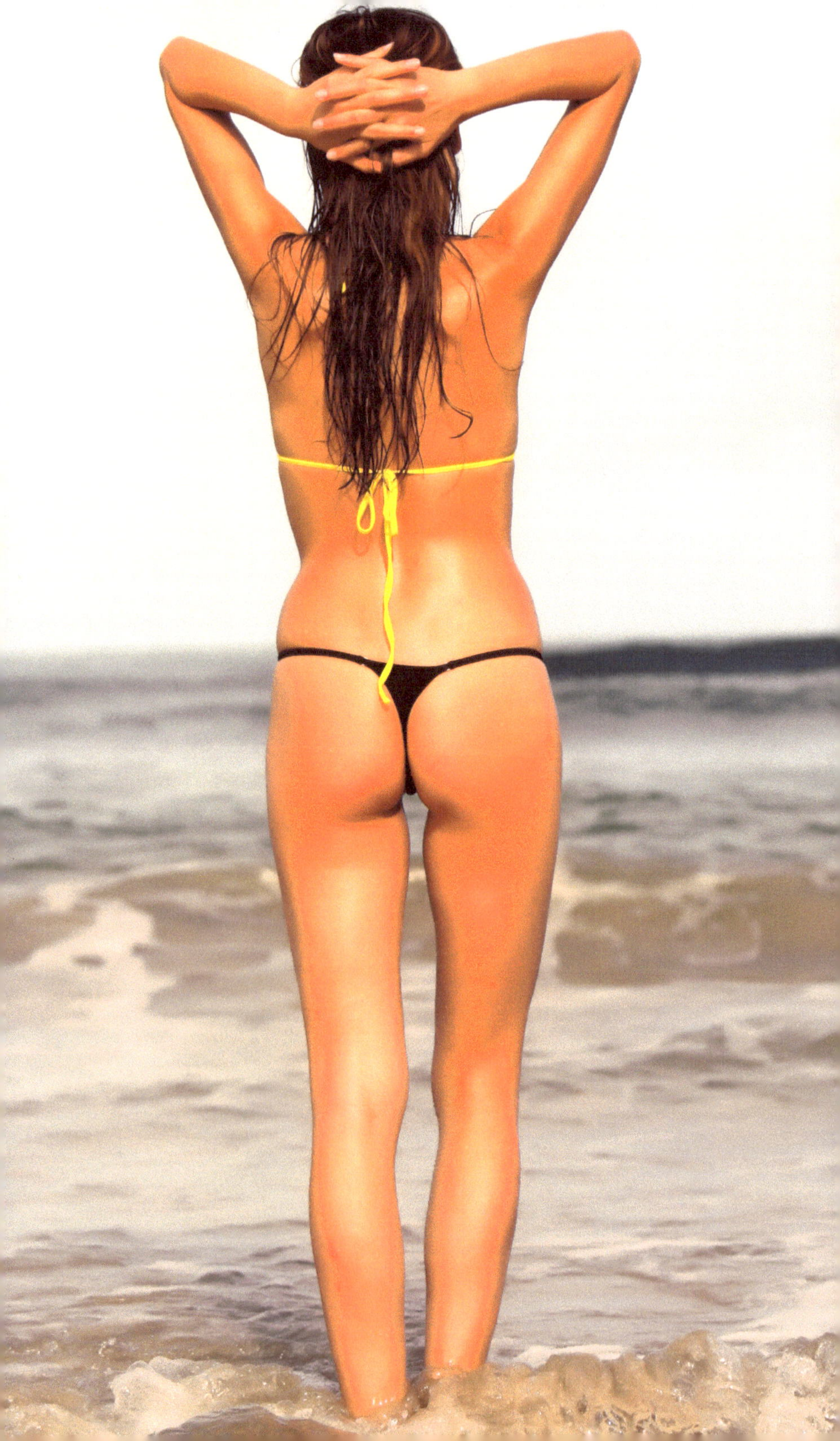

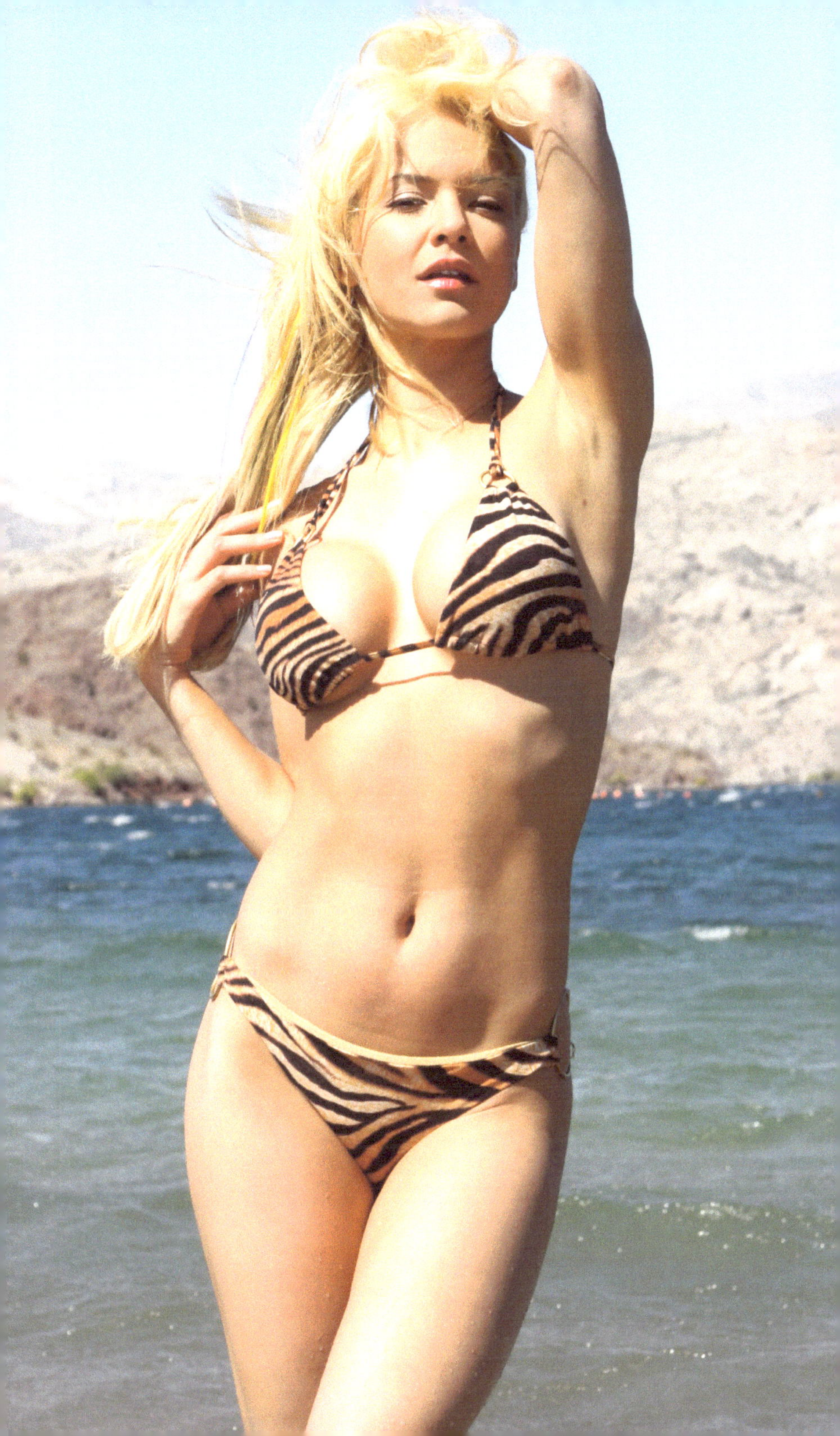

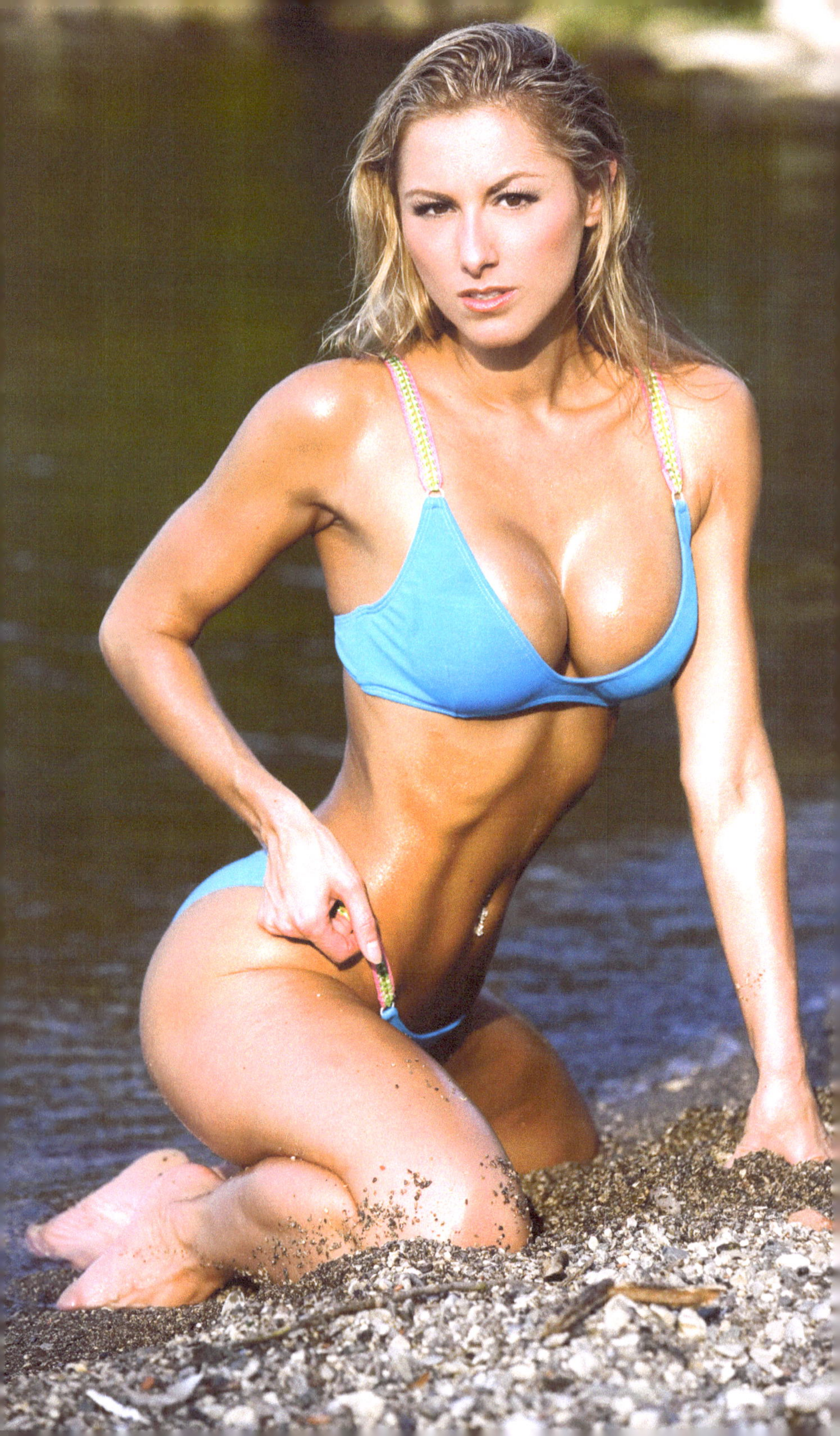

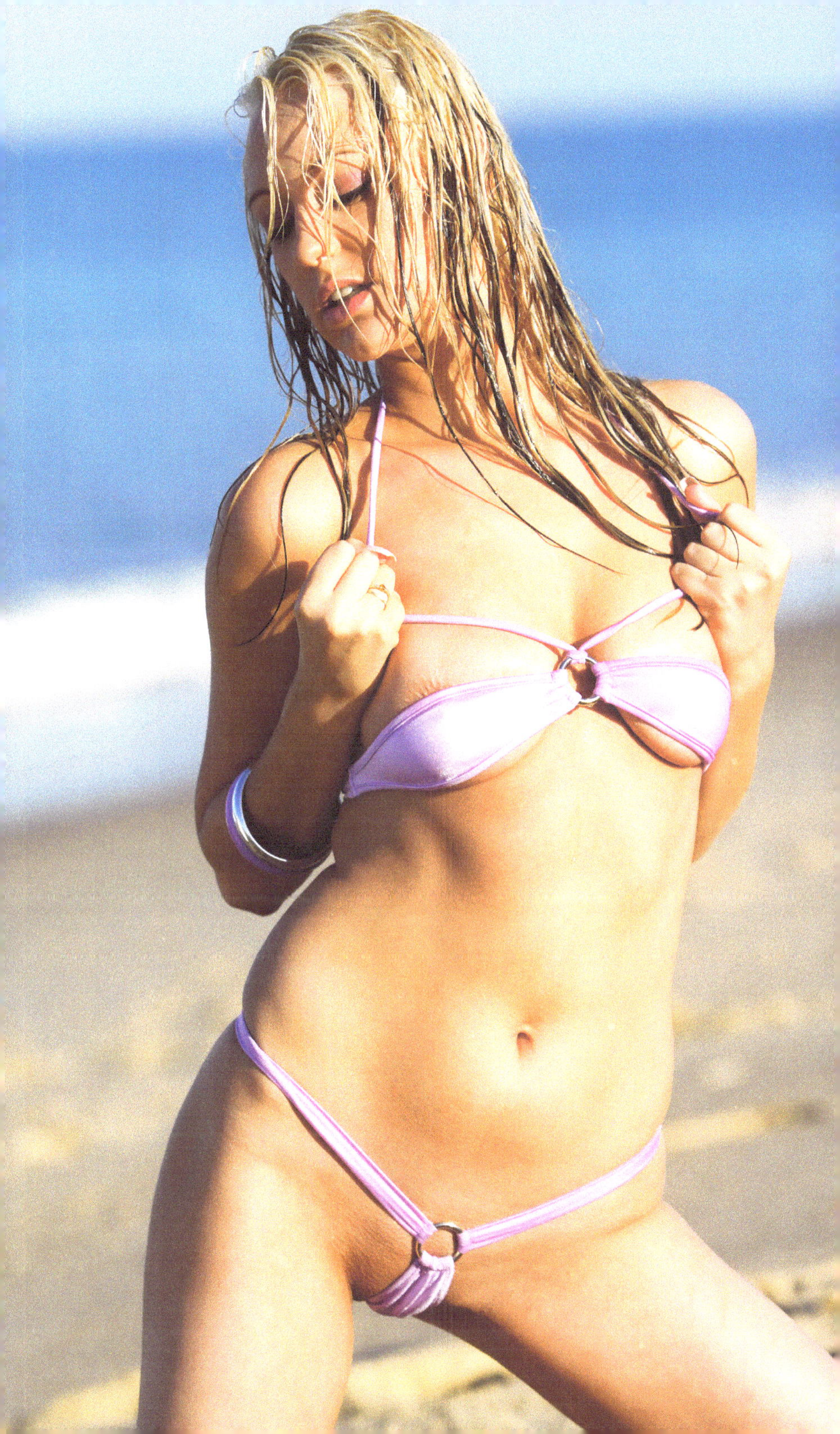

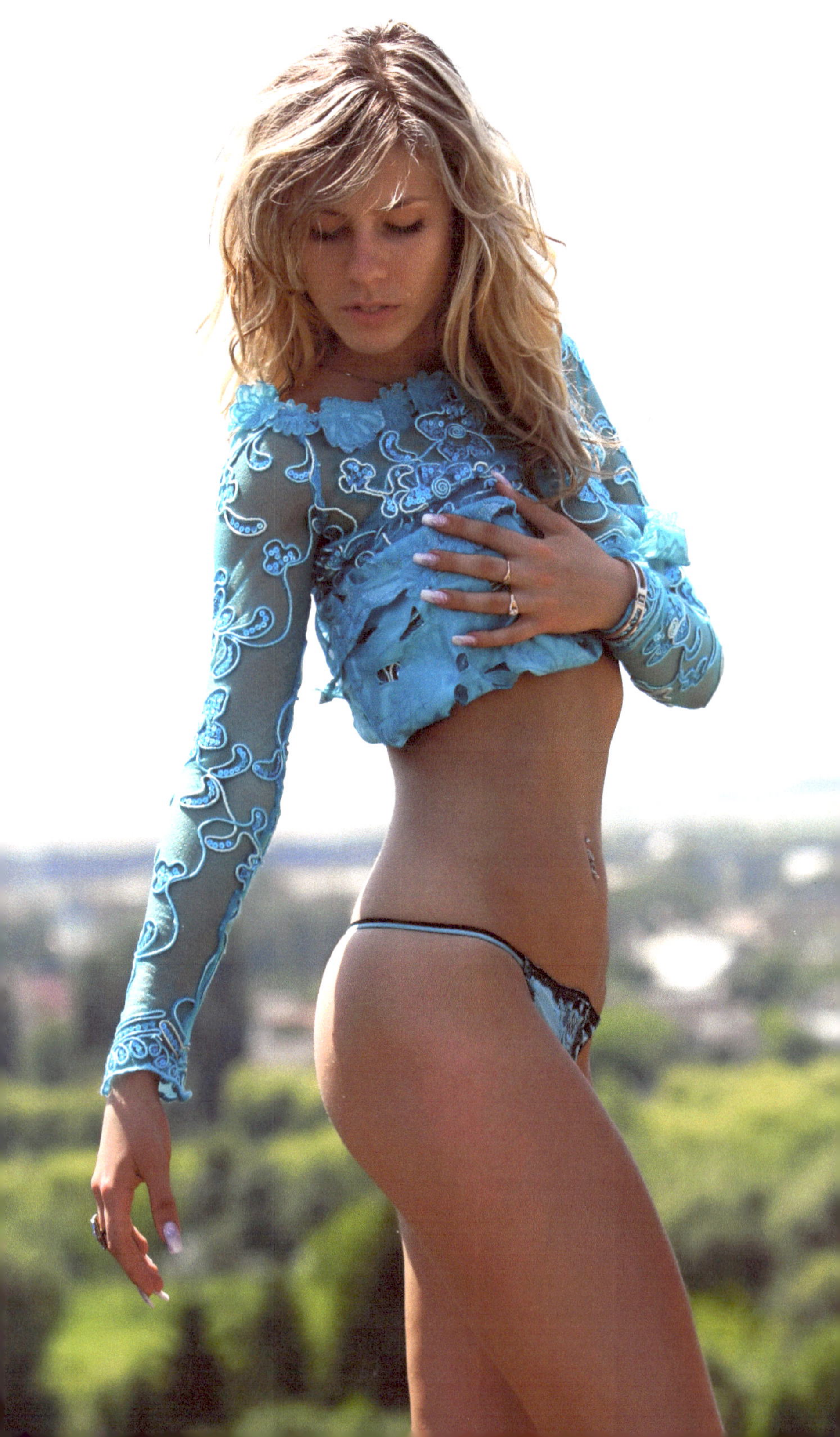

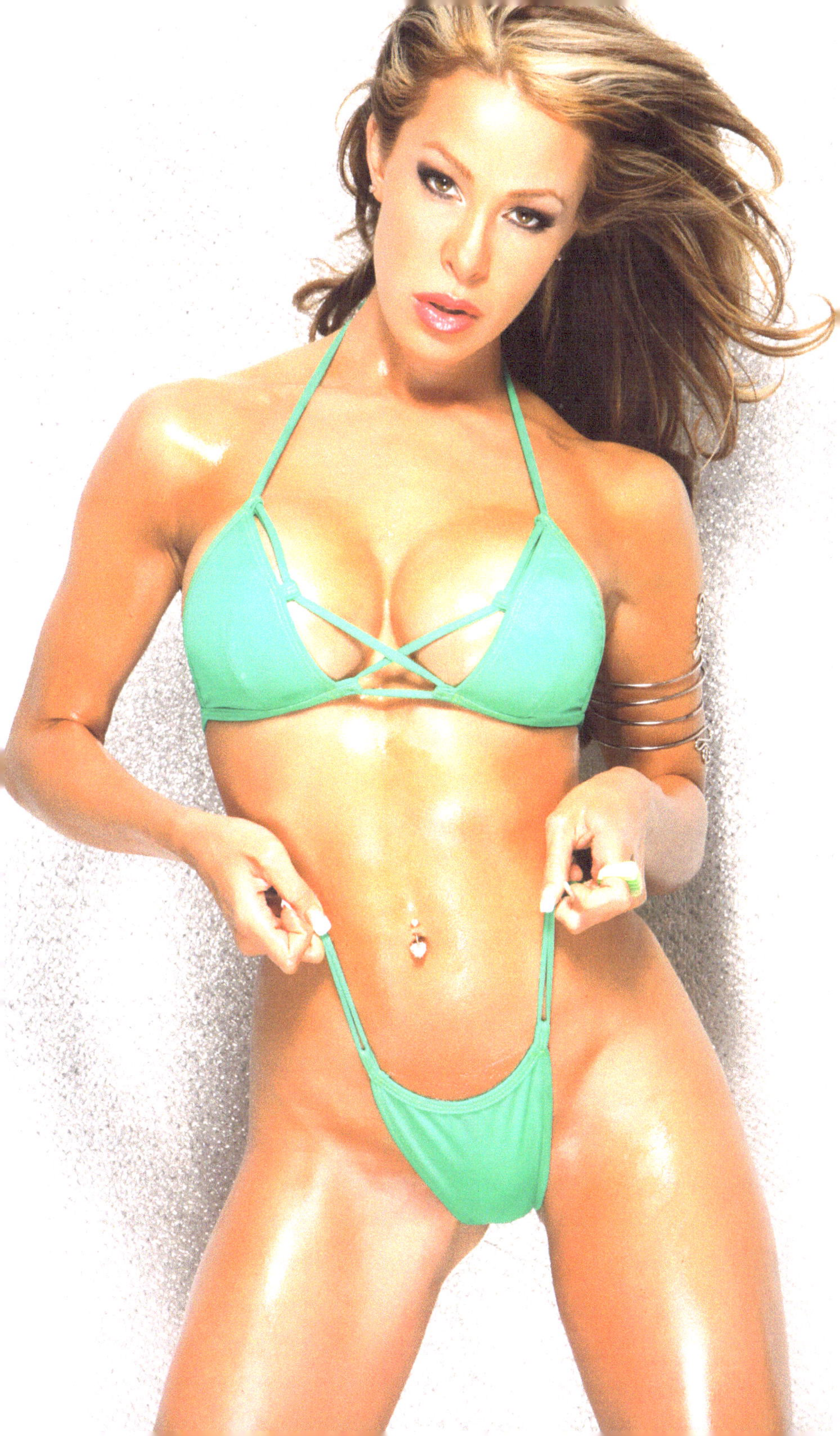

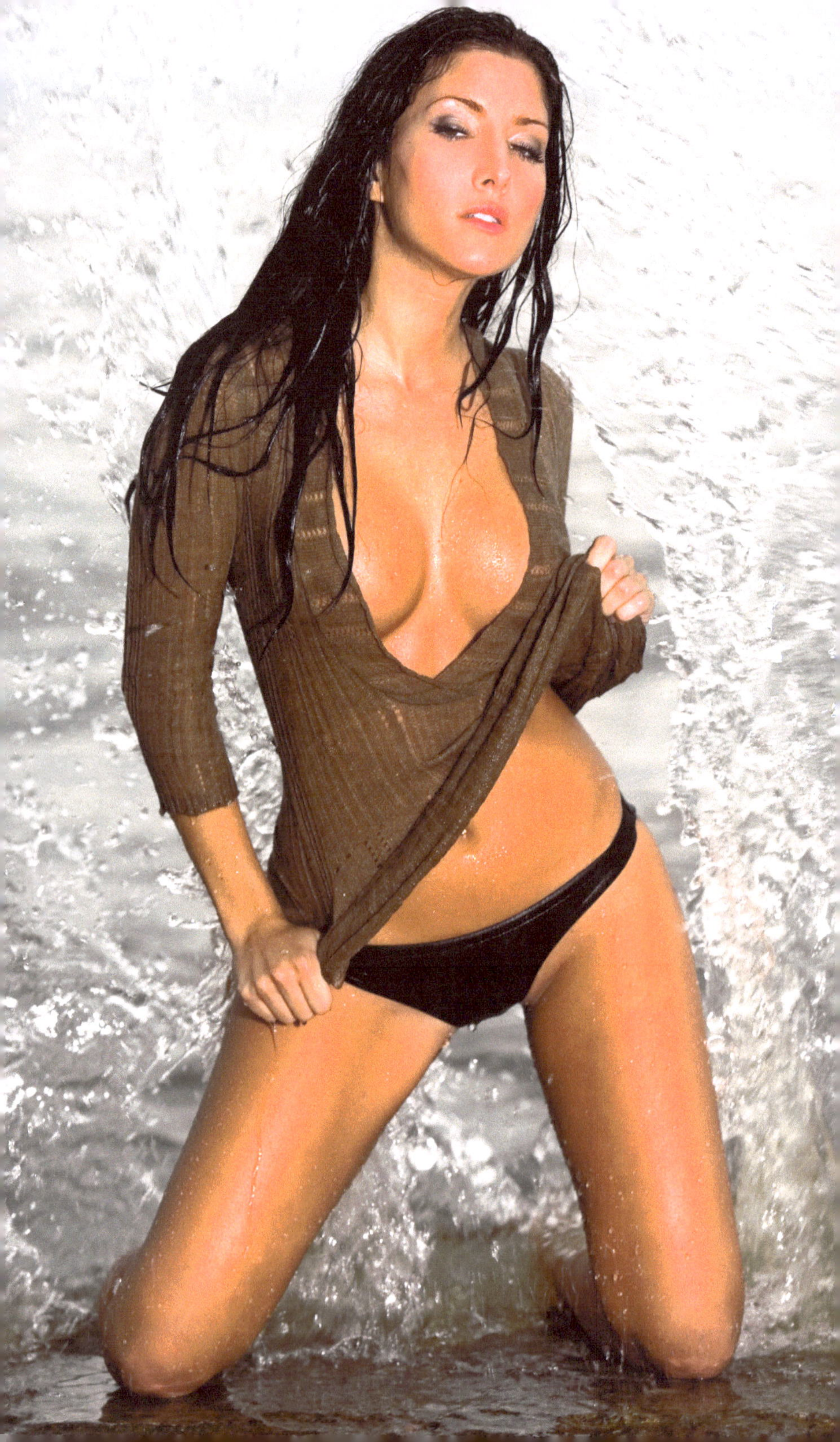

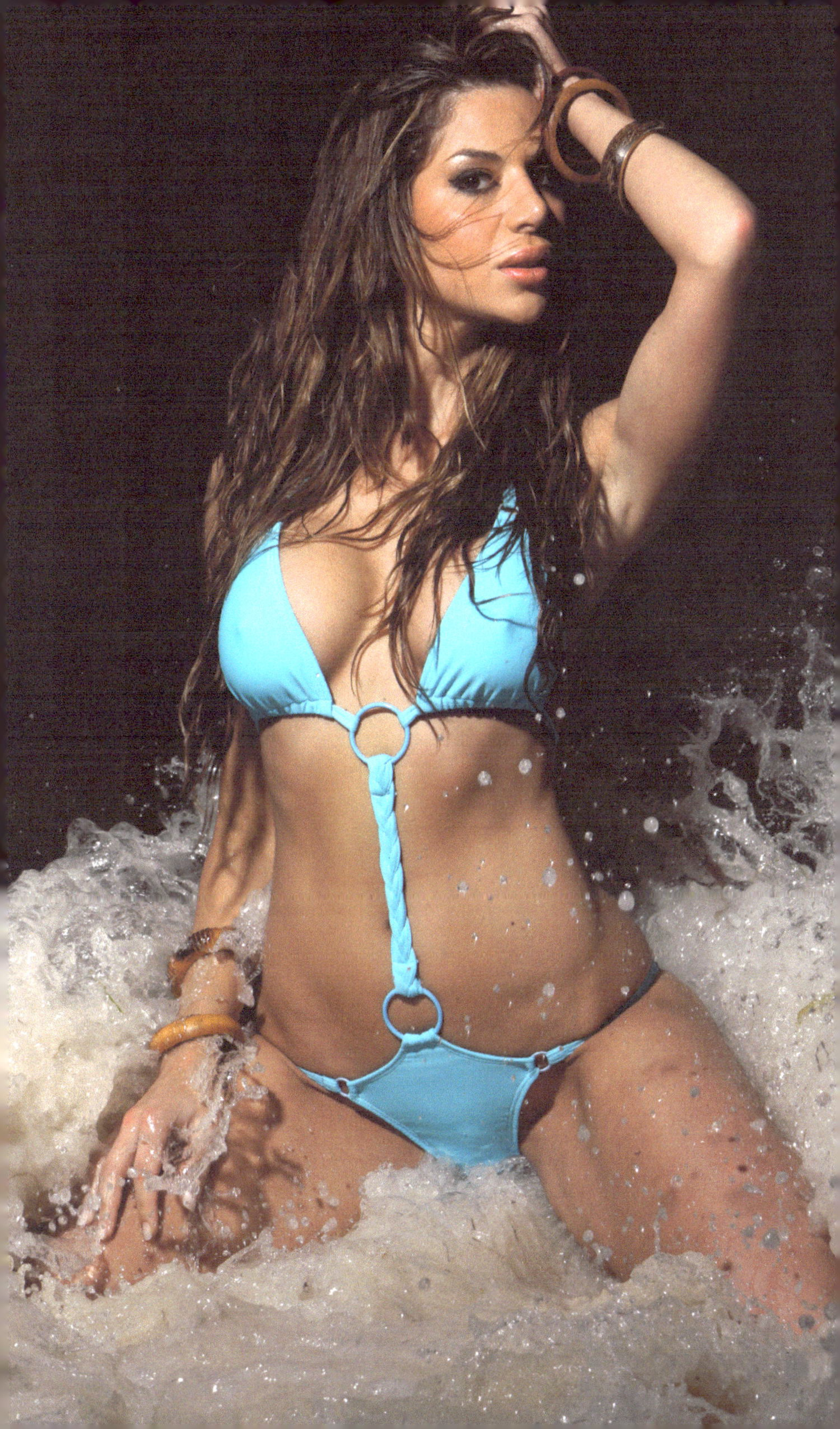

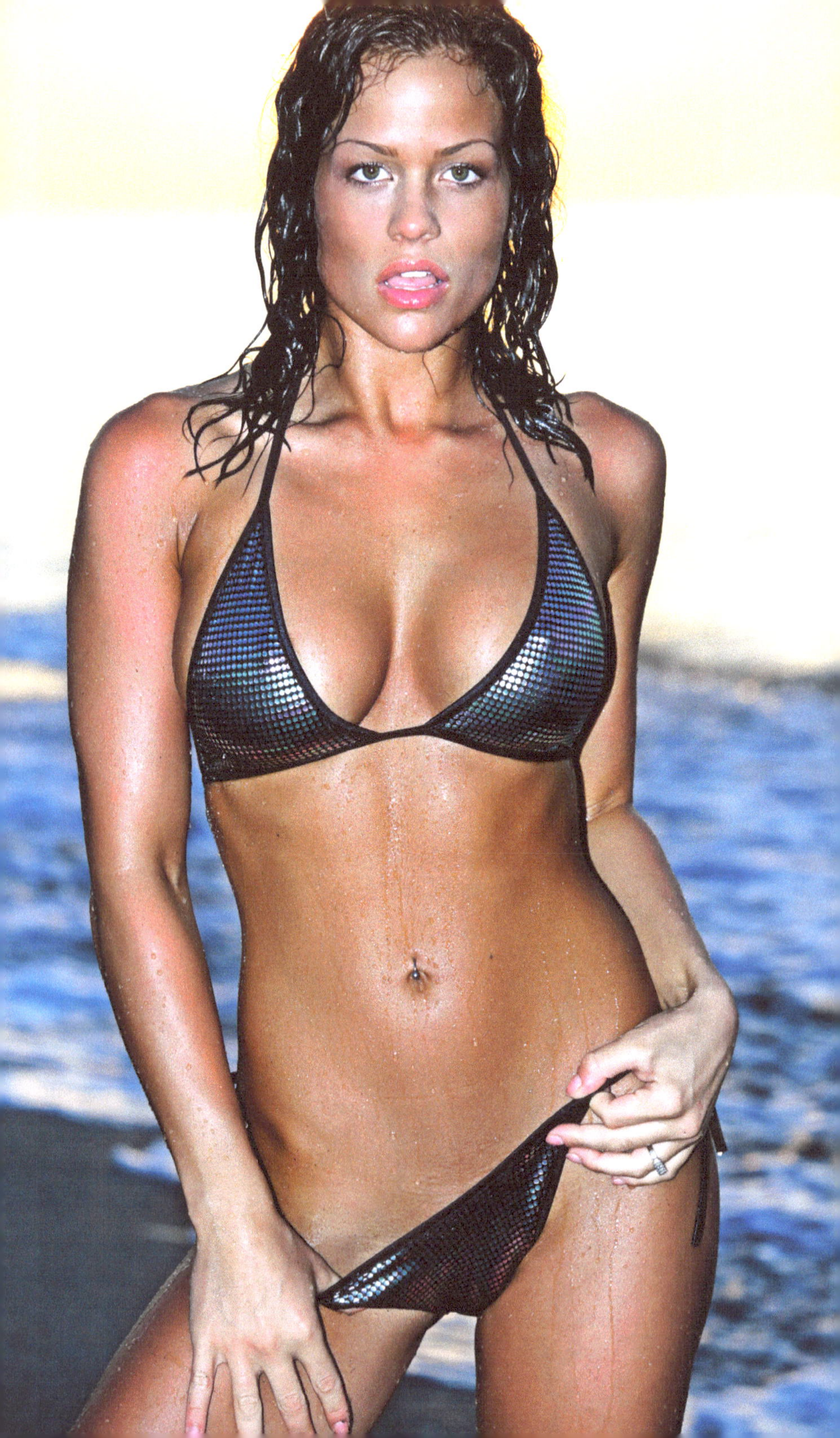

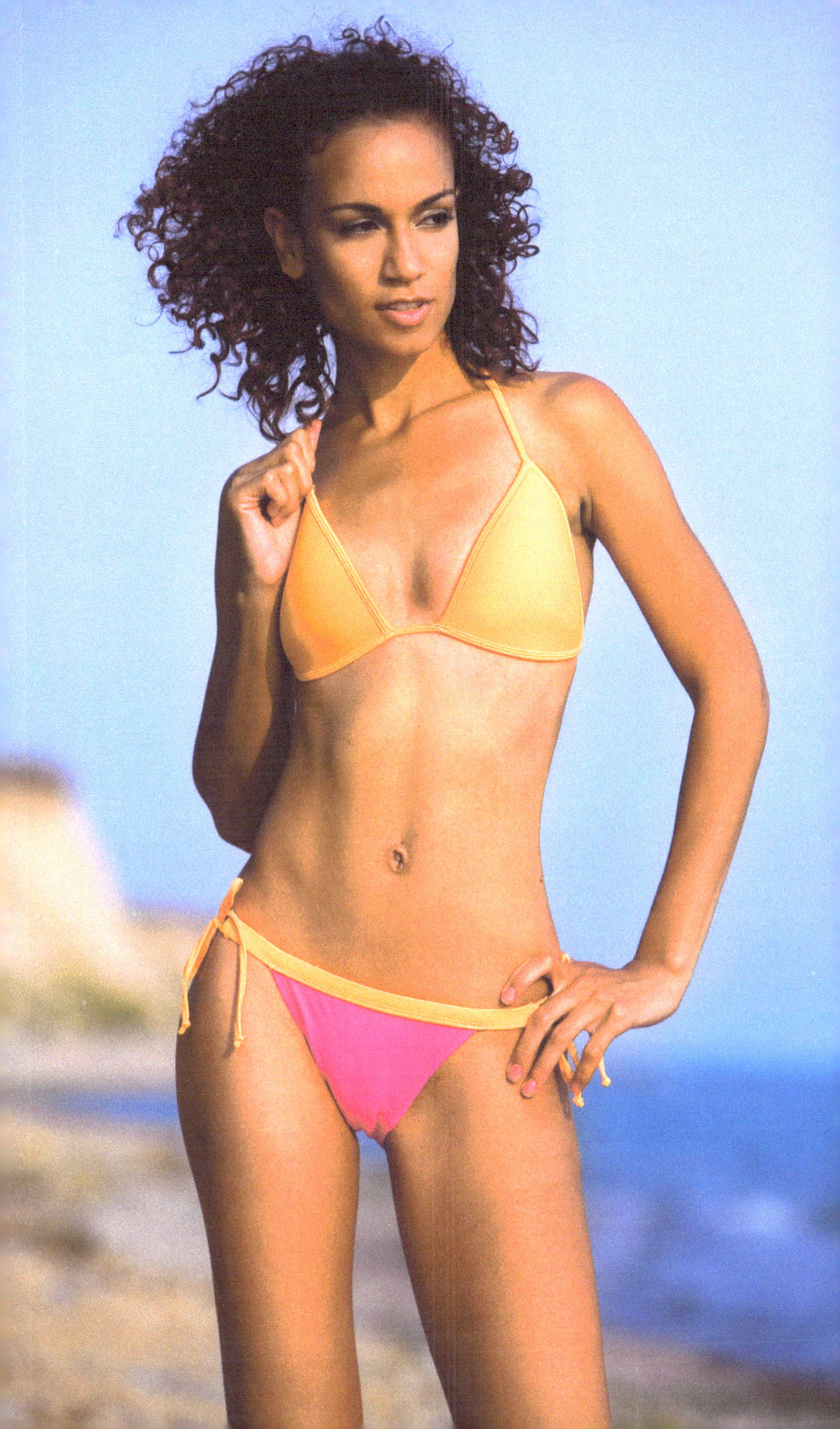

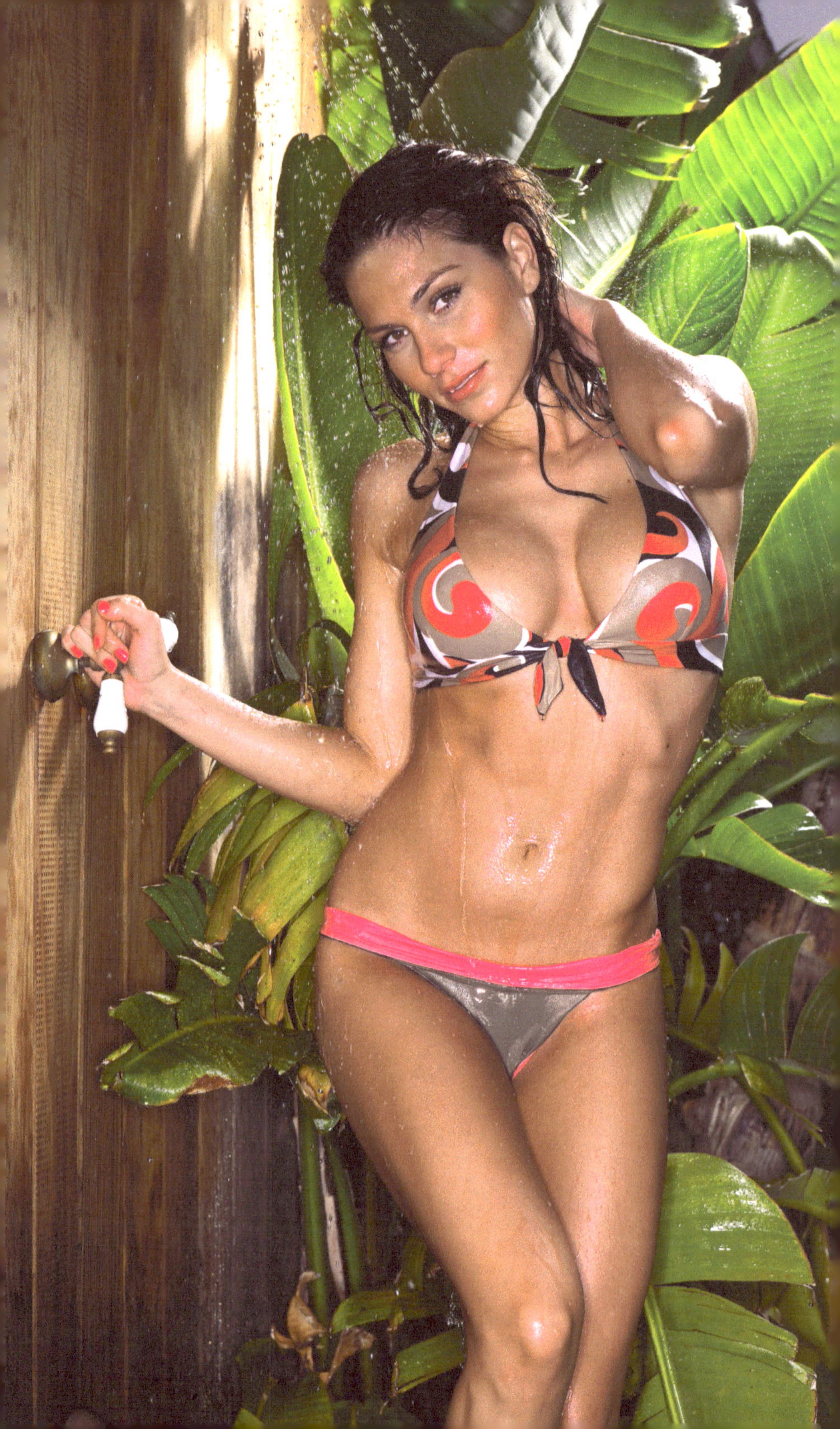

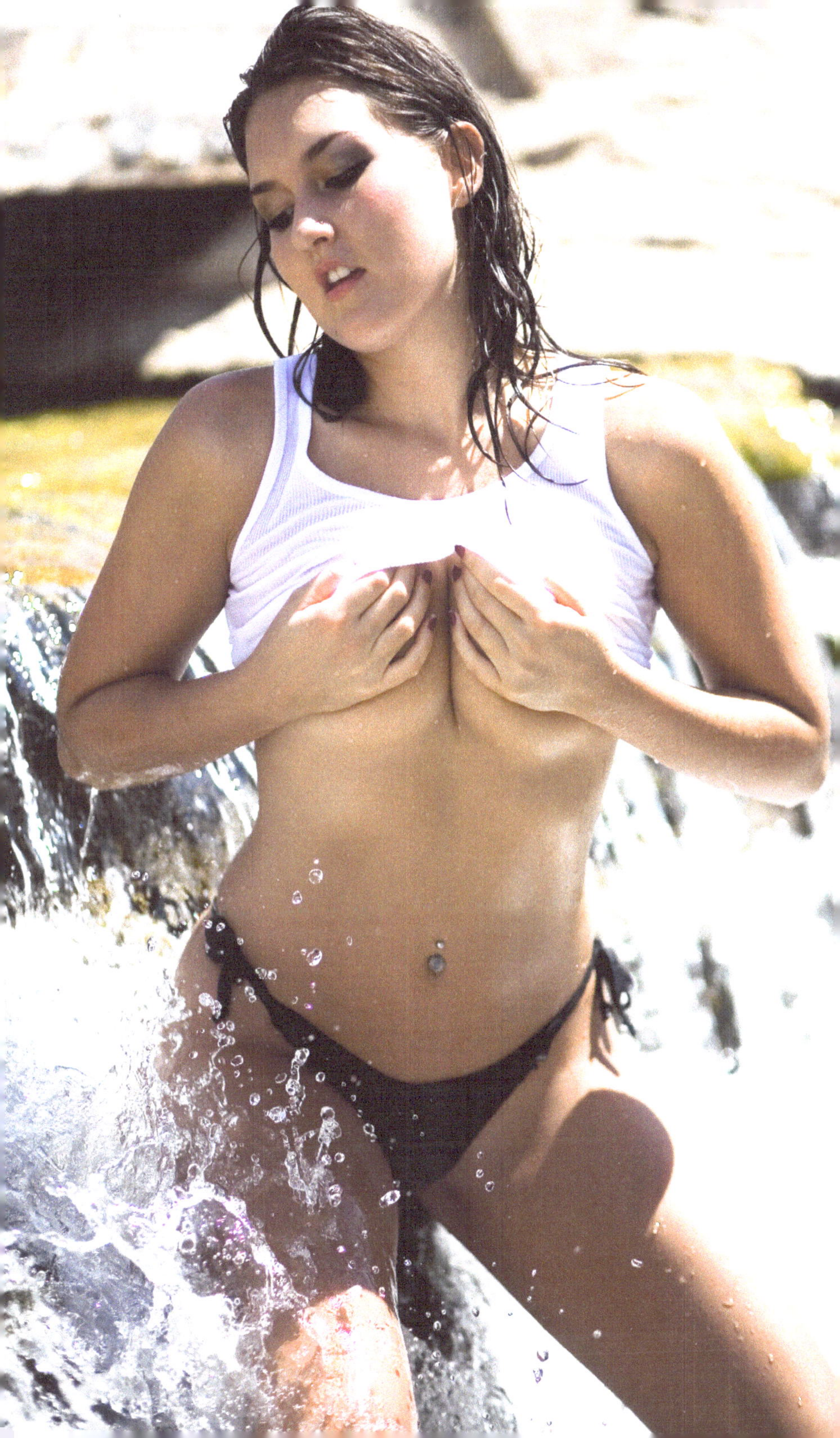

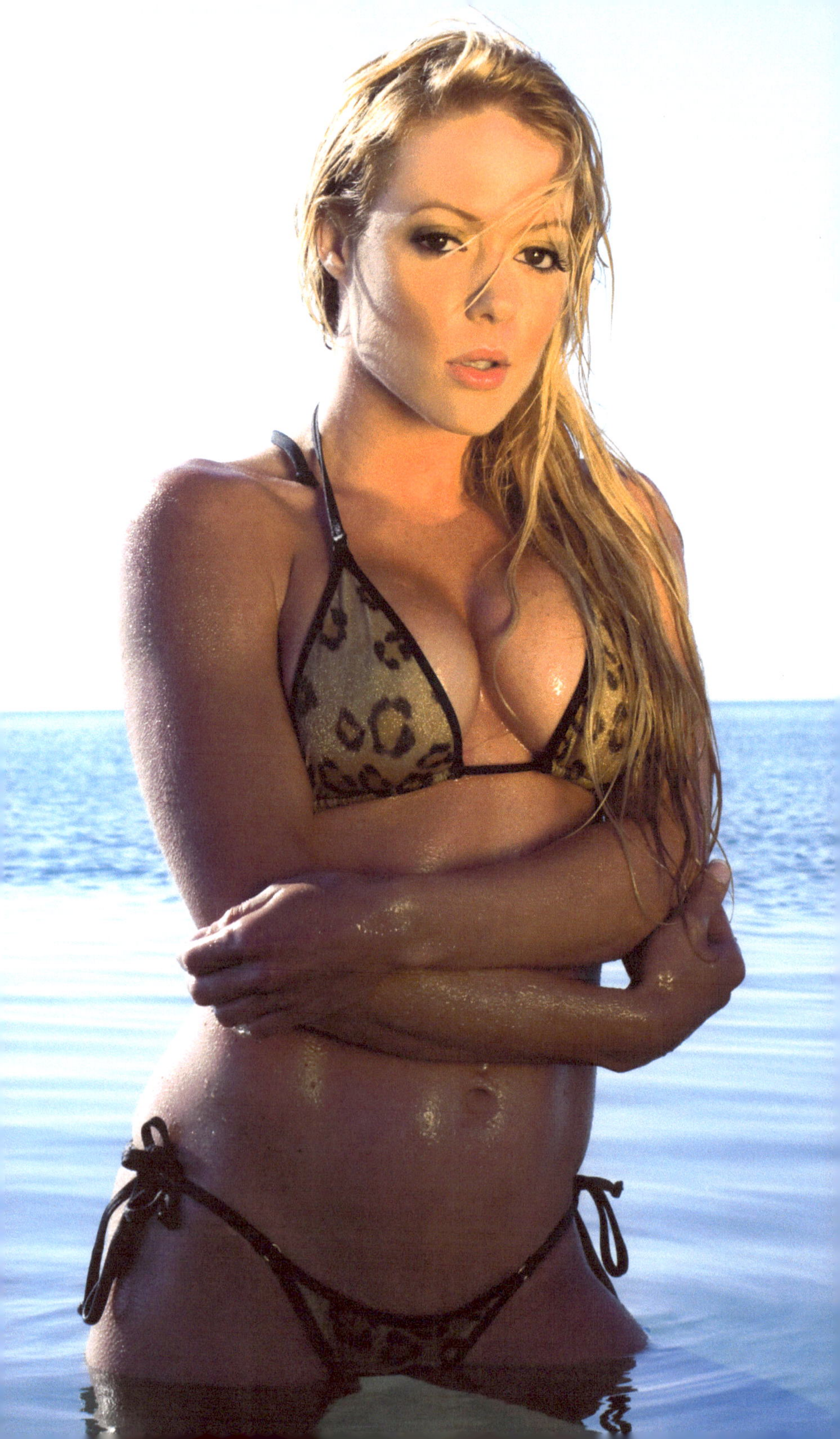

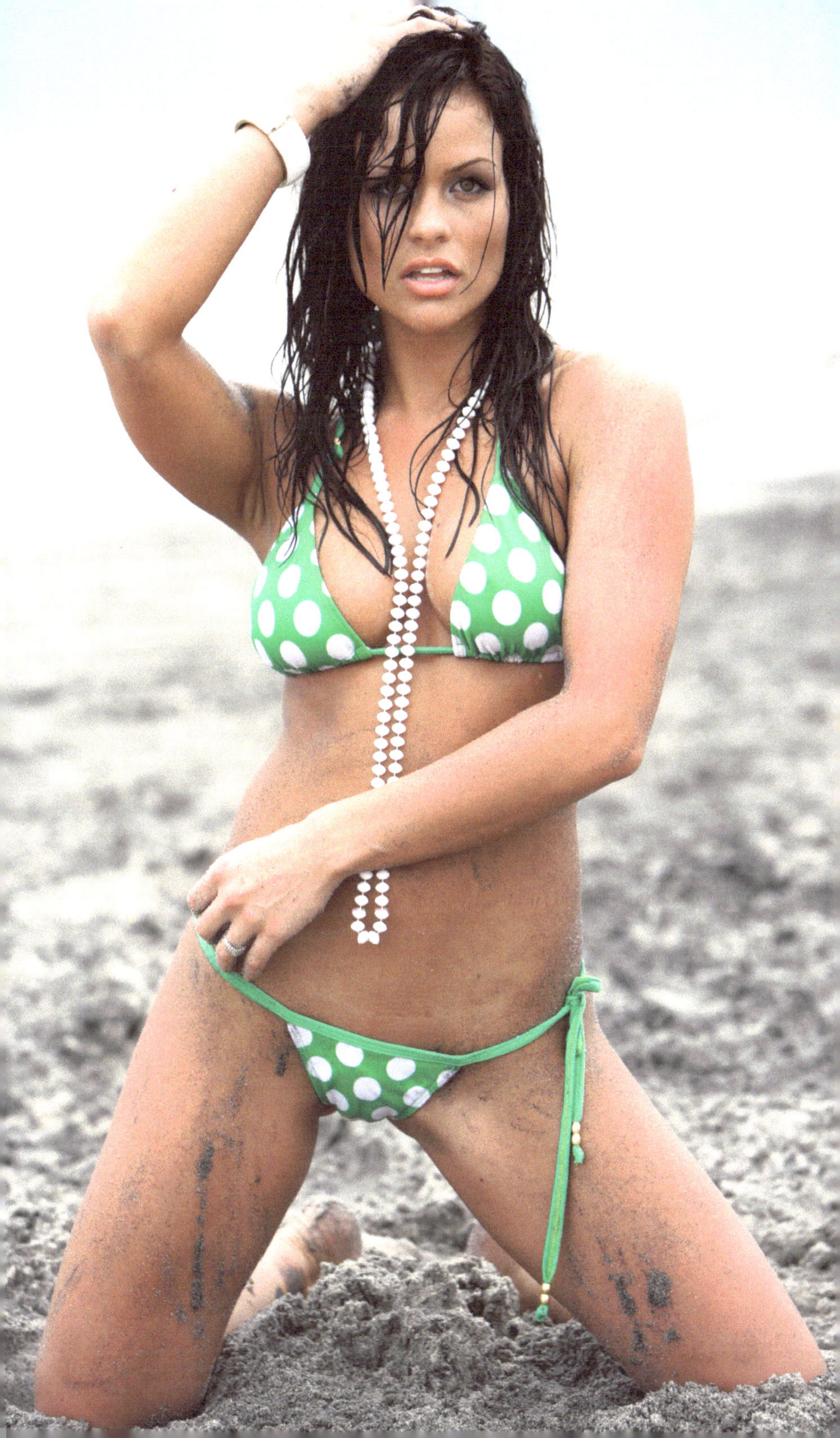

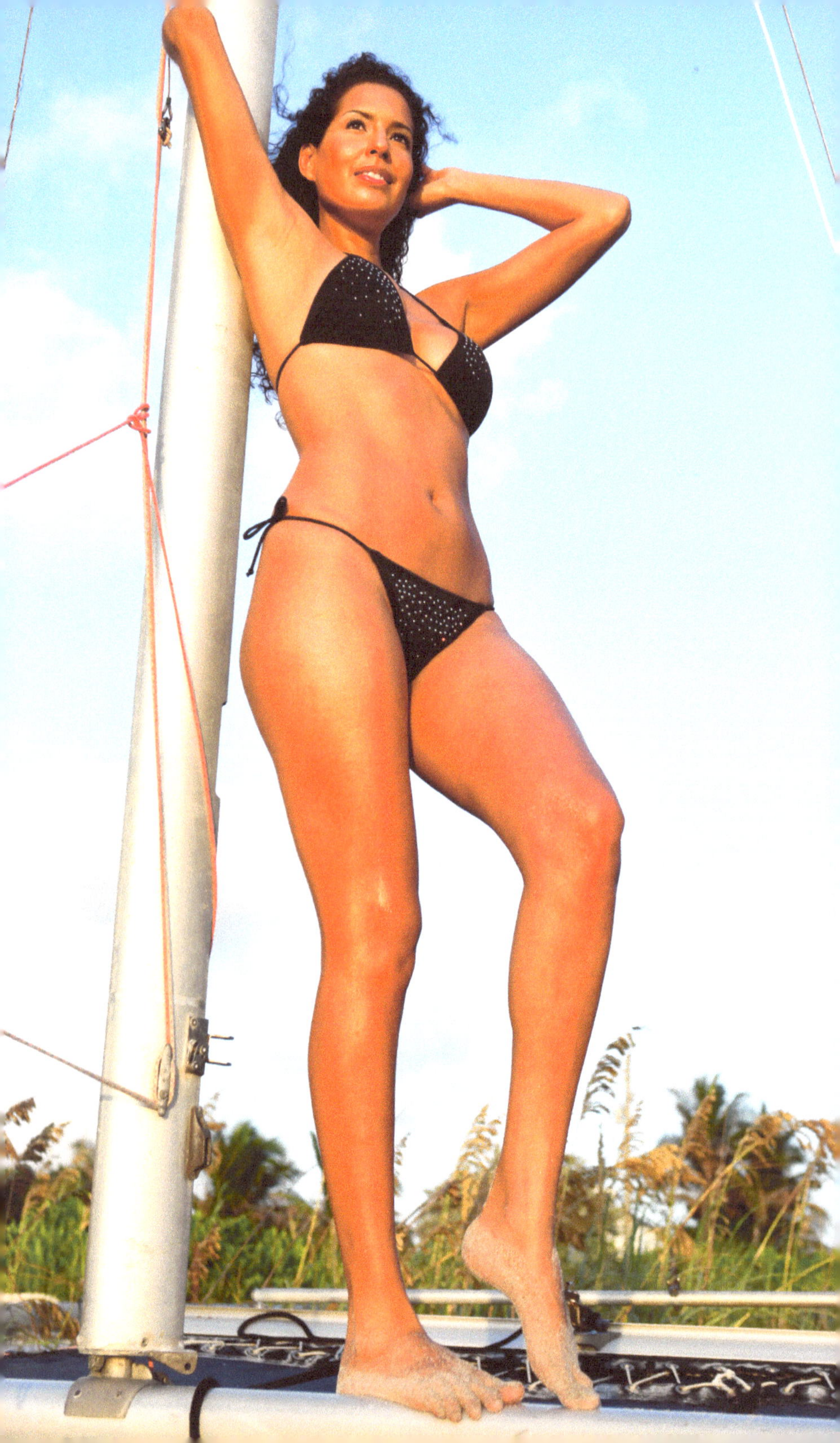

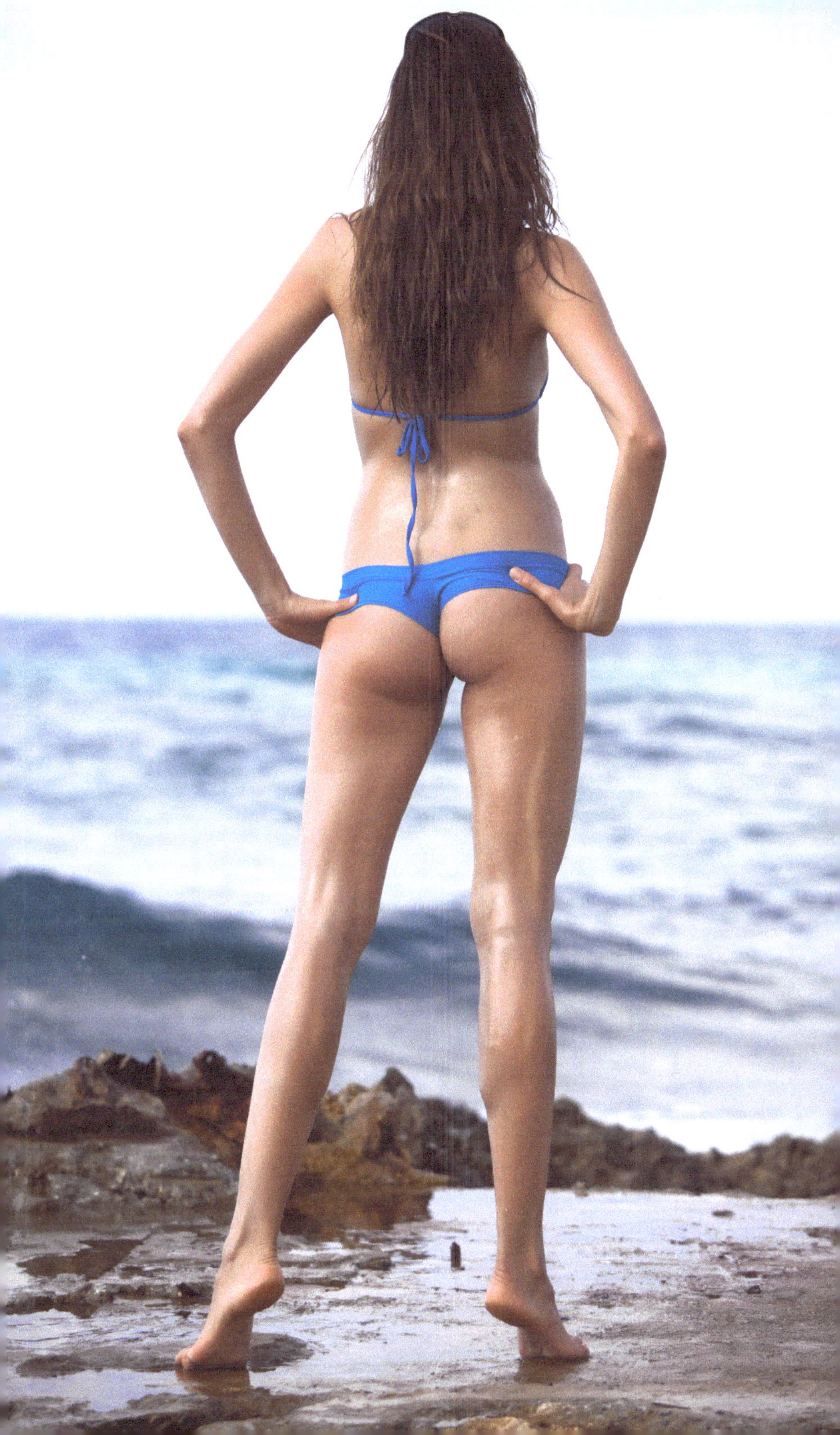

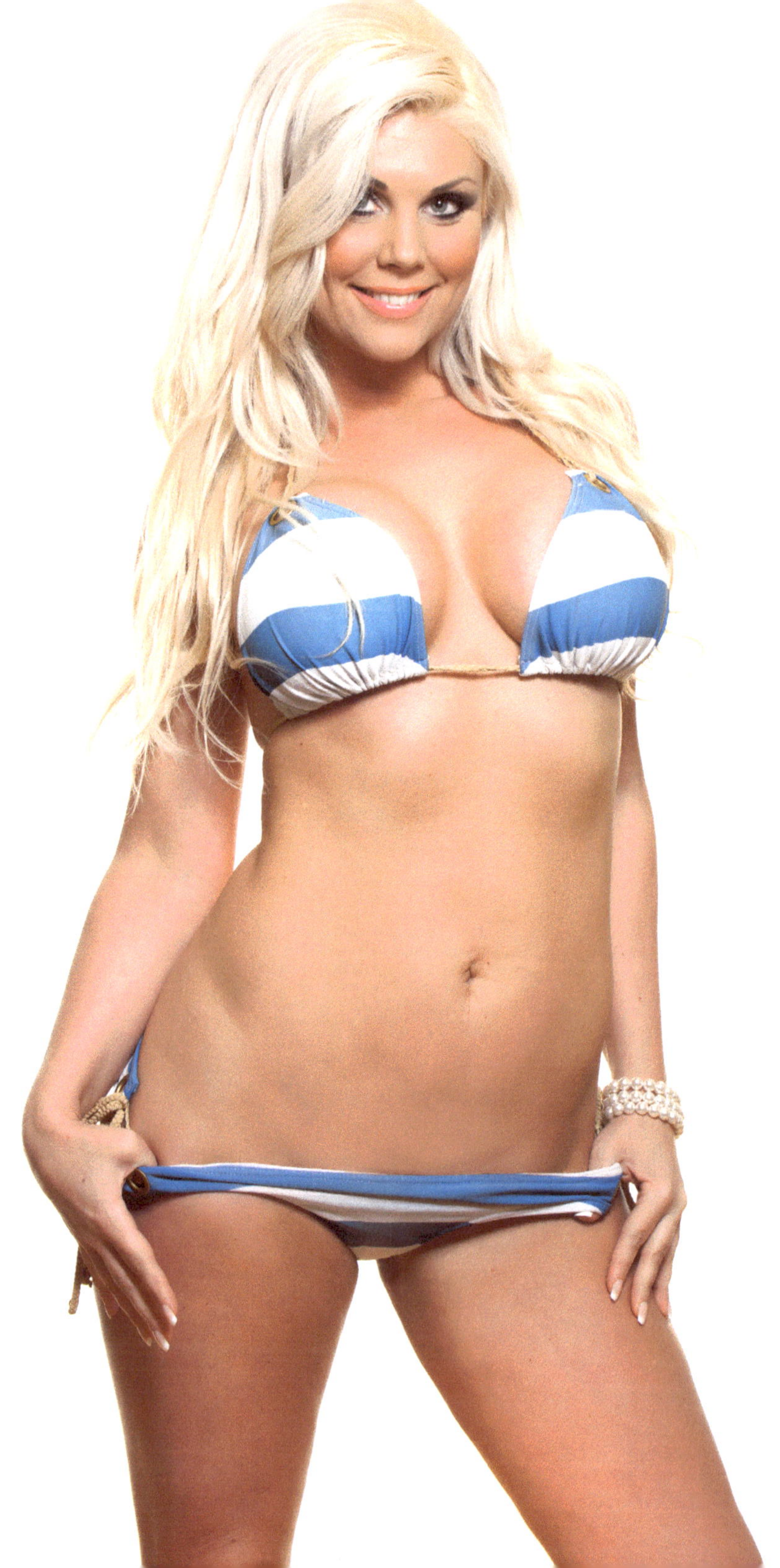

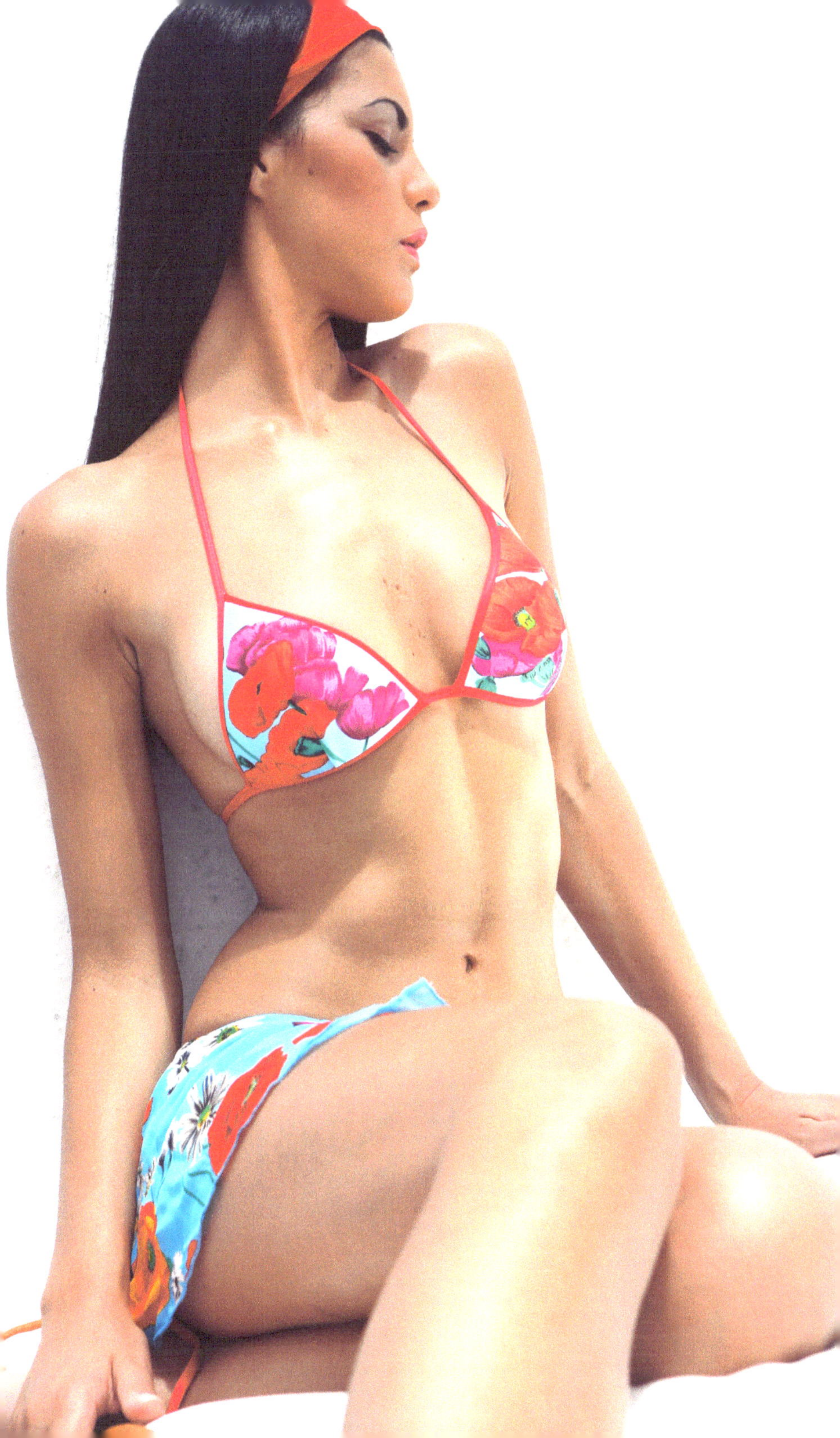

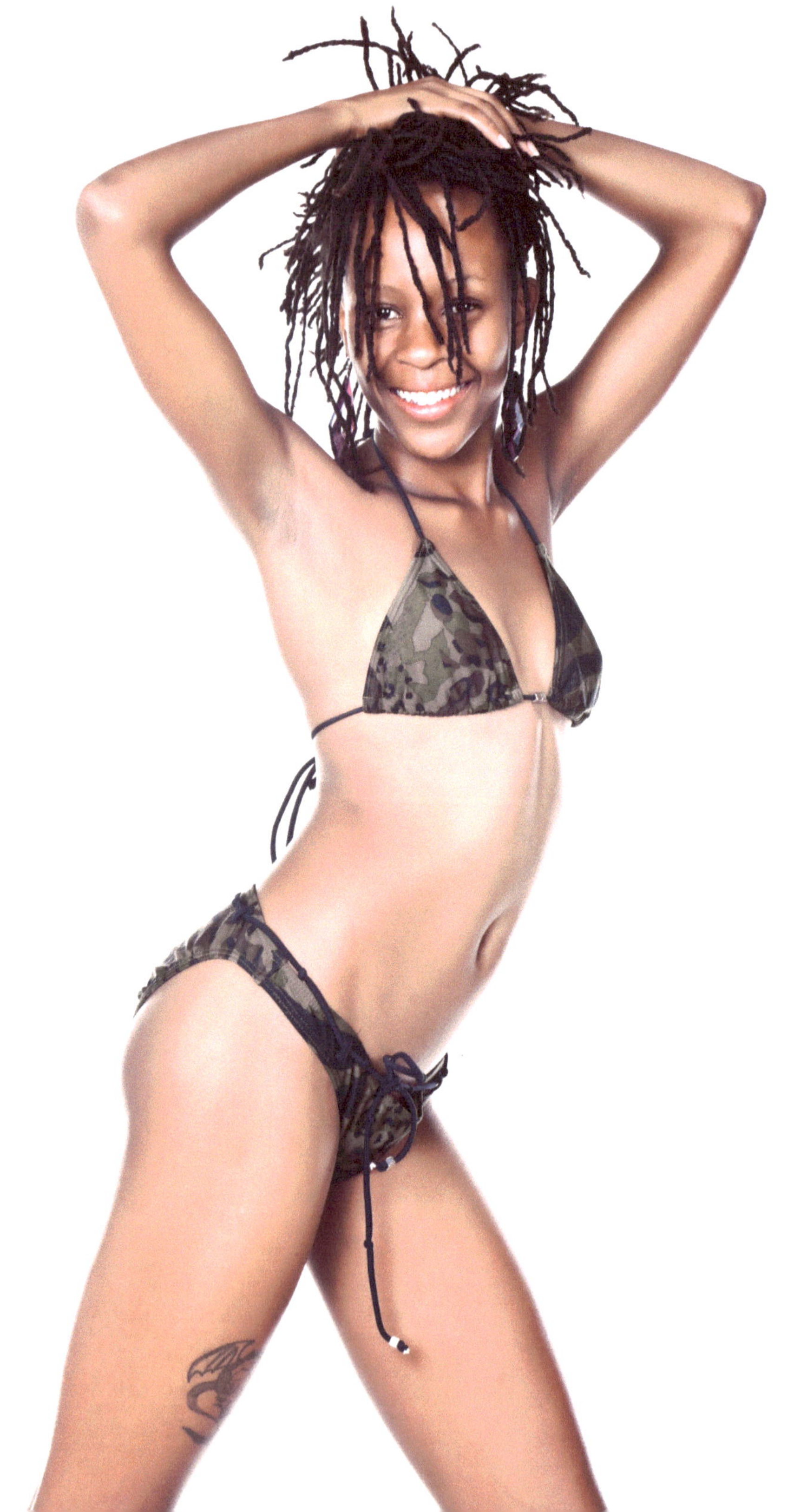

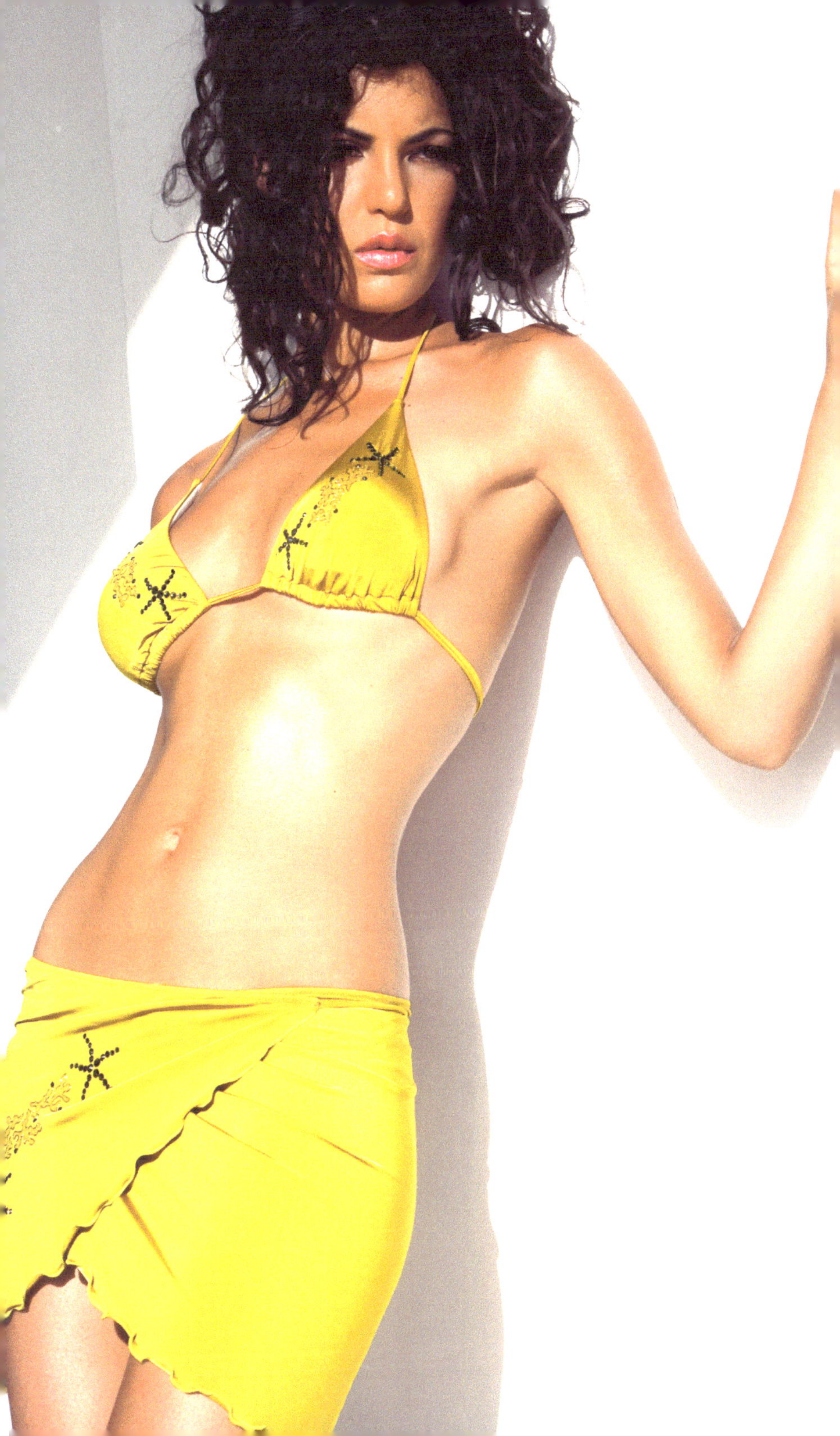

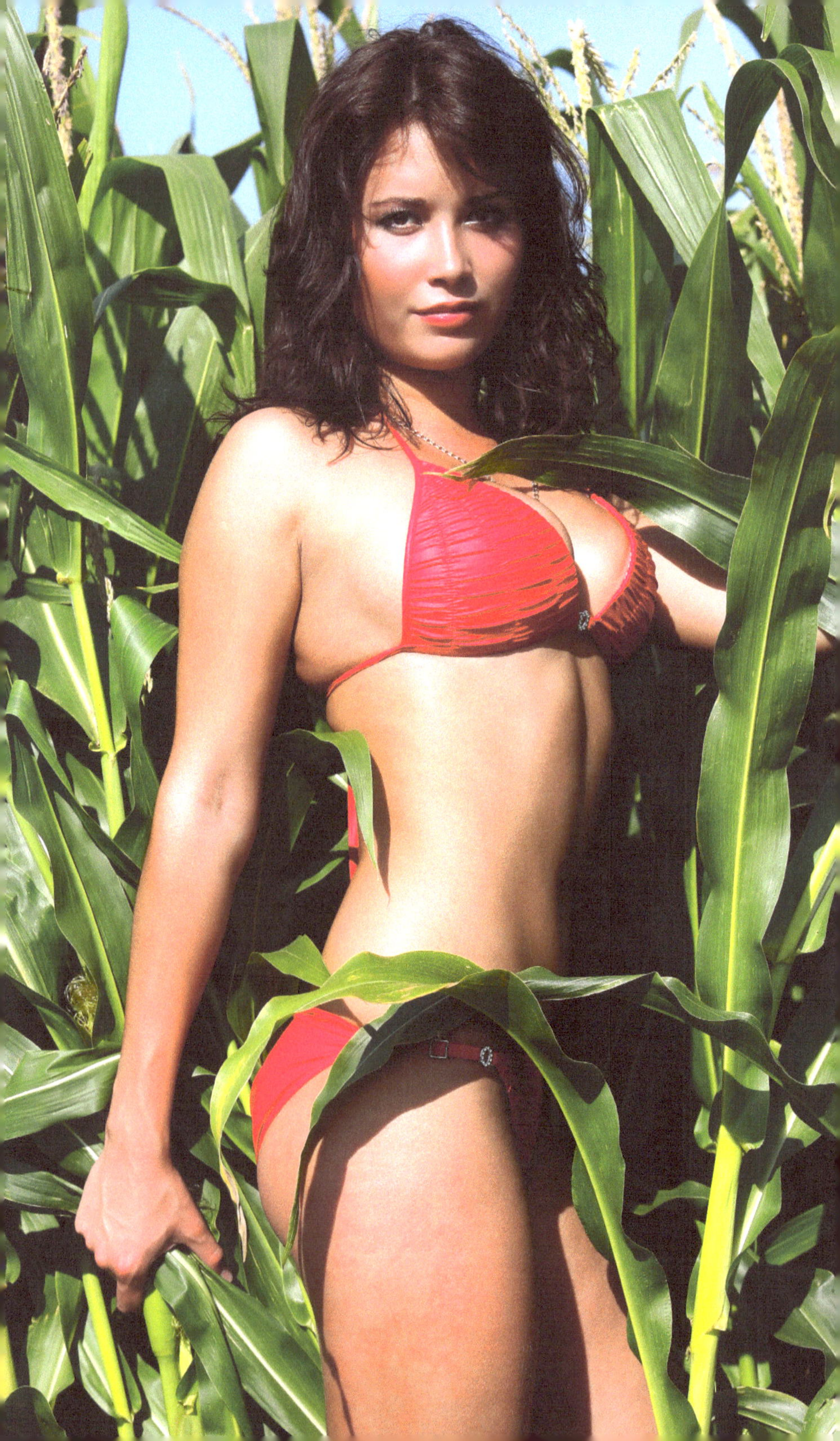

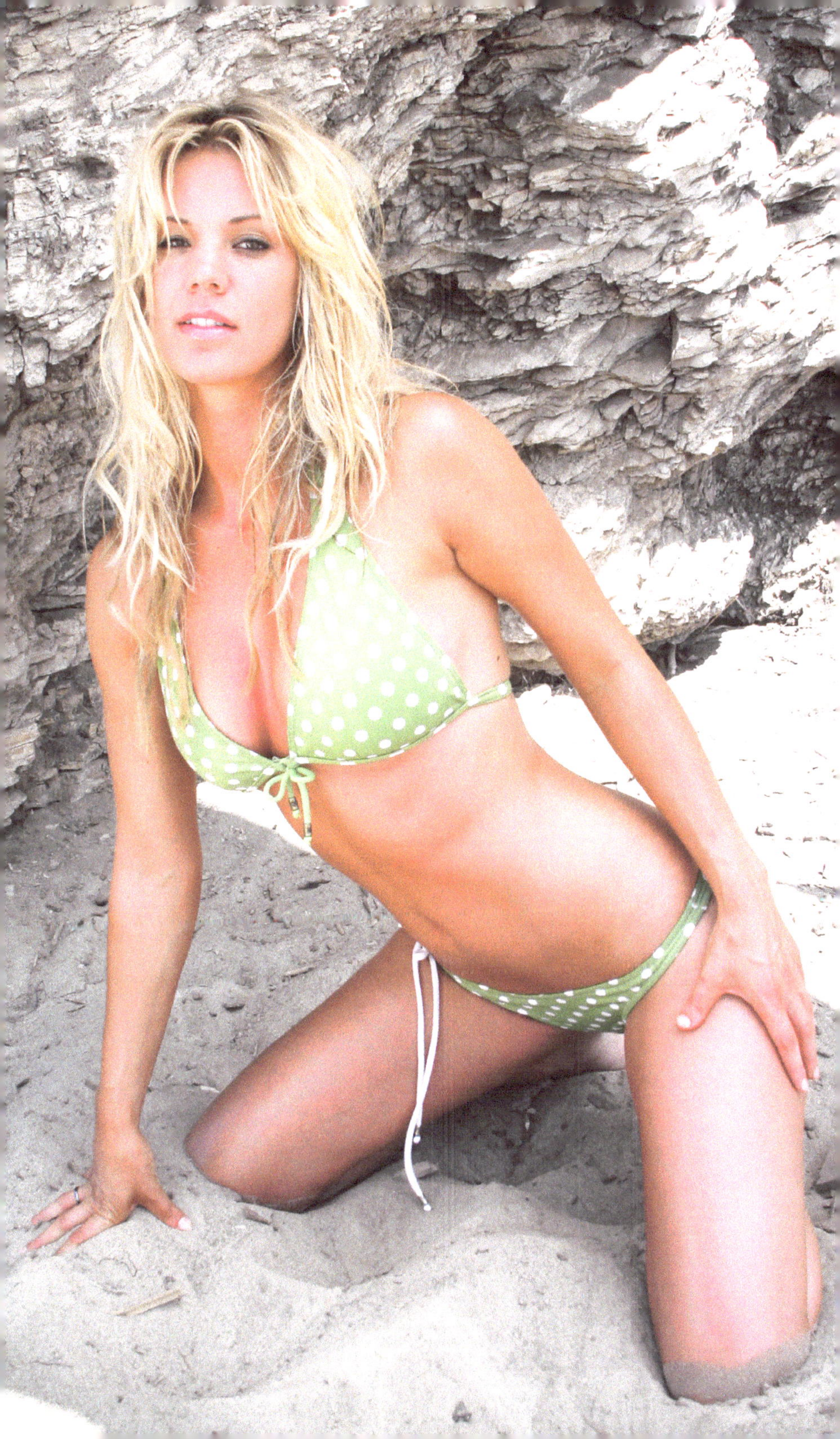

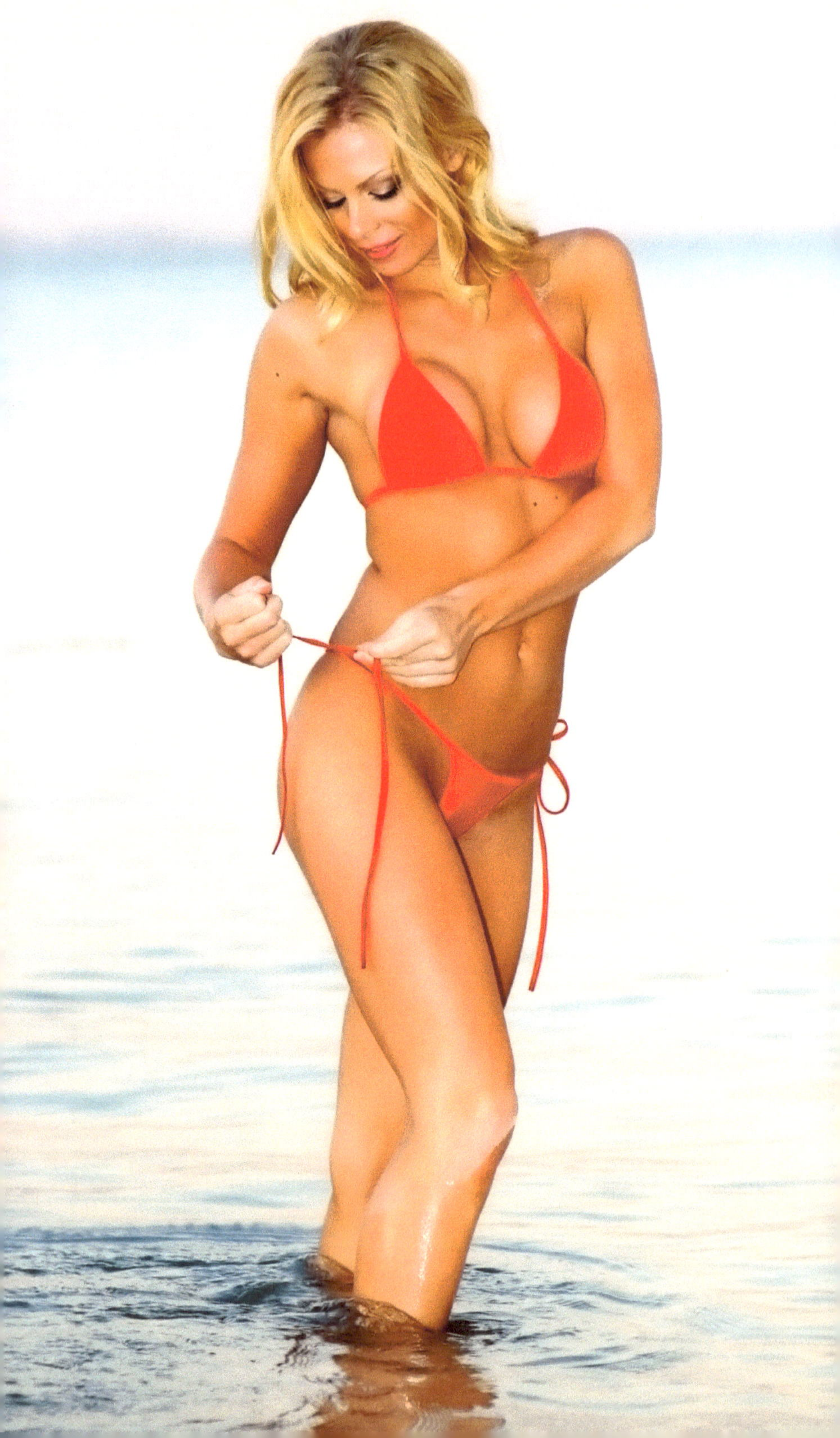

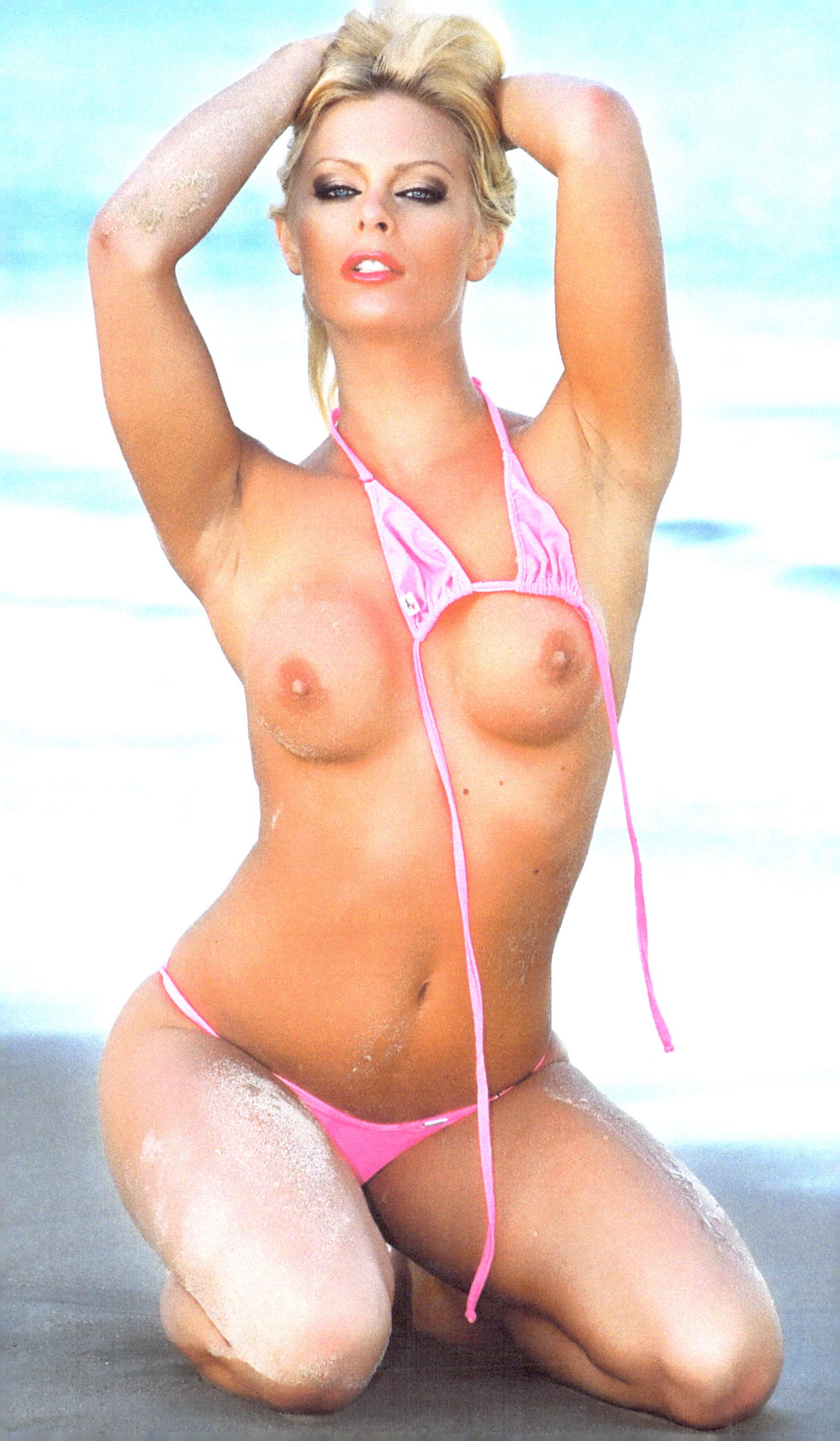

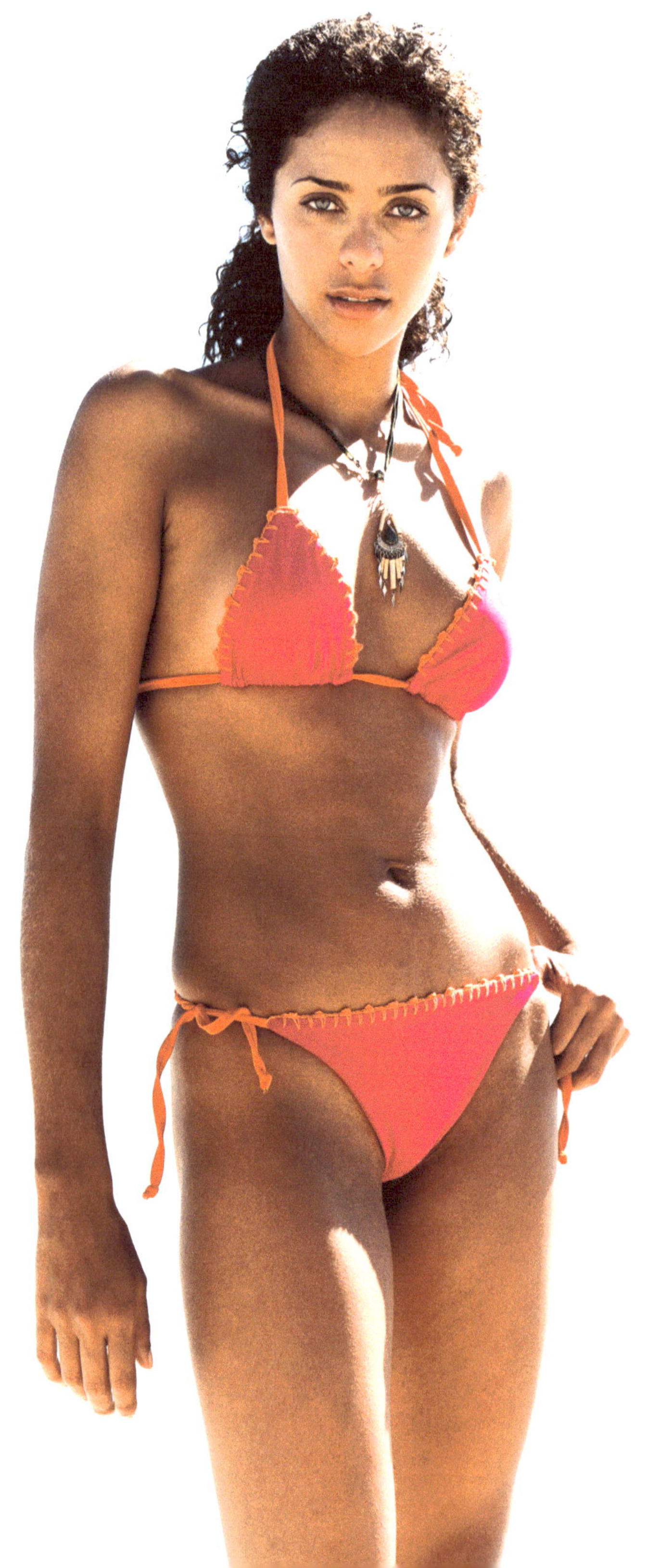

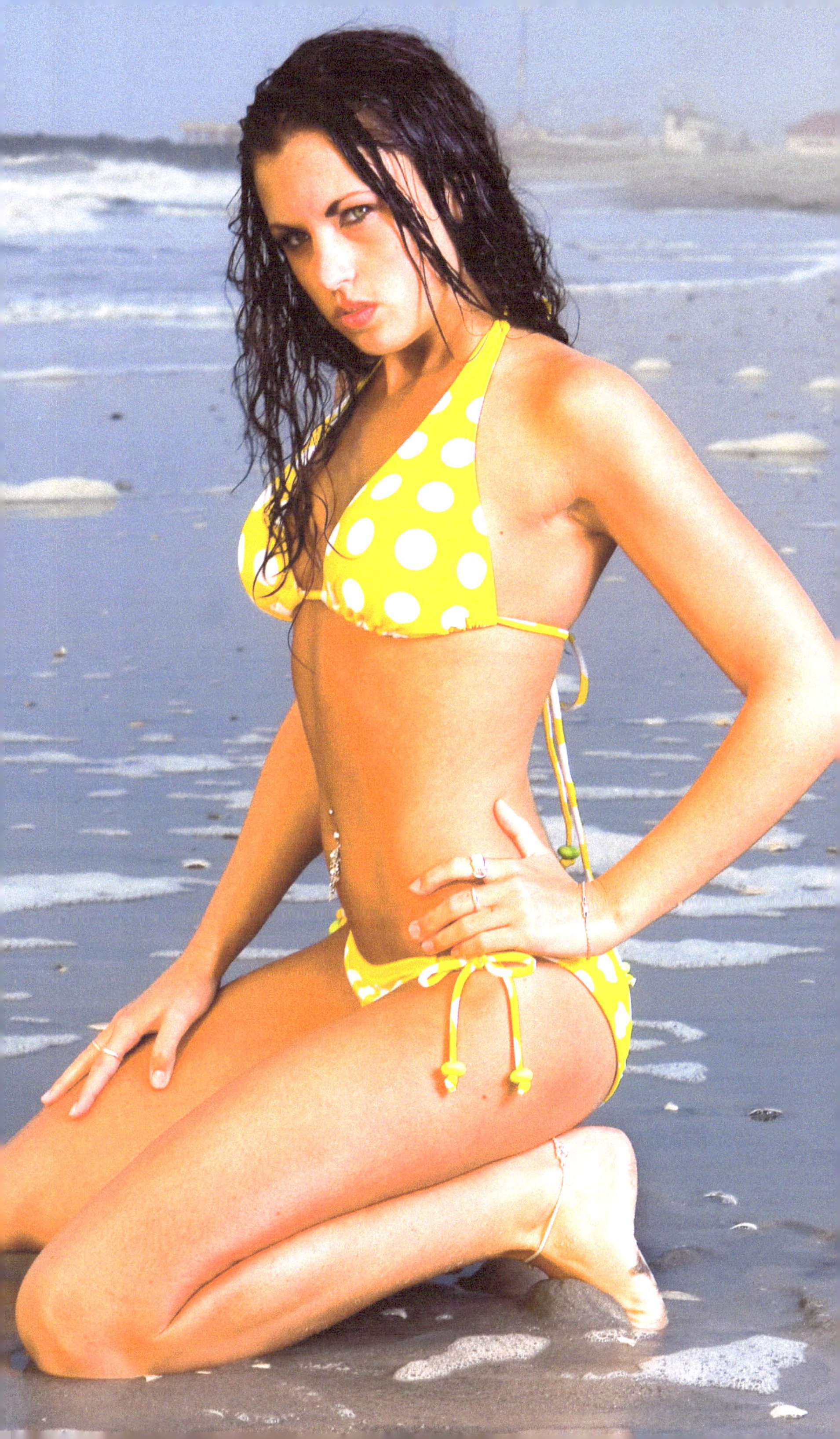

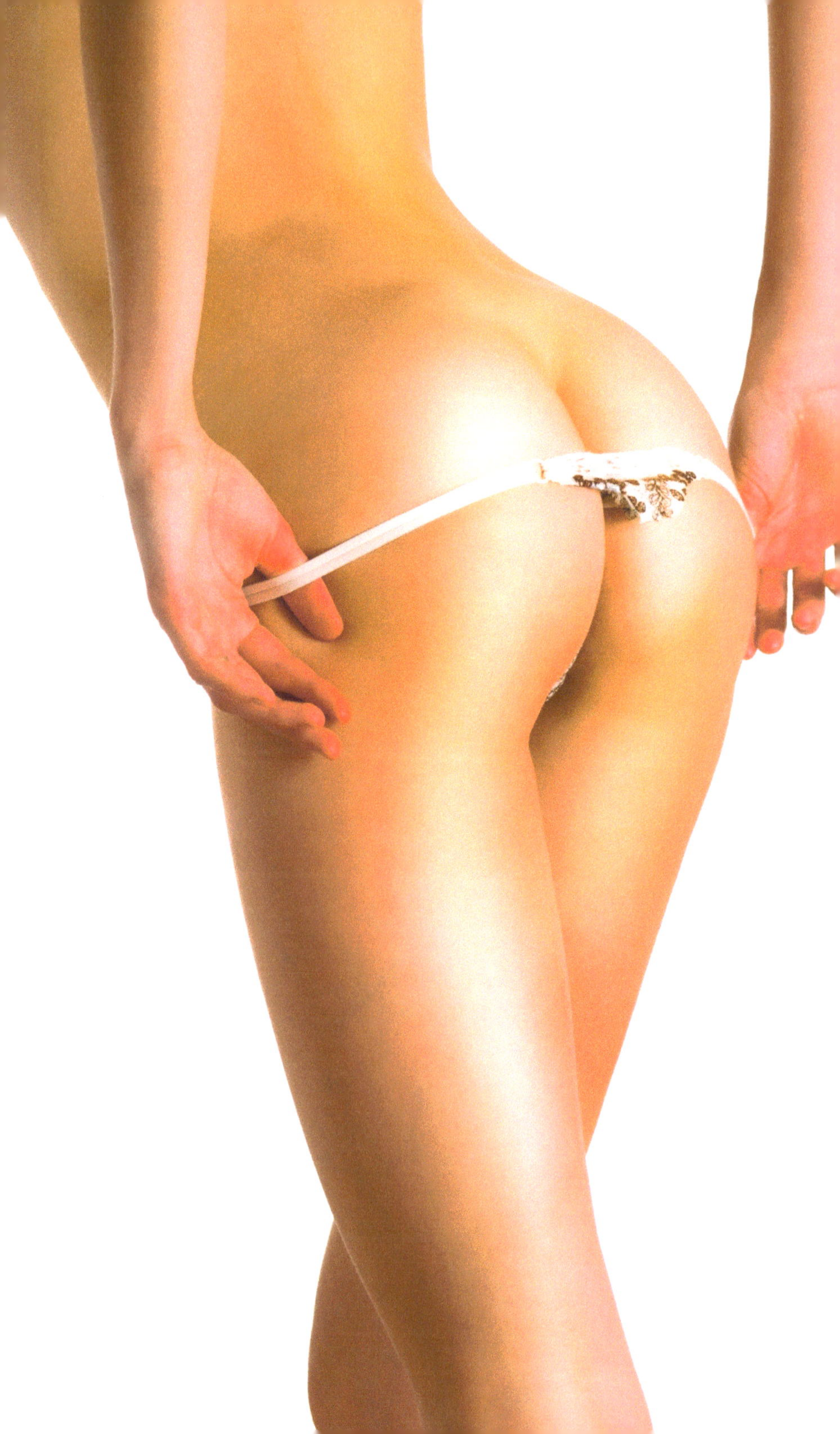

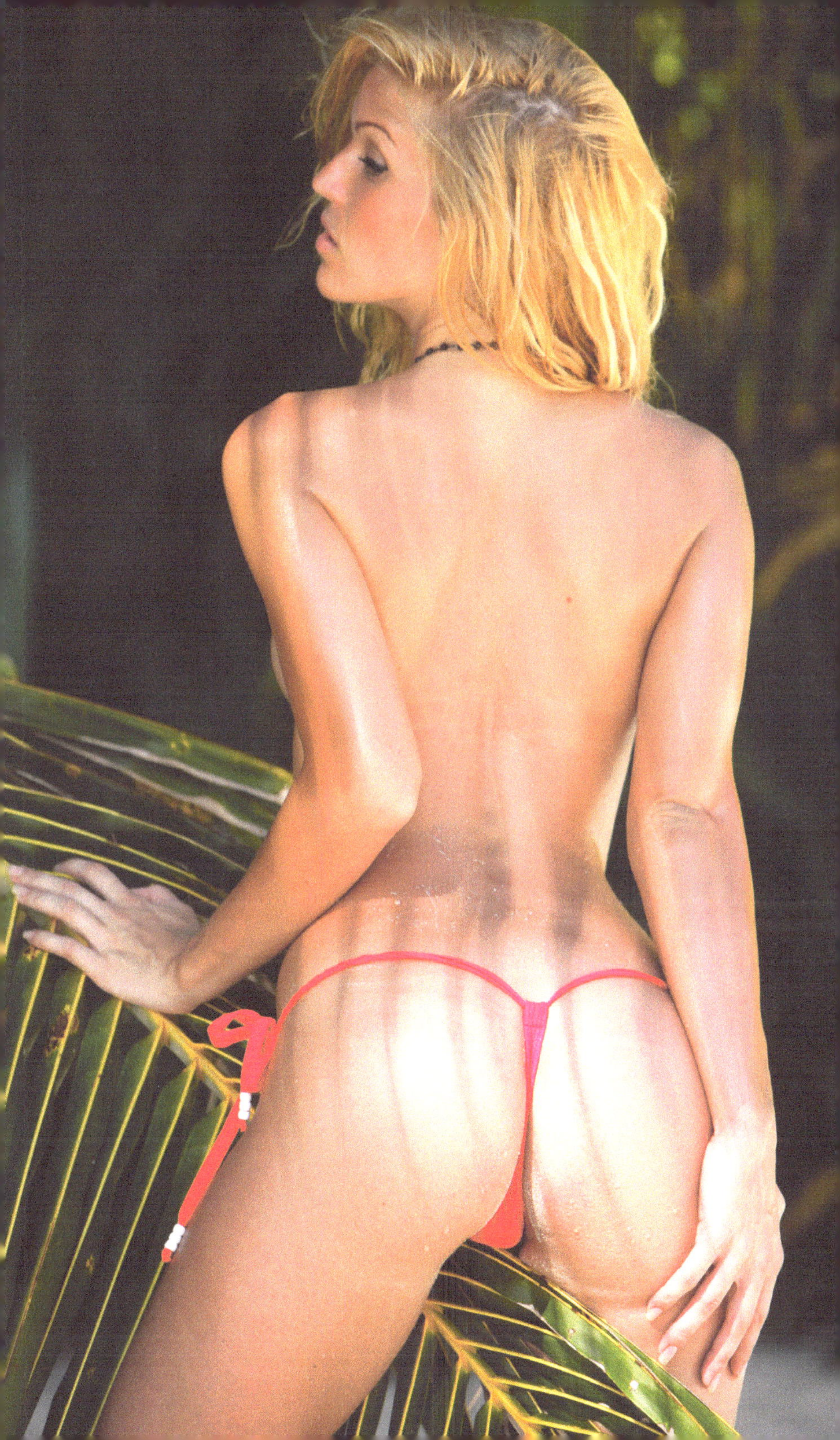

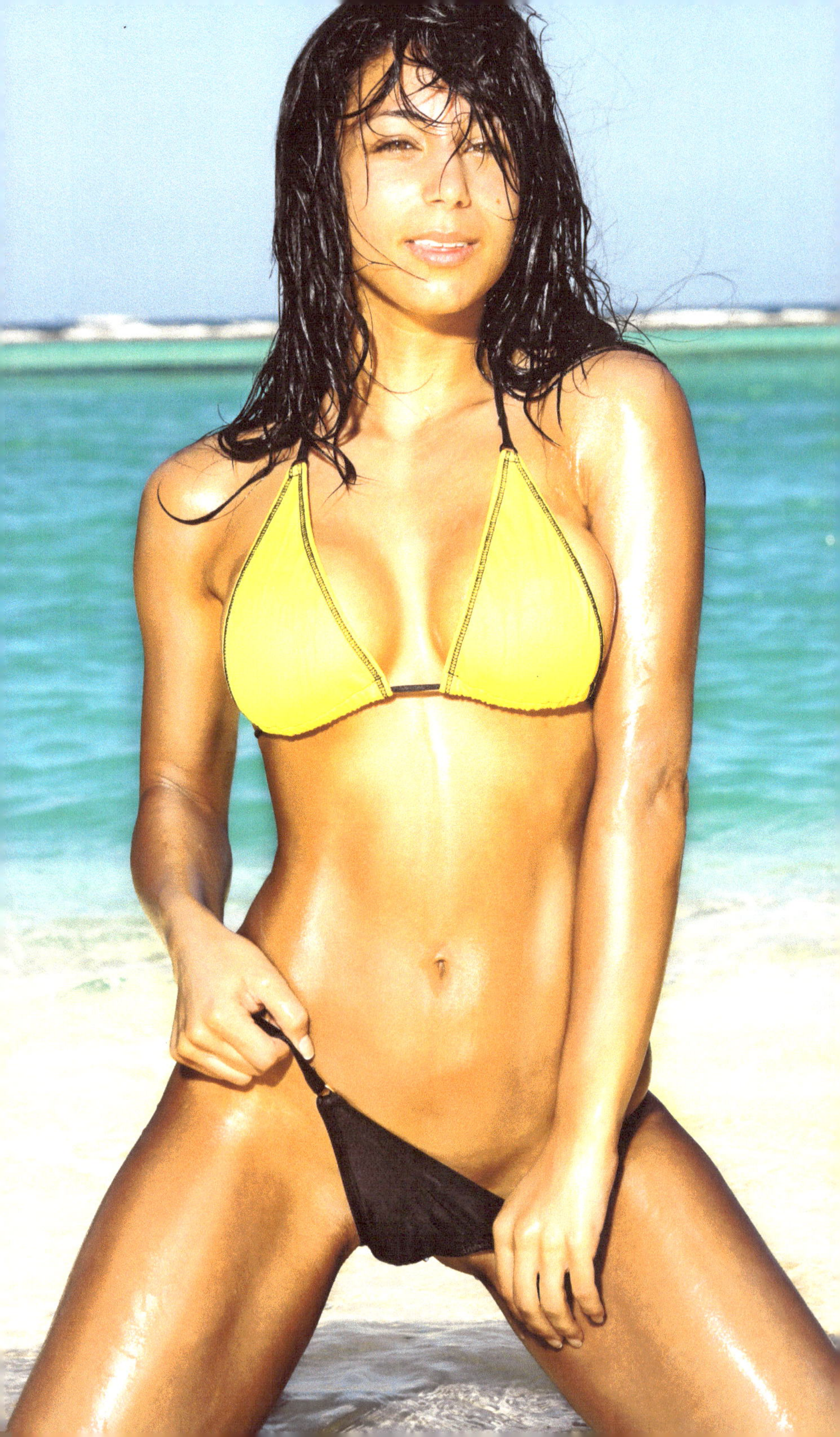

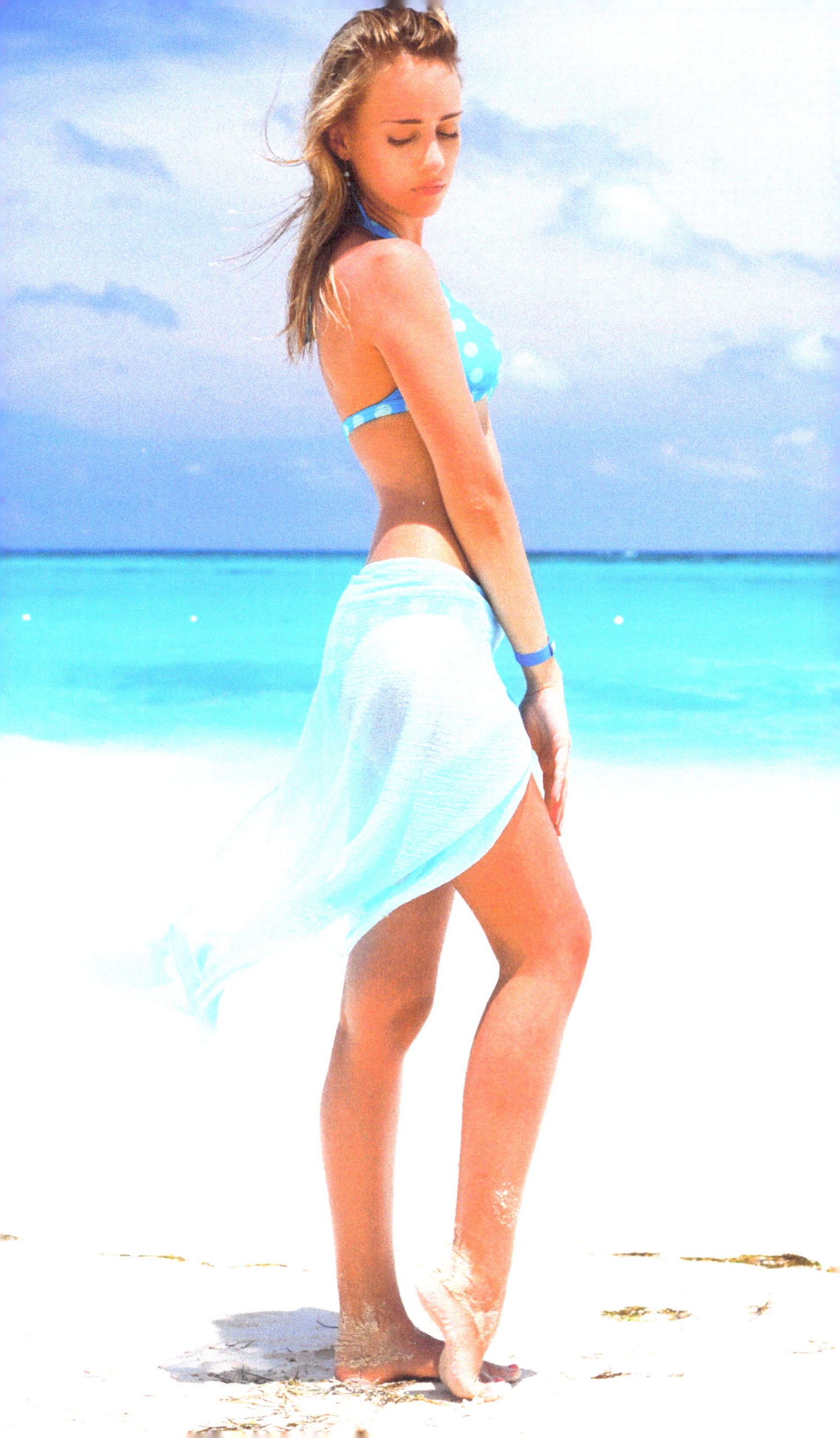

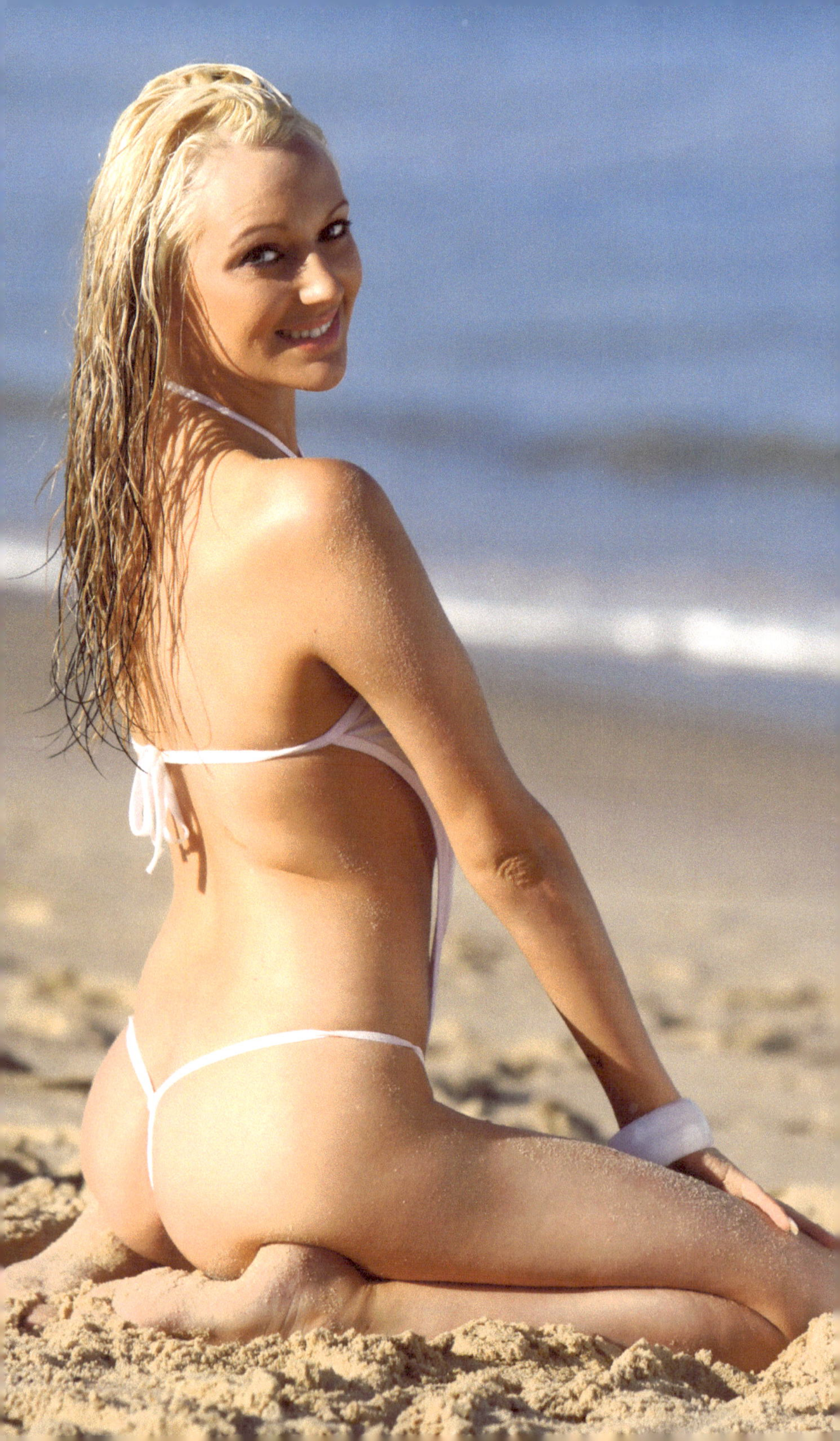

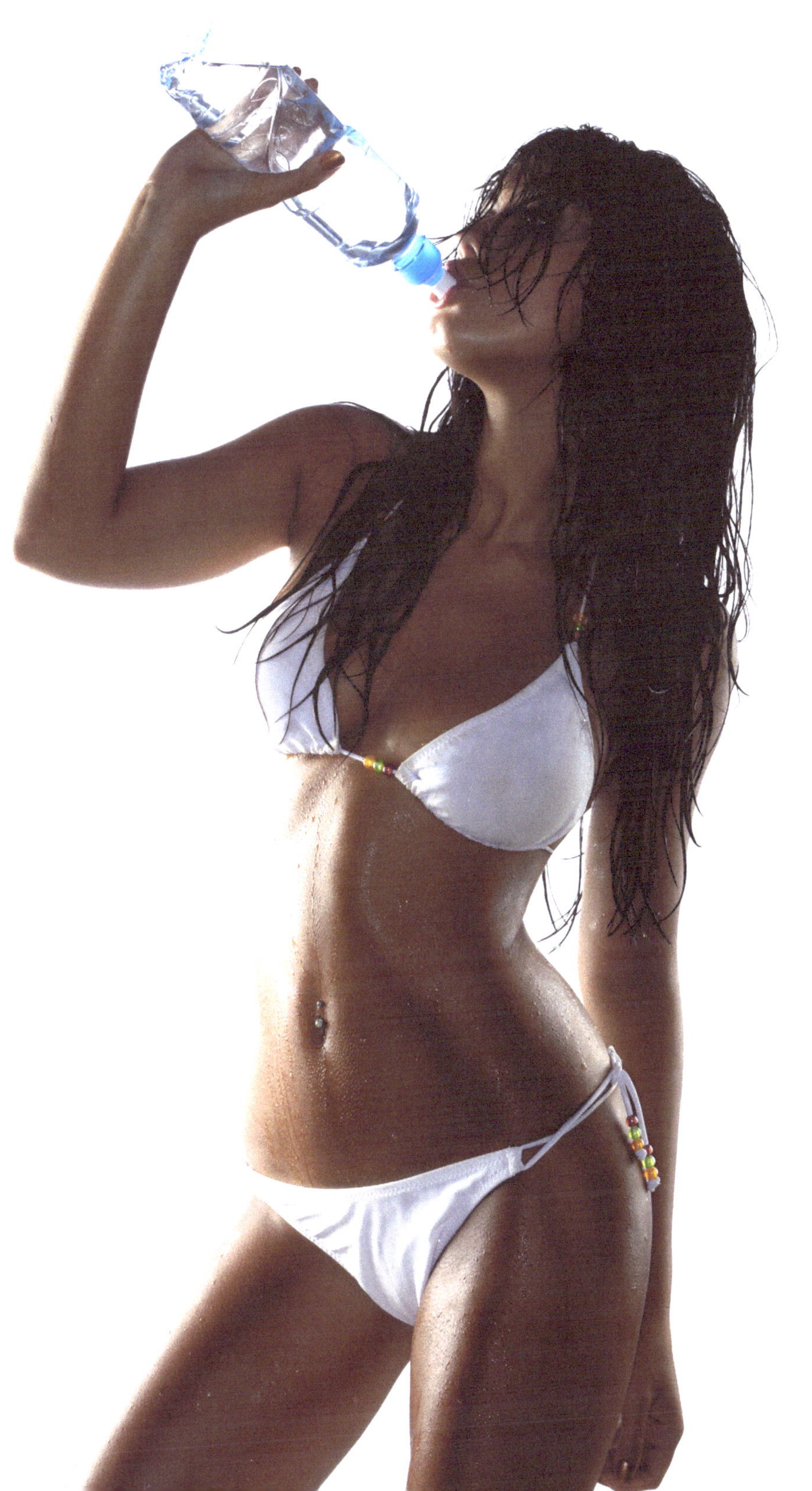

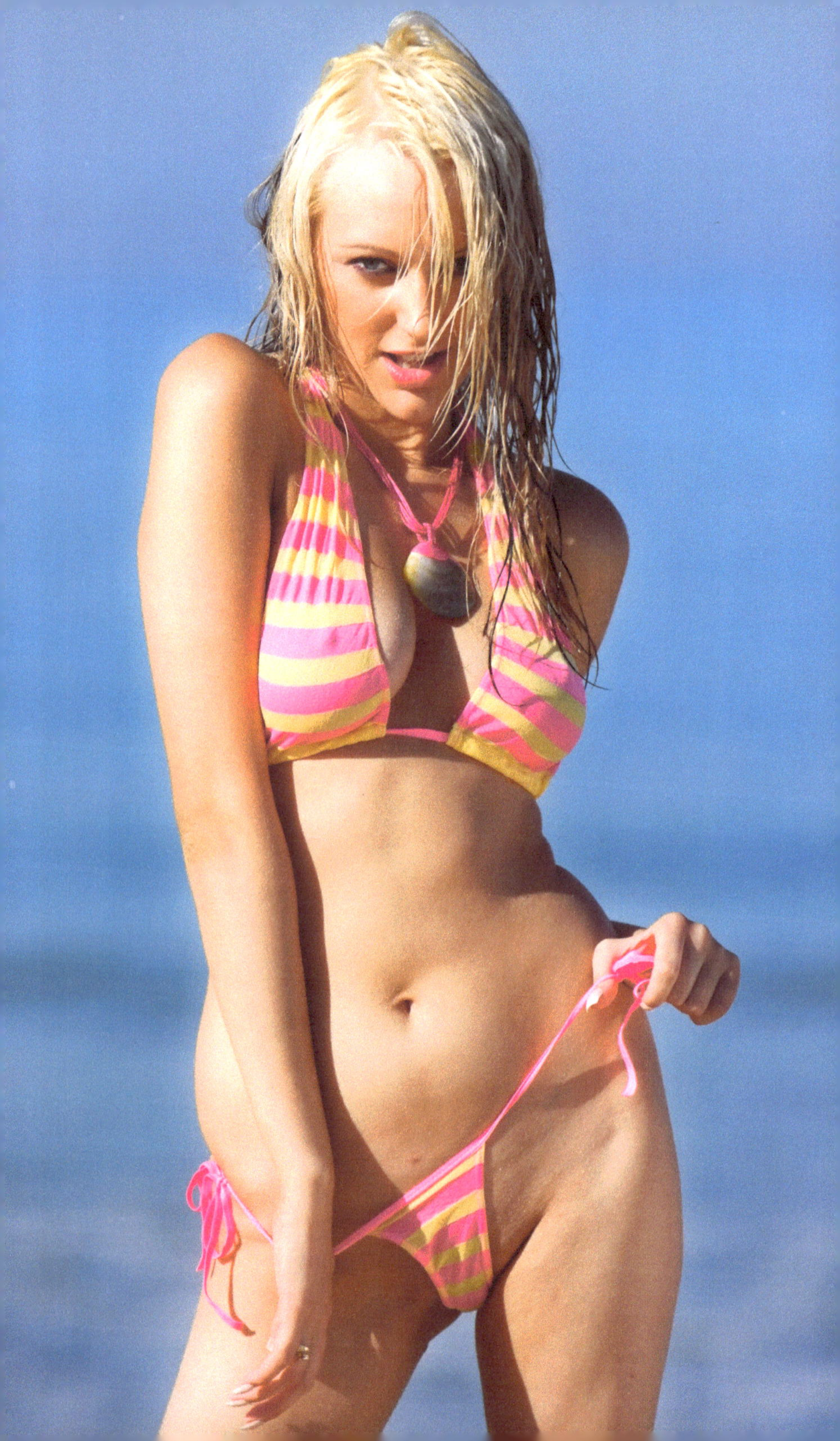

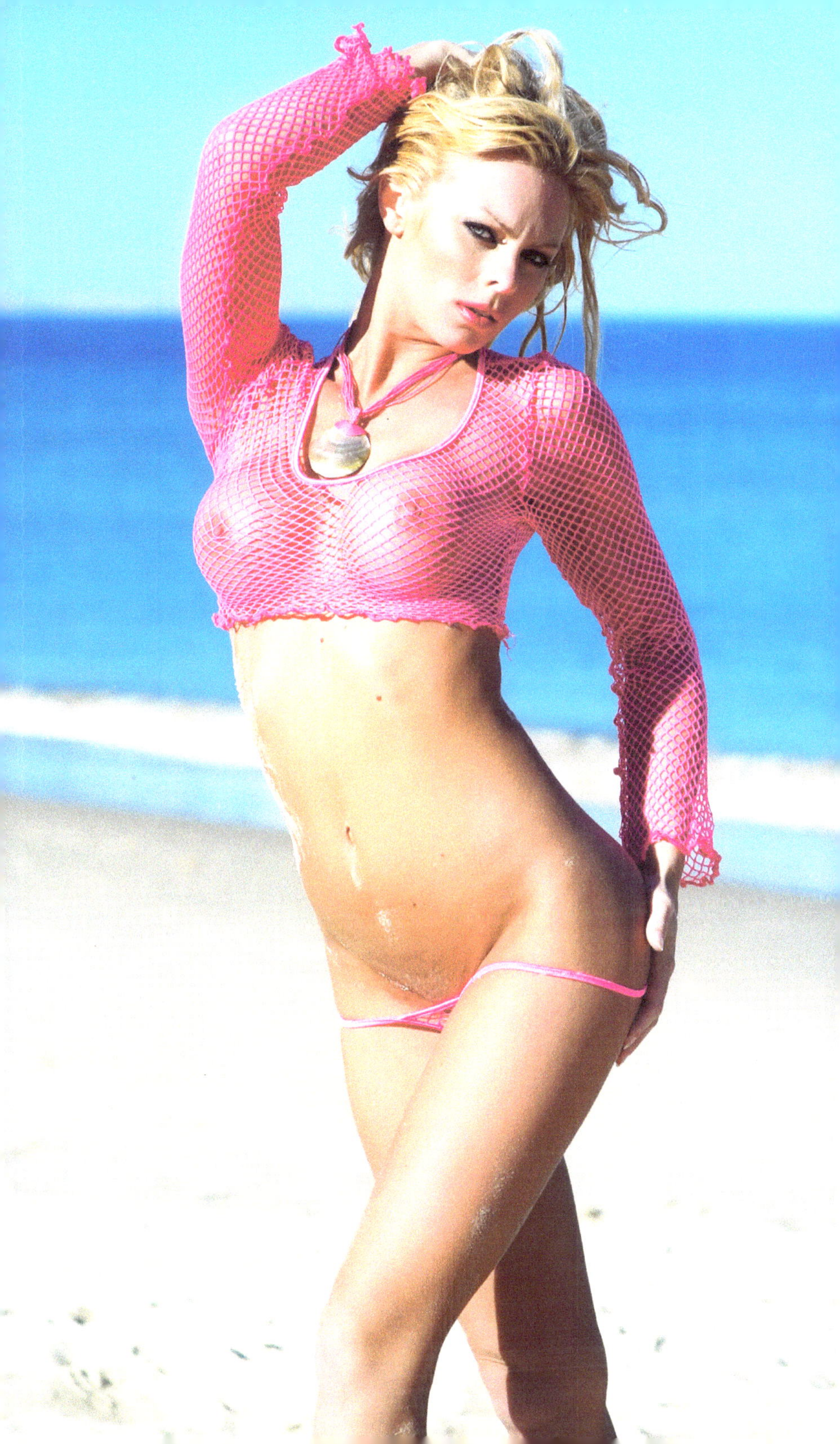

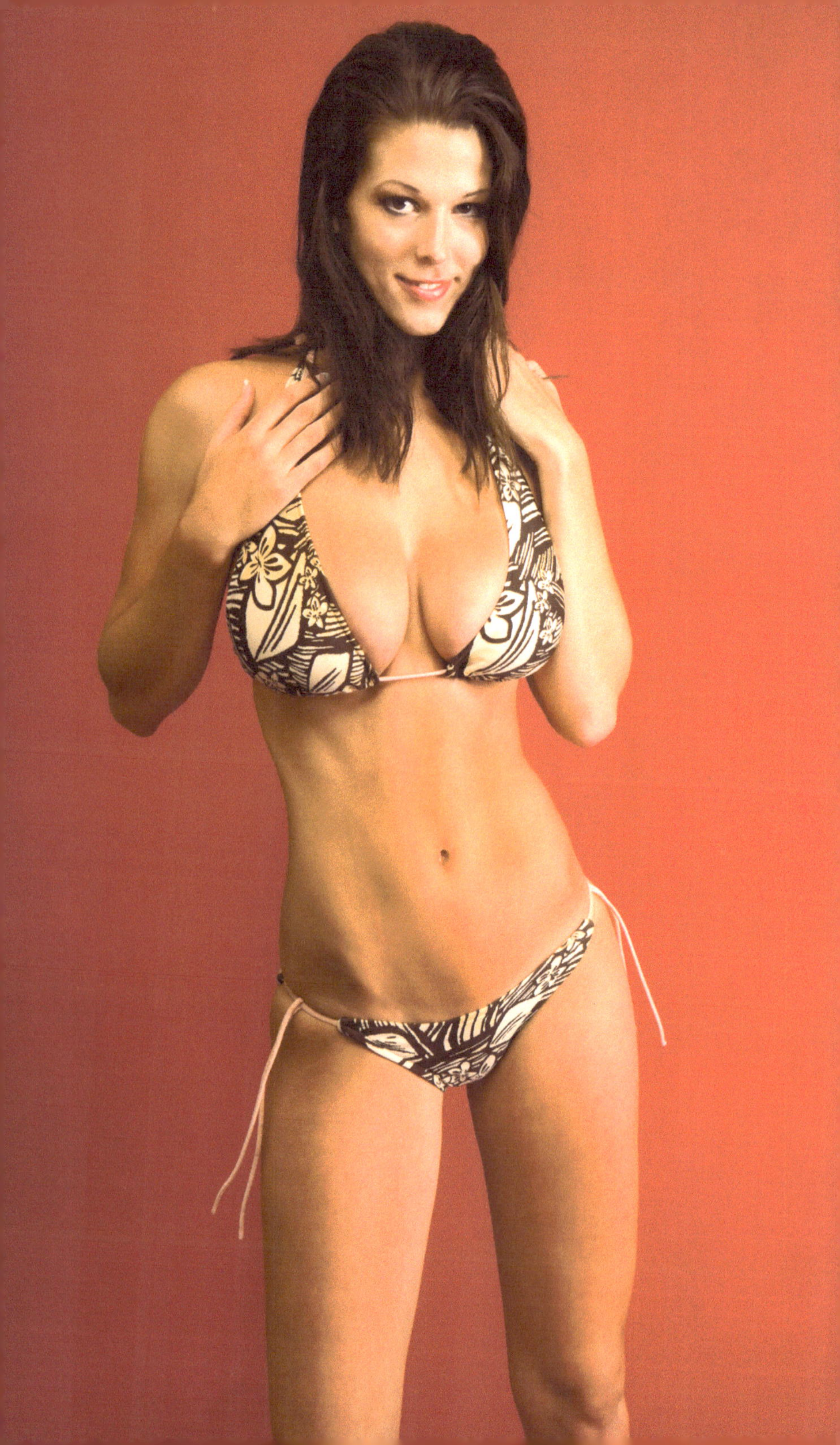

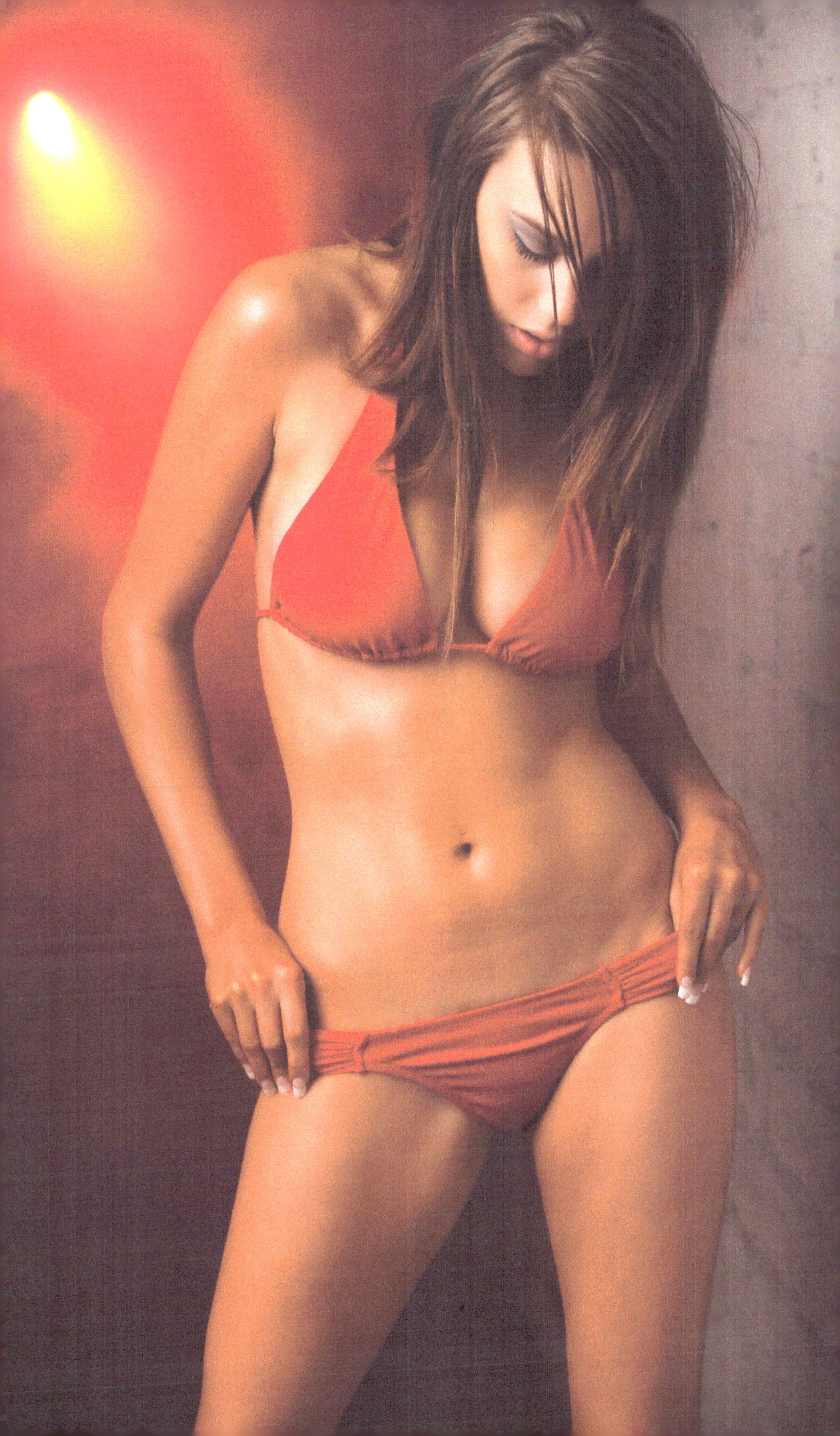

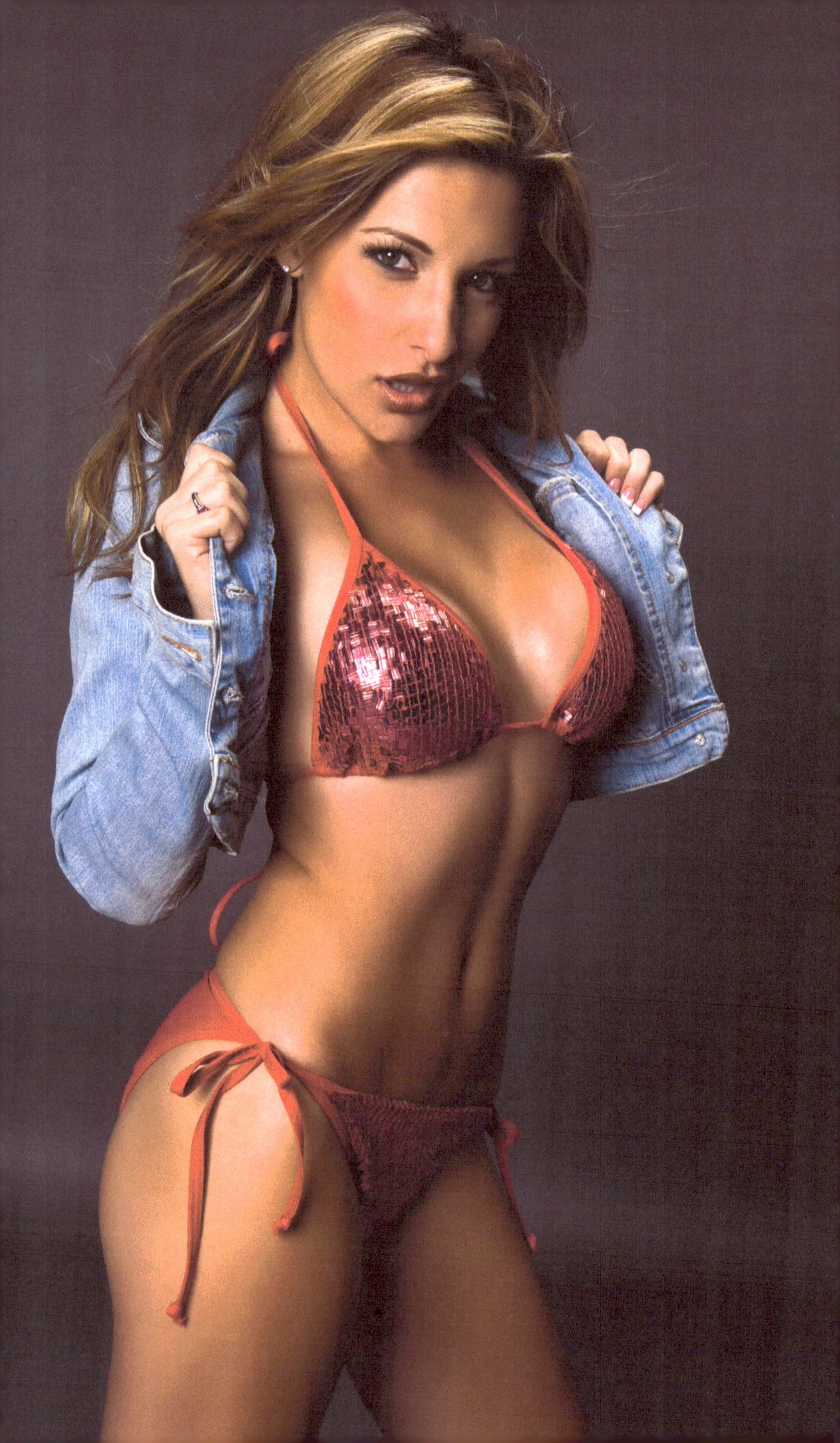

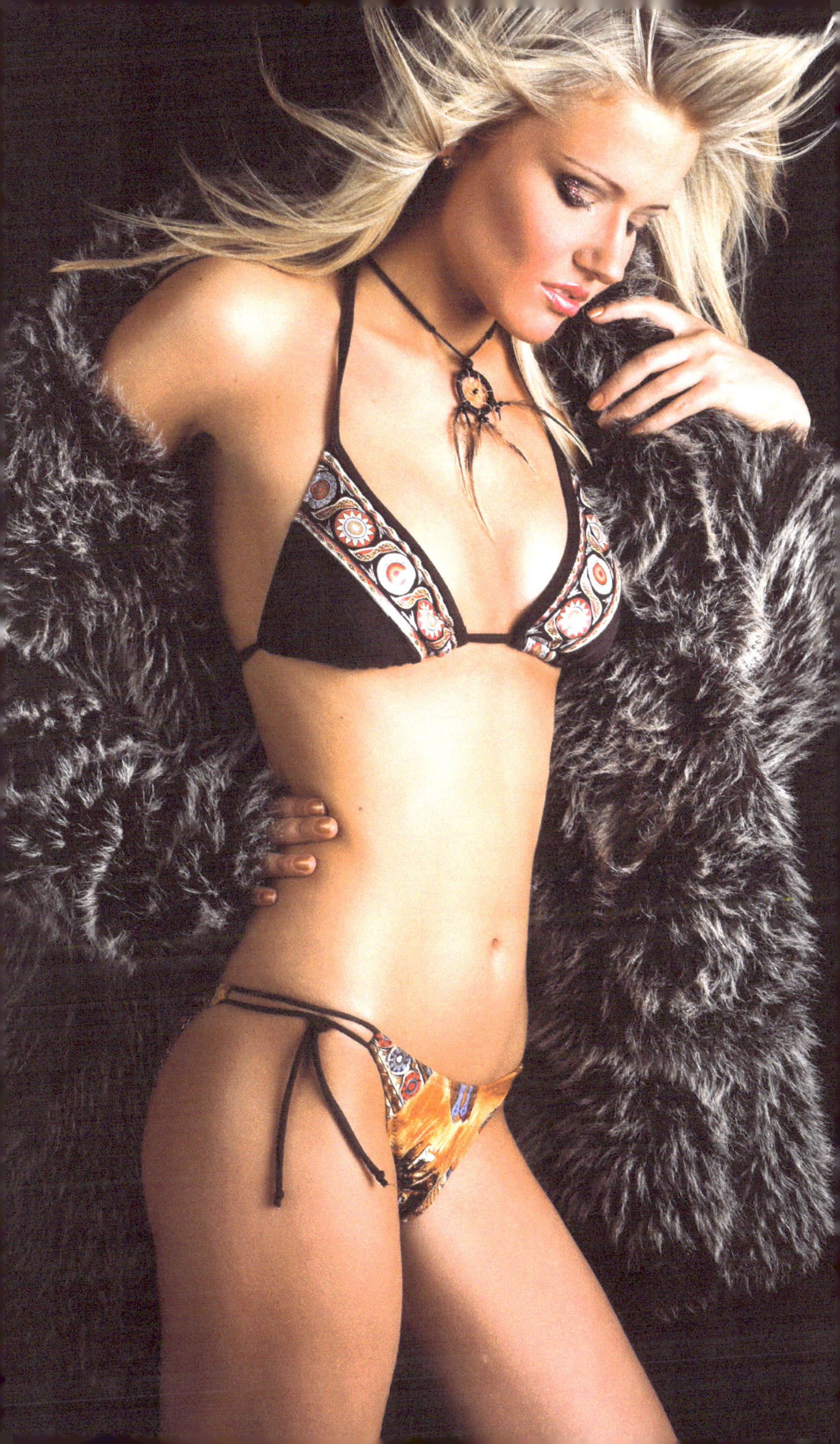

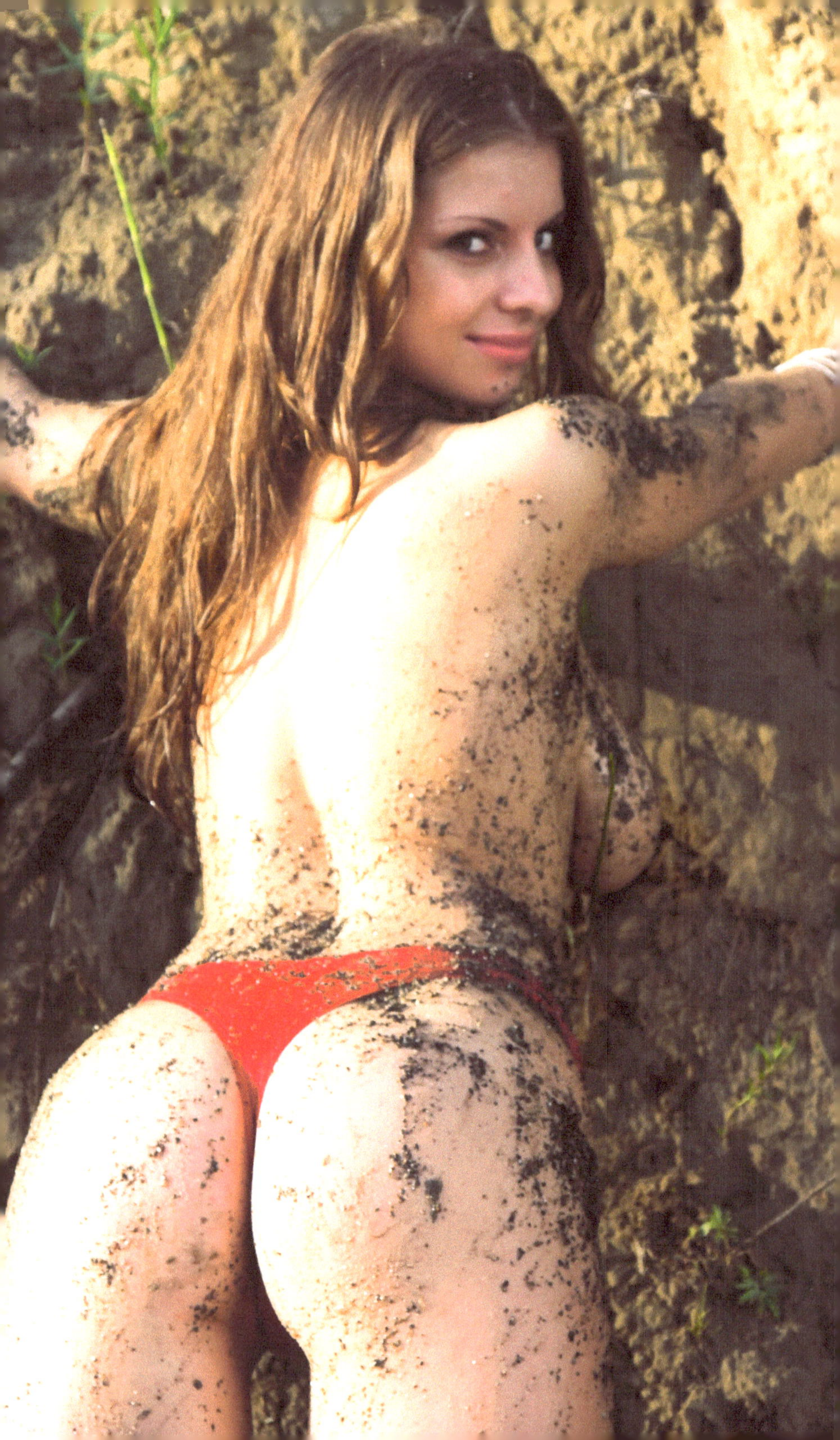

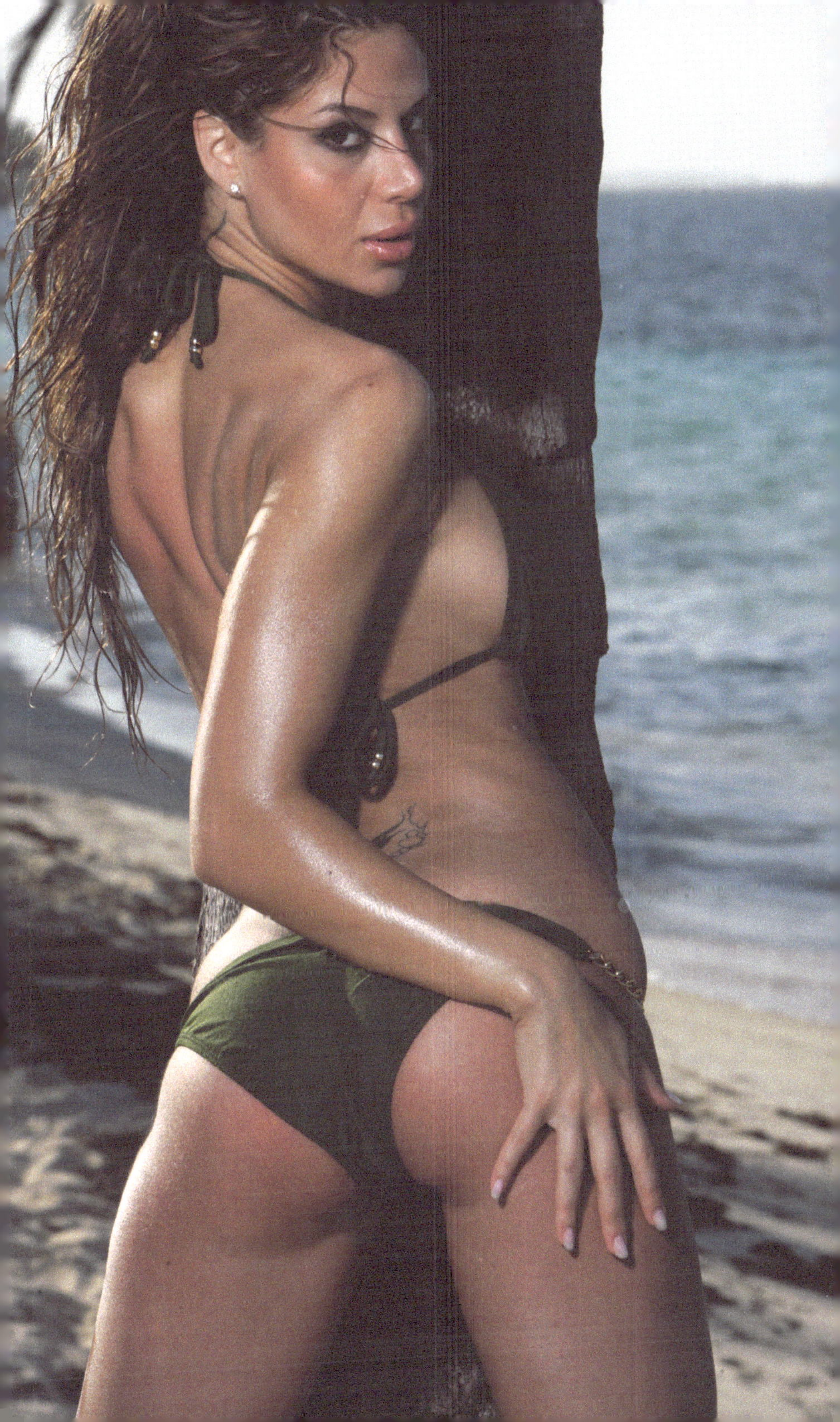

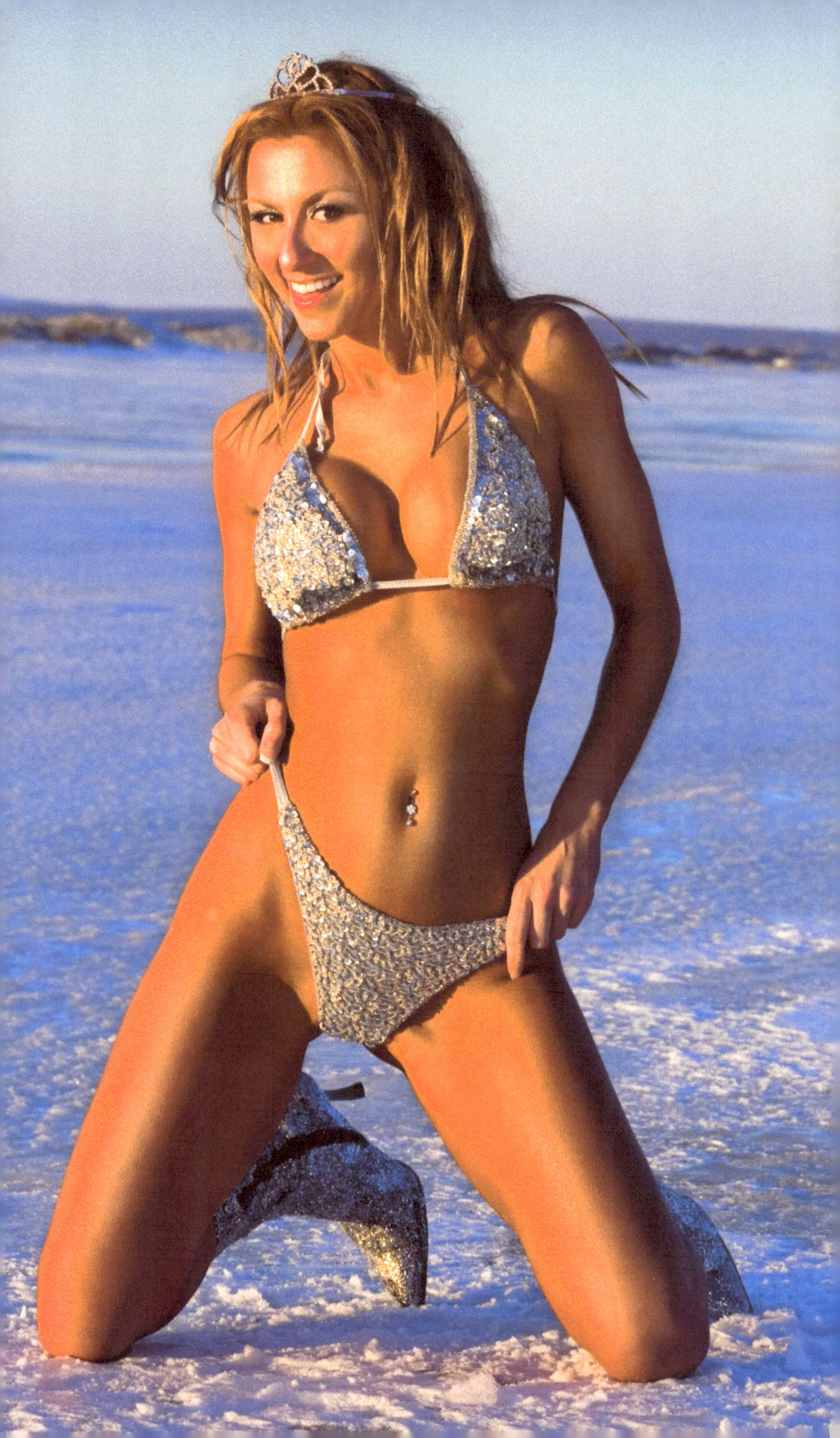

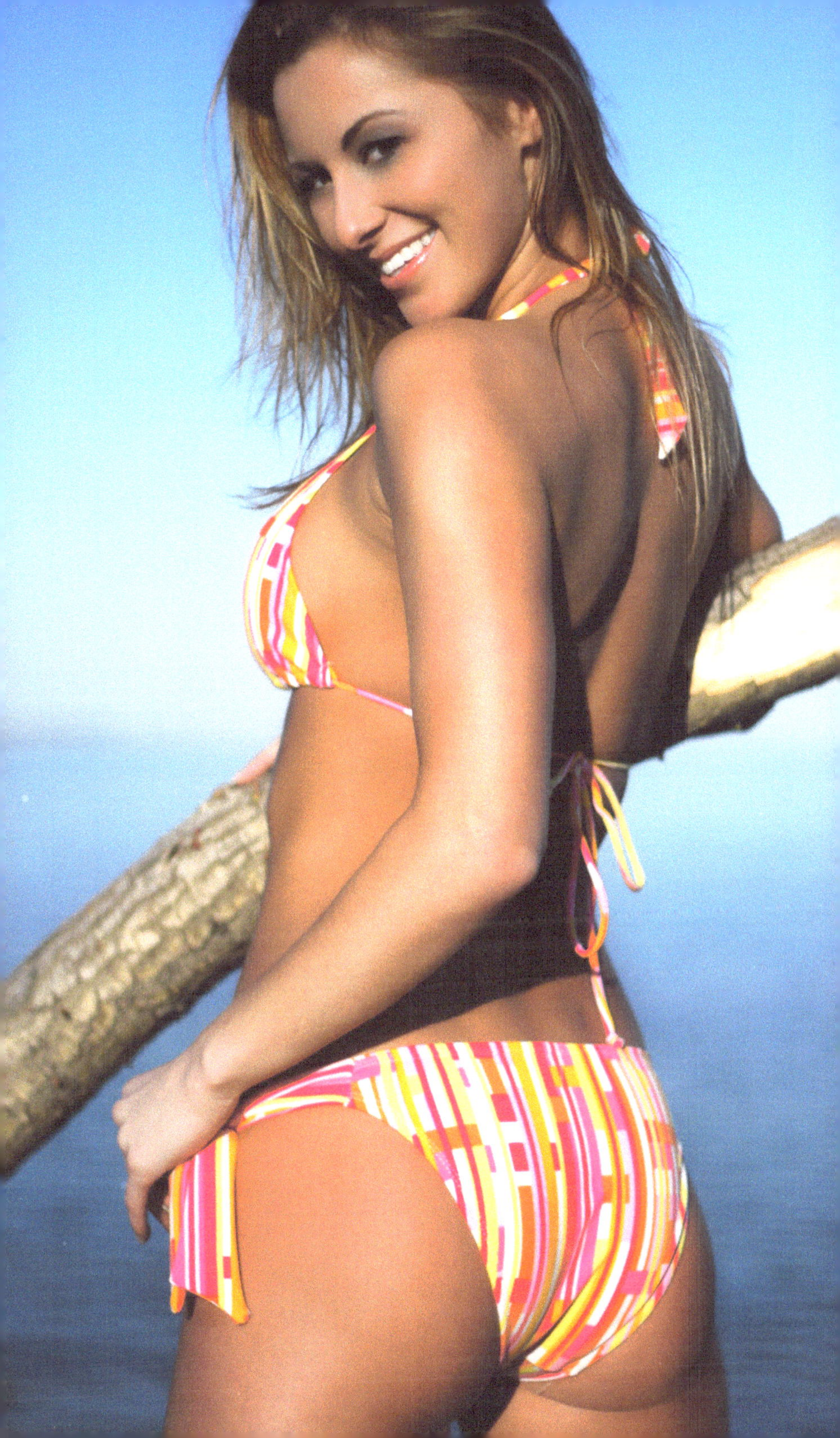

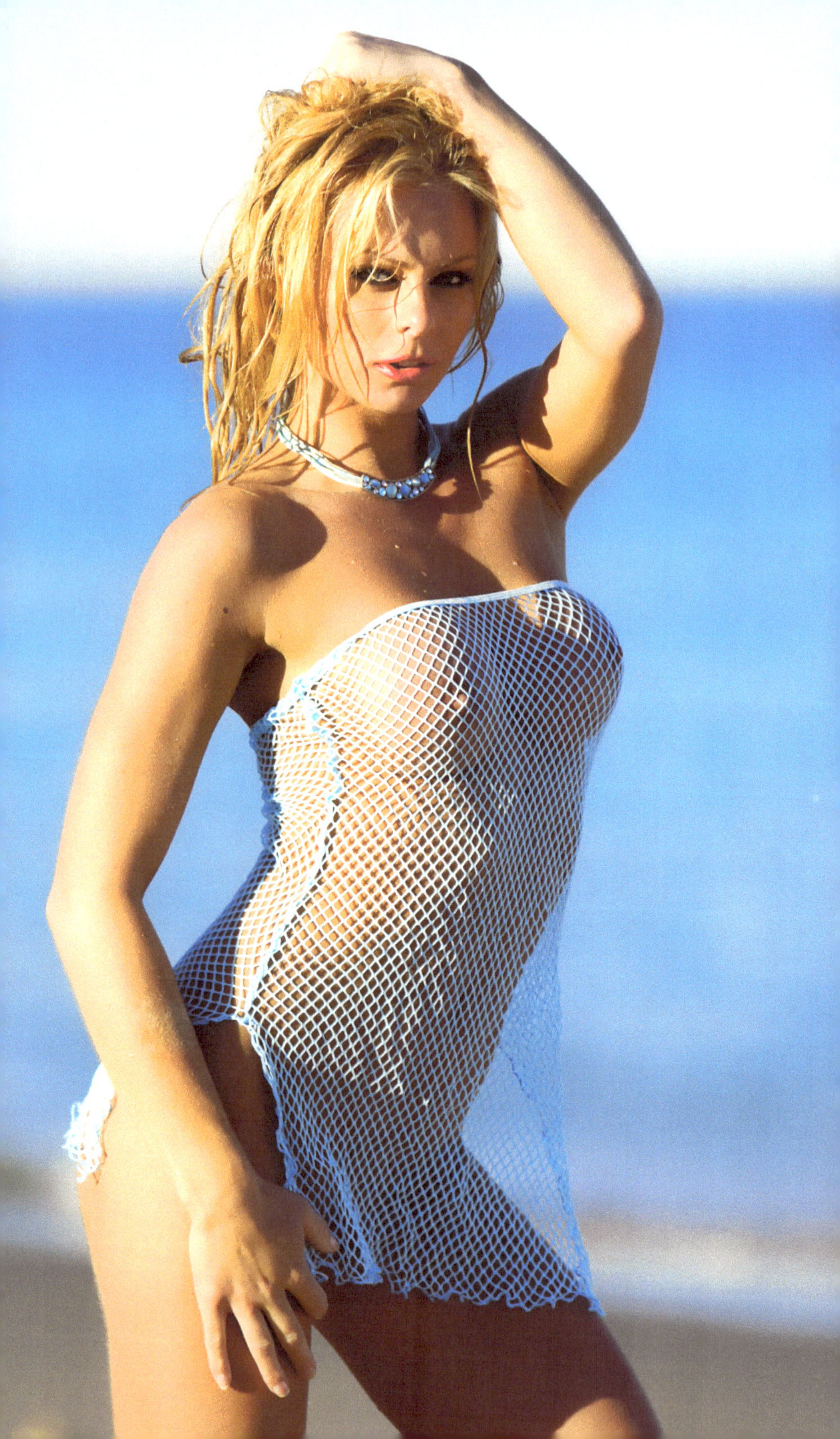

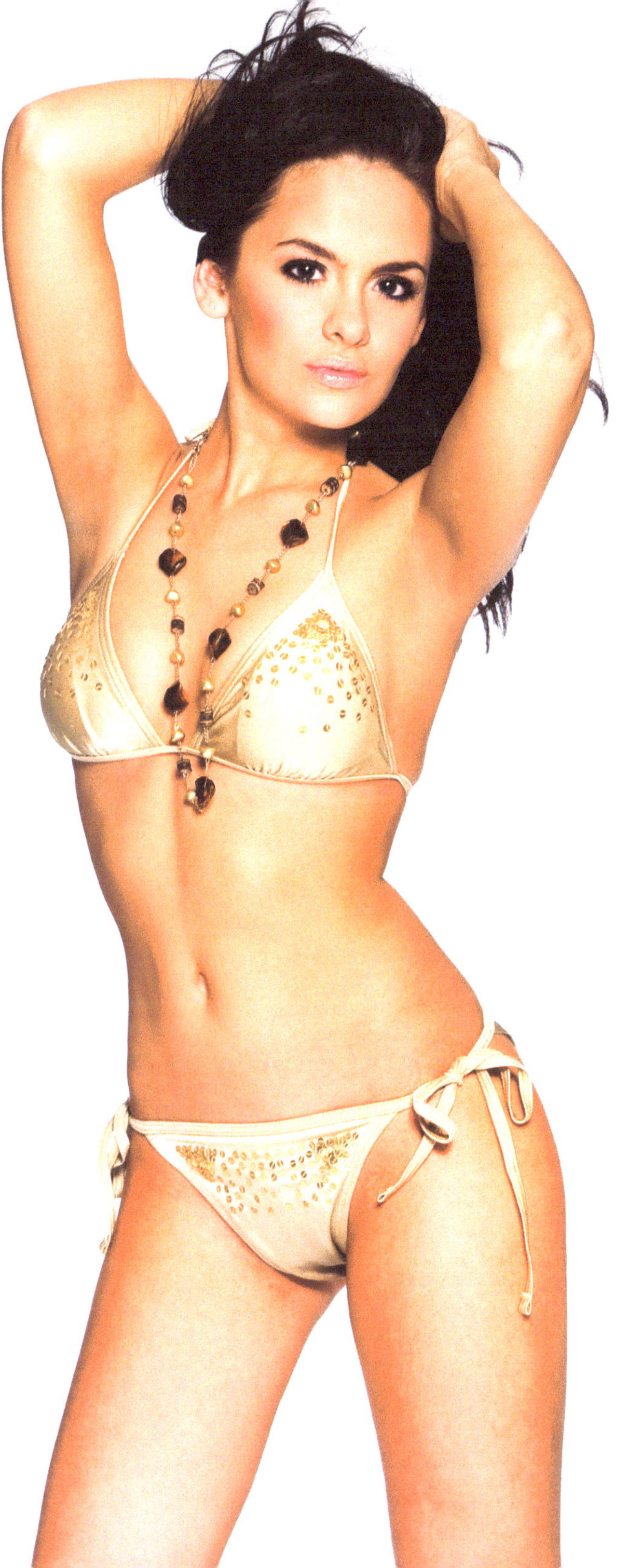

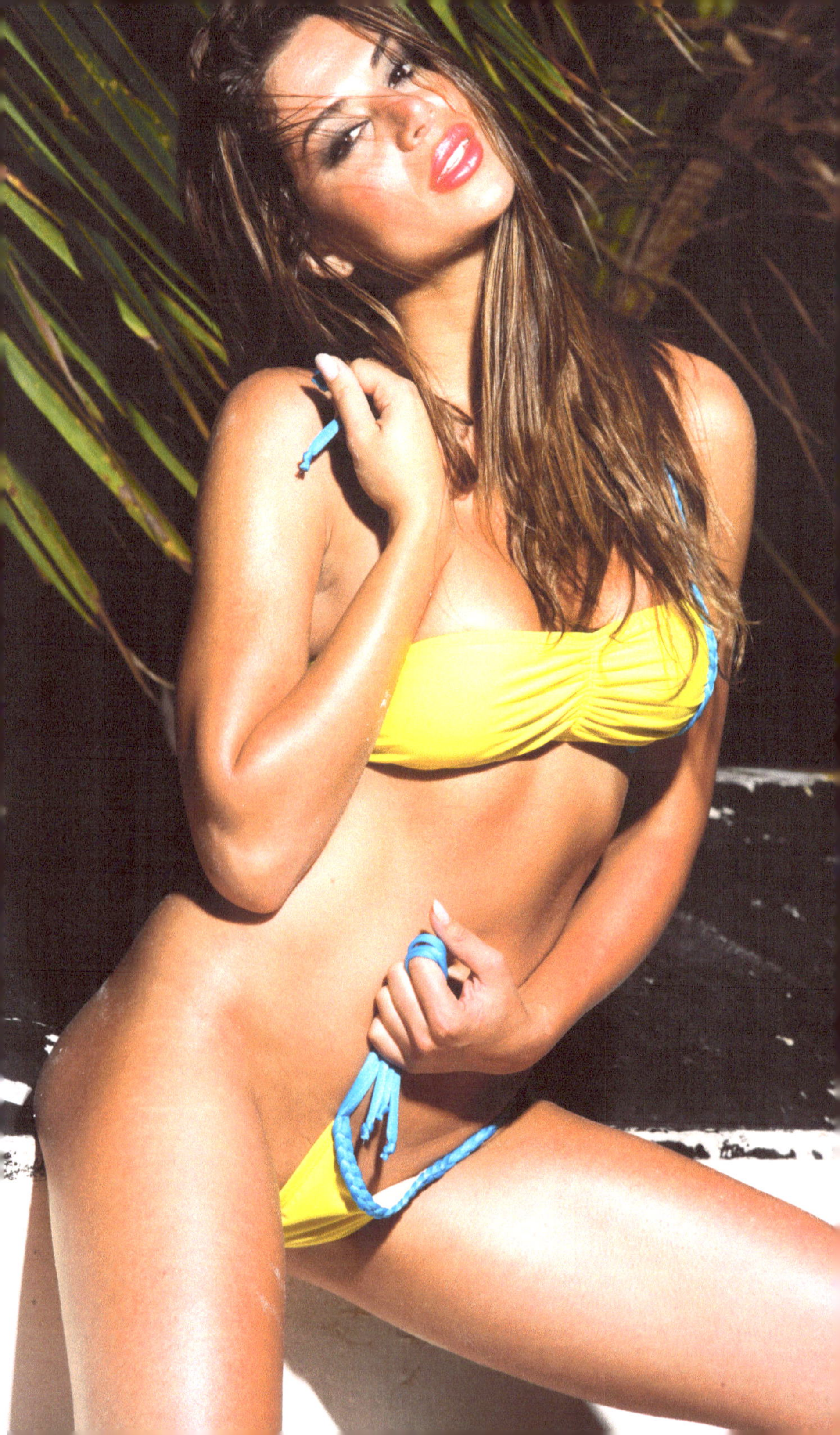

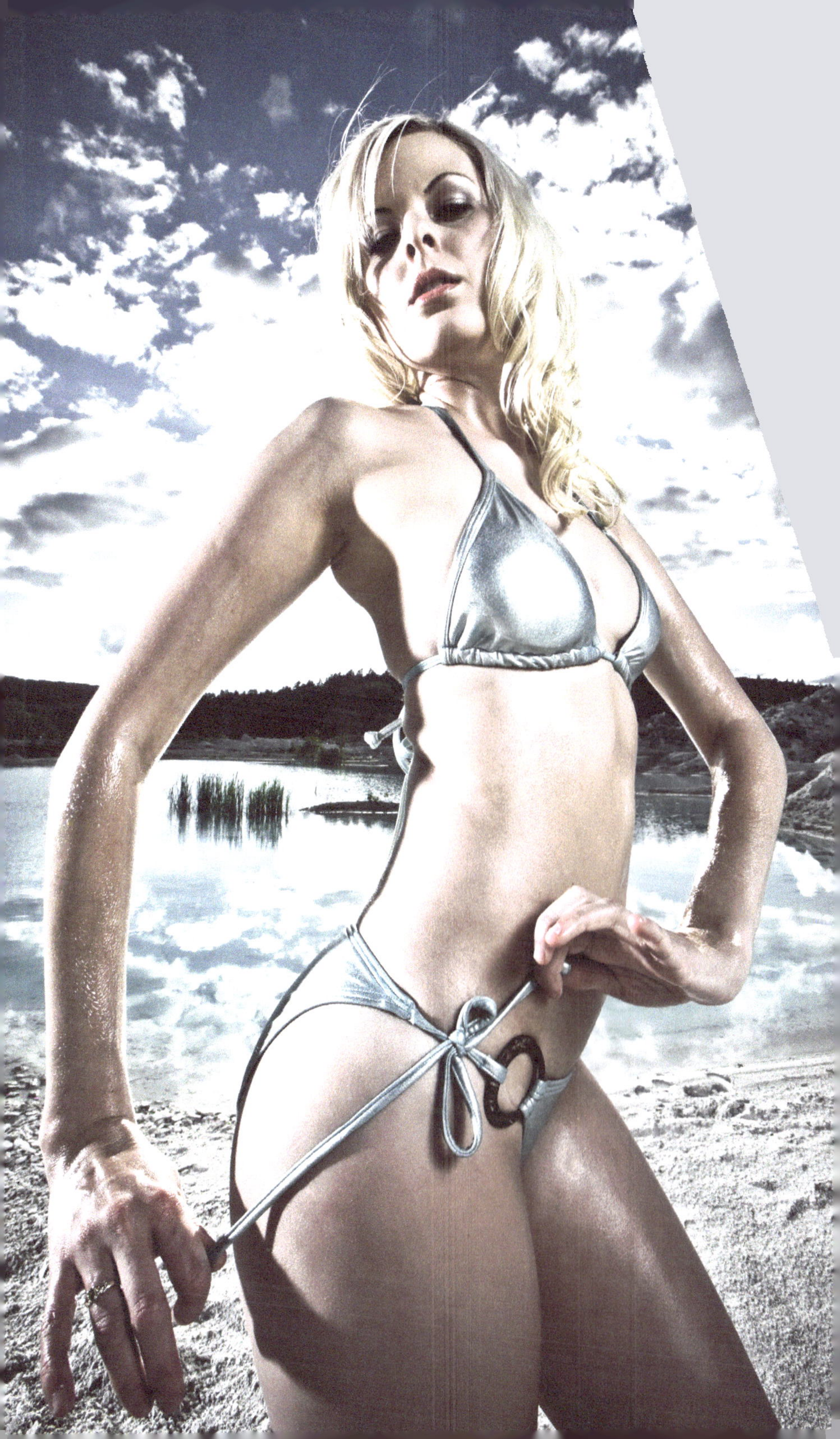

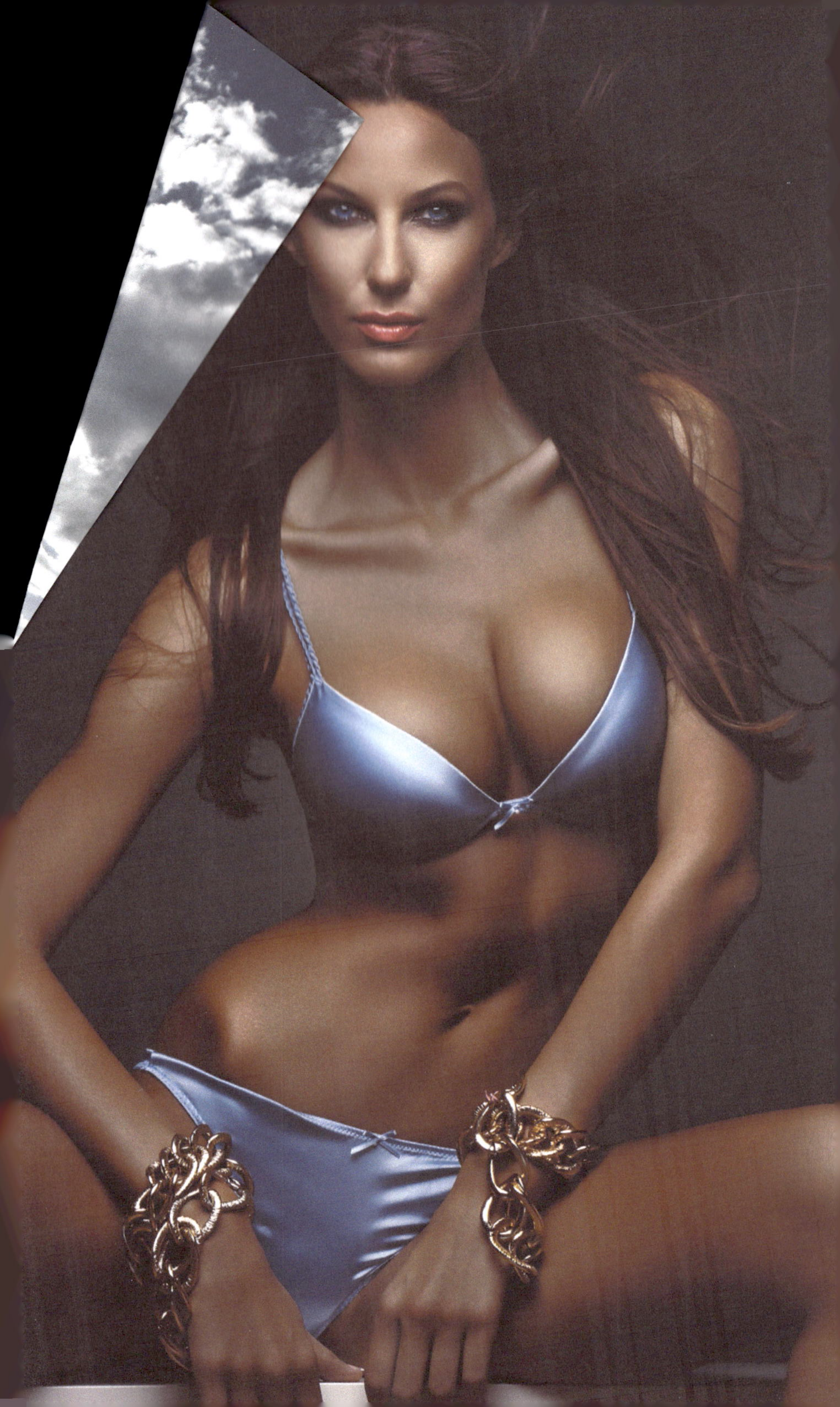

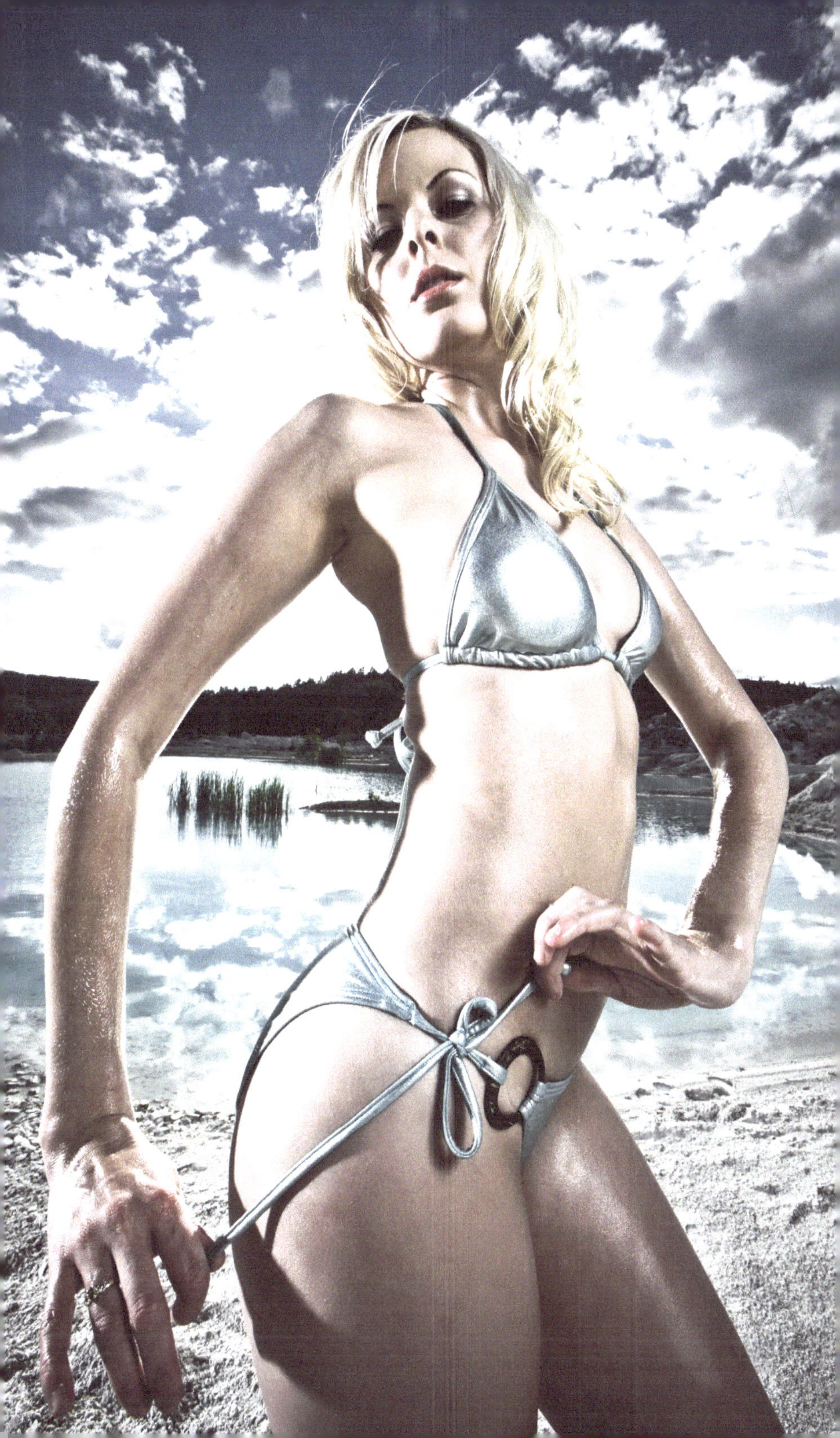

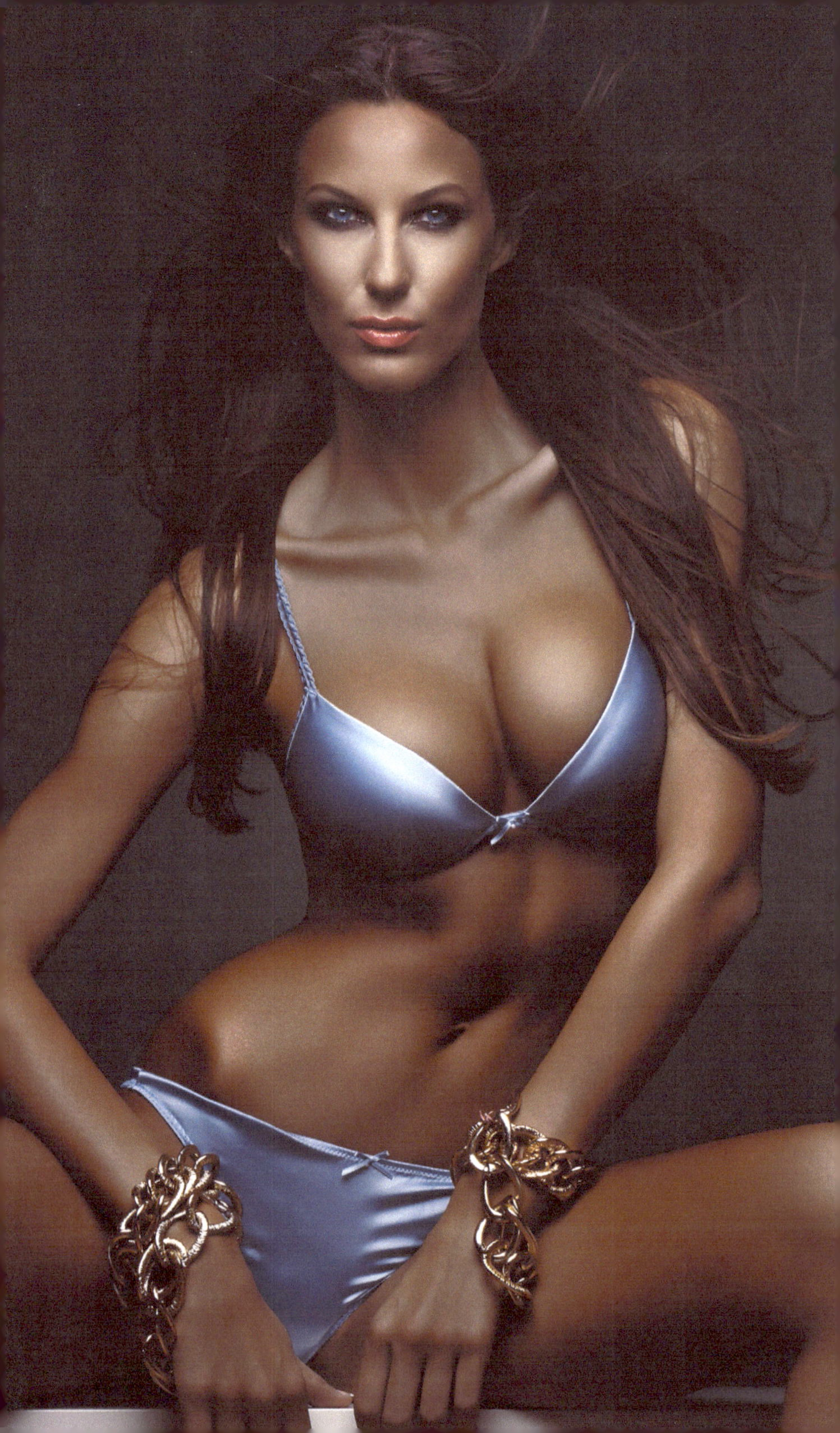